"This is easily the best prime
scholarly yet wide-ranging tre
makes *To Gaze upon God* a valuable resource and accessible
in a realist metaphysic, Parkison's moderate Reformed approach judiciously
encourages evangelicals to take seriously the tradition's teaching on the transformative vision of God. Parkison effectively puts to rest the notion that the Reformation did away with belief in the beatific vision. Here is a book sure to rekindle our longing for happiness in God."

Hans Boersma, Nashotah House Theological Seminary, author of *Five Things Theologians Wish Biblical Scholars Knew*

"This is a book written from the heart, and it demonstrates a fruitful reception of the Christian theological tradition on eternal life. Samuel Parkison has put his finger on a doctrine that should animate the entirety of Christian life. He shows beautifully why and how this is so. Guided by the scriptural and theological testimonies he adduces, let us strive to attain the beatific vision, by God's grace and through the saving cross of Christ."

Matthew Levering, James N. Jr. and Mary D. Perry Chair of Theology
at Mundelein Seminary

"What is the end—the telos—of classical theology? The beatific vision. What could give the weary pilgrim greater comfort and hope than this promise: one day we will see God. Sadly, the significance of the beatific vision for Christian theology has been lost on the modern imagination. But if anyone can recover this lost jewel of Christendom, it is Samuel Parkison, who is one of the best young theologians today. In a breakthrough book, Parkison lets the beatific vision's pedigree in the great tradition shine. With exegetical rigor and theological precision, he also demonstrates why the beatific vision puts all of Christian theology in motion, from creation to Christology to participation in God. No student of theology can afford to ignore Sam Parkison's invitation to retrieve the beatific vision. This book is an irresistible summons to contemplate the beauty of the Lord himself."

Matthew Barrett, professor of Christian theology at Midwestern Baptist Theological Seminary and author of *The Reformation as Renewal*

"Much of evangelical theology languishes in a captivity to a pragmatist and naturalist understanding of the nature of salvation. Thankfully, significant efforts are underway to recover the doctrine of the beatific vision as the supernatural end of our faith. Parkison lends his convincing and balanced voice to these efforts, arguing that the beatific vision is central to the biblical notion of salvation and consistent with Protestant and Reformed priorities."

Adonis Vidu, Andrew Mutch Distinguished Professor of Theology at Gordon-Conwell Theological Seminary

"This book traces the full, long lines of the beatific vision from the Bible to today, with special attention to the near side, where the classic doctrine makes direct contact with evangelical Protestant commitments such as *sola Scriptura* and imputed righteousness. Late in the book, Parkison asks himself, 'Is it right for a Baptist to talk in this way?' It is a question worth pressing, and this is the book that answers it with a carefully considered, critical, and clear 'yes!'"

Fred Sanders, systematic theologian and professor at the Torrey Honors College at Biola University

"This overview of the history of Christian reflection on the beatific vision is an extremely important study, for it rightly reveals the central place that the hunger to gaze upon God has had in Christian tradition. But this is a hunger that far too many Western evangelicals in this 'Secular Age,' as Charles Taylor has termed it, seem to have lost and even rejected as pie-in-the-sky pietism. May this study be used by God to reawaken this hunger and so empower our witness to the ever-present God in this day!"

Michael Haykin, professor of church history at The Southern Baptist Theological Seminary

Samuel G. Parkison

To GAZE UPON GOD

*The Beatific Vision in
Doctrine, Tradition, and Practice*

ivp
Academic

An imprint of InterVarsity Press
Downers Grove, Illinois

InterVarsity Press
P.O. Box 1400 | Downers Grove, IL 60515-1426
ivpress.com | email@ivpress.com

©2024 by Samuel Guy Parkison

All rights reserved. No part of this book may be reproduced in any form without written permission from InterVarsity Press.

InterVarsity Press® is the publishing division of InterVarsity Christian Fellowship/USA®. For more information, visit intervarsity.org.

Scripture quotations, unless otherwise noted, are from The Holy Bible, English Standard Version, copyright © 2001 by Crossway Bibles, a division of Good News Publishers. Used by permission. All rights reserved.

The publisher cannot verify the accuracy or functionality of website URLs used in this book beyond the date of publication.

Cover design: David Fassett
Interior design: Daniel van Loon

ISBN 978-1-5140-0766-2 (print) | ISBN 978-1-5140-0767-9 (digital)

Printed in the United States of America ∞

Library of Congress Cataloging-in-Publication Data
Names: Parkison, Samuel G., author.
Title: To gaze upon God : the beatific vision in doctrine, tradition, and
  practice / Samuel G. Parkison.
Description: Downers Grove, IL : IVP Academic, [2024] | Includes
  bibliographical references and index.
Identifiers: LCCN 2024005633 (print) | LCCN 2024005634 (ebook) | ISBN
  9781514007662 (print) | ISBN 9781514007679 (digital)
Subjects: LCSH: Beatific vision. | God
  (Christianity)–Knowableness–History of doctrines. | BISAC: RELIGION /
  Christian Theology / History | RELIGION / Christianity / Orthodox
Classification: LCC BT98 .P36 2024 (print) | LCC BT98 (ebook) | DDC
  231.7/4–dc23/eng/20240505
LC record available at https://lccn.loc.gov/2024005633
LC ebook record available at https://lccn.loc.gov/2024005634

In honor of

CRAIG BOWEN (1956–2022)

"I have fought the good fight,
I have finished the race,
I have kept the faith."

2 TIMOTHY 4:7

CONTENTS

Acknowledgments   *ix*

1 What Is the Beatific Vision?   *1*

2 Biblical Foundations for the Beatific Vision   *22*

3 A Cloud of Witnesses, Part One   *61*
   Pre-Reformation Historical Witness

4 A Cloud of Witnesses, Part Two   *104*
   Reformation and Post-Reformation Historical Witness

5 Retrieval for Reformed Evangelicals   *138*

6 The Beatific Vision and the Christian Life   *178*

   Postscript   *211*
   The Beatific Vision and Global Christianity

Bibliography   *215*

General Index   *225*

Scripture Index   *229*

ACKNOWLEDGMENTS

THIS BOOK HAS EASILY been one of the most enriching and worshipful projects I have ever undertaken, and as such, I am brimming with far more gratitude than I can adequately express. Still, I should like to try. I am grateful to God, first and foremost, for the bounty of grace he has given me, not only in saving me in Christ and granting me the precious promise of the beatific vision, but also for generously giving me such an abundance of earthly kindnesses "in the meantime." I am grateful for my dear wife, Shannon, who is my best friend and the supportive engine behind this book and everything I do. She is unimaginably more than I deserve, and she has all my affection. I am also grateful for the future men the Lord has entrusted to my care: my sons, Jonah, Henry, and Lewis. I am beyond proud of them, and I pray they come to cherish the beatific vision as their ultimate and absolute hope.

Additionally, I cannot express enough what a joy it is to live and minister to the church of Jesus Christ in the Middle East. I am thankful for my pastor, Aubrey Sequeira, who has not only fed my soul week in and week out from the pulpit but has also significantly encouraged me in this project. I also wish to thank my students—many of whom received a sampling of this book's contents in the form of an elective theology course I taught in May 2023—whose love for the Scriptures and the contemplation of God inspires and enriches me. I am thankful, also, for Eric Zeller, the president of my institution, The Gulf Theological Seminary, who has shown nothing but encouragement for my ministerial efforts—whether in the classroom or on paper.

I also must thank Matthew Barrett, who is in no small measure responsible for this volume. Not only did he provide valuable feedback that made the book better than it would otherwise be, he also facilitated conversation with the good people at IVP Academic, an introduction for which I cannot thank him enough. Along the lines of helpful feedback, I would also like to thank my colleague, Adam Brown, for carefully reading an early draft of this manuscript and offering substantial feedback (particularly in chap. 2), and for his general enthusiastic encouragement surrounding this book. Adam is one of the best scholars and educators I have the privilege of knowing, and I count it a gift not only to serve with him here in the UAE but also to call him my friend. Ryan Sclater also has my thanks for combing through an early draft of the book and offering up thorough editorial notes. The editorial team at IVP will perhaps never realize how much help they received from this brother at no cost. In addition to these people, I offer my thanks to Harrison Perkins, N. Gray Sutanto, Ronni Kurtz, and Craig A. Carter, each of whom offered clarity on portions of the first draft of this book. They have my thanks for taking the time to briefly engage my work.

I feel I should also acknowledge, with gratitude, Hans Boersma, whose work on the beatific vision has made this book possible. While I differ from his conclusions at various points, it was his work that brought this doctrine on the map for me, and his work that raised my affections for Christ and desire for the beatific vision. For that, I am humbly indebted to him. Along these lines, although he is so seldom mentioned in this book, John Piper also deserves my acknowledgment. In a real way, his influence on my life is manifest on every page of this book. Over the years, it was his preaching ministry that awakened my desire for the beatific vision, even before I had language to articulate that this was, in fact, what he was doing. I consider my unabashed love for the doctrine of the beatific vision to be nothing other than a well-informed expression of my thoroughgoing "Christian hedonism," which, by God's grace, was brought about in my life by the Christ-savoring sermons and talks of Piper.

Before concluding this section of acknowledgments, I would like to say a word about its dedicant. William "Craig" Bowen was a faithful husband, father, and pastor in a small town in the Midwest. I came to know Craig through one of his children, who was a church member of a congregation I pastored for several years. For the last couple years of Craig's life, as he was dying of terminal cancer, I had the weighty privilege of pastoring one of his adult children through a very difficult time (unrelated to his illness, but nevertheless requiring regular communication with him and his family). This difficult season with his child afforded me the opportunity to discover what kind of a man Craig was. And Craig was truly a great man—a servant of the Lord Jesus Christ, who quietly gave his life to shepherding the flock of God. Let me offer some examples. Every week, for sixteen years as a pastor, Craig would take time to translate his biblical passage from the original languages as he prepared faithful, expositional sermons—a labor I am certain few of his members knew he undertook on their behalf. In those sixteen years, Craig counseled members with the Scriptures, officiated weddings, officiated funerals, sat with the sick at their hospital beds, mentored young men in the faith, and toward the end of his life, left an indelible witness of Christ's worth by the way he faced his trial of terminal cancer with nobility and devotion to his Savior. He suffered, but in his suffering, he followed honorably in the footsteps of Paul: "Therefore I will boast all the more gladly of my weakness, so that the power of Christ may rest upon me. For the sake of Christ, then, I am content with weaknesses, insults, hardships, persecutions, and calamities. For when I am weak, then I am strong" (2 Cor 12:9-10).

Craig's church was small and did not begin to see its modest growth until the last years of his life—up to that point, he faithfully sowed the seed of the Word, trusting God to deliver the produce. During that time, he lovingly cared for his wife, as they raised and devoted themselves to their five children and ten grandchildren. In many ways, so much of the fruit of Craig's faithful ministry was not felt until after he died (in fact, his ministry will no doubt yield much more fruit in the years to come). In other words, Craig was a model pastor.

He died on Sunday, May 8, 2022, with family surrounding him, reading Scripture and singing his favorite hymns. Craig Bowen exemplified the Christian life I aspire to live. He exemplified the kind of piety I pray this meditation on the beatific vision will engender in my readers. Craig prized, over all, the things above. Christ was his chief treasure, and his life was a marked blessing to everyone around him as a consequence of this heavenward gaze. This book is dedicated to Craig because his life and death preached the central claim of this book more powerfully than I could ever hope to accomplish in the written word: to live is Christ, to die is gain. Craig knew this to be true until the last moments of his earthly pilgrimage and beyond. He knows it still today. May it be so for us as well.

1

WHAT IS THE BEATIFIC VISION?

WHAT MAKES HEAVEN, HEAVEN? Christianity's resounding answer to that question throughout the centuries has been the beatific vision. This is no exaggeration. In fact, the beatific vision is one of the few doctrines that can truly boast ecumenical status; it is not the exclusive doctrine of Eastern Orthodoxy, nor Roman Catholicism, nor Protestantism—the beatific vision is the blessed hope of the one, holy, catholic, and apostolic church. This is not to suggest that each of these traditions has no unique contribution to make. As we will see in this book, there are variations of how the beatific vision is articulated within the various rooms of mere Christianity's house (to use C. S. Lewis's analogy).[1] But for all its variegated formulations to the precise nature of the beatific vision, Christian tradition speaks in unison when it declares that the hope of heaven is the blessed vision of God. The overwhelming majority of Christians throughout the ages have said with Paul, "For now we see in a mirror dimly, but then face to face. Now I know in part; then I shall know fully, even as I have been fully known" (1 Cor 13:12).[2] What makes heaven, heaven is that there we shall see the face of God. That blessed vision is the culmination of all our godly enjoyments in this life and the satiation of all our desire. That blessed vision is the Promised Land we march on toward, and the

---

[1] C. S. Lewis, *Mere Christianity* (New York: HarperCollins, 2001), xiii-xiv. We will concern ourselves with the distinct contributions of various Christian traditions in chap. 3.
[2] Unless otherwise indicated, all Scripture citations are taken from the English Standard Version (ESV).

consolation that sustains us on our pilgrimage. We shall see God. While Christians have many desires and aspirations, the central point of every single one of them is the same as David's: "One thing have I asked of the Lord, that will I seek after: that I may dwell in the house of the Lord all the days of my life, to gaze upon the beauty of the Lord and to inquire in his temple" (Ps 27:4).

In this sense, the book you hold in your hand is a (small "c") catholic book. My prayer is that the majority of what I write here will elicit a hearty "amen" from all Christians. In another sense, however, it has a narrower focus. I write as a Reformed evangelical, and it is other Reformed evangelicals I particularly address.[3] This is fitting, in part, because the widespread Christian consensus on the beatific vision I describe here is only true if we use the wide-angled lens of two millennia. If our focus is on the past couple hundred years of evangelicalism, and indeed, the status quo over the past couple of decades, we will find a conspicuous absence of discussion on beatific vision. There are many reasons for this, and we shall address them in due course (particularly in chap. 5), but here we must simply acknowledge that the beatific vision is bound to be a new doctrine for many an evangelical. So, while this book is broad in the sense that I hope to retrieve a catholic doctrine that has enjoyed far-reaching consensus for the majority of the church's history, it is narrow in the sense that I hope to apply it in the particular context of Protestant and Reformed evangelicalism. This will simultaneously allow for us evangelicals to remember our catholic heritage,

---

[3]To give some specific examples of what I mean by this designation, I subscribe to the 1689 Second London Baptist Confession of faith, which puts me squarely within the confessional Reformed tradition. As to what I mean by *evangelical*, I served for nearly five years at a Southern Baptist Church, graduated from a Southern Baptist seminary, and now serve as a theology professor at a seminary who has ties to several Southern Baptist seminaries as well as non-denominational free church seminaries. In other words, I see myself in the descriptions of David W. Bebbington's *The Evangelical Quadrilateral: The Denominational Mosaic of the British Gospel Movement* (Waco, TX: Baylor University Press, 2021) and Thomas S. Kidd's *Who Is an Evangelical?: The History of a Movement in Crisis* (New Haven, CT: Yale University Press, 2019).

while also contributing to that catholic tradition by connecting the beatific vision with our theological distinctives (particularly, our soteriological distinctives).

In this present chapter, I will develop the theological foundations that support the beatific vision, as well as lay out the broad contours of the doctrine itself. As a final word of preface, it is worth mentioning that while evangelicals (particularly of the Reformed variety like myself) may be unfamiliar with the doctrine of the beatific vision consciously speaking, they are probably already primed and ready to embrace it. In fact, they may even believe it without knowing as much. "Christian hedonists" who have learned from John Piper that "God is most glorified in us when we are most satisfied in him"—those who have come to agree with Piper that the chief delight of the soul is "seeing and savoring Christ"—are ready to embrace the beatific vision.[4] If one has learned from C. S. Lewis to ache for "the stab of joy,"[5] to reject playing with mud-pies in the slums for the sake of a holiday at sea,[6] and to go joyfully "further up and further in" to Aslan's country forever,[7] one is ready to embrace the beatific vision. If one has learned from Jonathan Edwards that heaven is "a world of love," one is ready to embrace the beatific vision.[8] If one has learned to pray with Augustine, "Thou hast made us for Thyself, and our hearts are restless until they find their rest in Thee,"[9] one is ready for the beatific vision. All of these lessons that so many Reformed evangelicals have learned traffic in the

---

[4]See John Piper, *Desiring God: Meditations of a Christian Hedonist*, rev. ed. (Colorado Springs: Multnomah, 2011).
[5]See C. S. Lewis, *Surprised by Joy: The Shape of My Early Life* (Orlando, FL: Harvest, 1958).
[6]See C. S. Lewis, *The Weight of Glory* (New York: HarperCollins, 2001).
[7]This reference is, of course, referring to Lewis's name for "heaven" in his fantasy children's novels, the Chronicles of Narnia. Since the talking lion, Aslan, is the Christ figure of these novels, it is fitting to call heaven *his* country. See C. S. Lewis, *The Last Battle* (New York: HarperCollins, 1994).
[8]See Jonathan Edwards, *The Works of Jonathan Edwards Online*, 72 vols. (New Haven: Jonathan Edwards Center at Yale University, 2009), 8:367-97.
[9]Augustine of Hippo, *Confessions* 1.1.5. Unless otherwise specified, all citations of the church fathers are taken from the *Nicene and Post-Nicene Fathers: First and Second Series*, 28 vols., ed. Philip Schaff (Grand Rapids, MI: Eerdmans, 1956).

blessed hope of the beatific vision. They may therefore proceed in confidence.

Why a Book on the Beatific Vision?

There are reasons why this doctrine, and indeed, this *way* of talking about heaven, feels so foreign for us who live in the twenty-first century. The radical individualism produced by the Enlightenment has yielded strange fruit that may lead us to think that any examination of the beatific vision is irrelevant today. In his brief and infamous essay, "What Is Enlightenment?," Immanuel Kant (1772–1804) answers his own question in this way:

> Enlightenment is man's leaving his self-caused immaturity. Immaturity is the incapacity to use one's intelligence without the guidance of another. Such immaturity is self-caused if it is not caused by lack of intelligence, but by lack of determination and courage to use one's intelligence without being guided by another. *Sapere aude!* ["Dare to know!"] "Have the courage to use your own intelligence" is therefore the motto of the enlightenment.[10]

Tradition, according to the spirit of Enlightenment, is a straight jacket, confining the would-be liberated intellect to immaturity. Growing into intellectual adulthood, for Kant, is one and the same with waking from one's dogmatic slumber and voyaging out on an open-ended quest for independent thought.

One of the surprising fruits of this "motto," so aptly summarized by Kant, is the fundamentalist-biblicist misrepresentation of *sola Scriptura*. I say "misrepresentation" because the Reformers never intended for the doctrine of *sola Scriptura* to sever Christians from their heritage. "Far from undergirding an individualistic or biblistic portrayal of Christianity," note Michael Allen and Scott Swain, "*sola Scriptura* operated within a catholic context that shaped the confessional, catechetical, and liturgical life of the early Reformed

---

[10]Immanuel Kant, "An Answer to the Question, What Is Enlightenment?" in *Practical Philosophy,* ed. Mary J. Gregor (New York: Cambridge University Press, 1996), 16-17.

churches."[11] No, the contemporary antipathy for tradition that often accompanies fundamentalism and a biblicist approach to theology did not come from *sola Scriptura*; modernity and the Enlightenment are to blame for this aberration from historic Christianity. This means that the problem with fundamentalism is not that it is too conservative but rather that it is not nearly conservative enough; it is willing to conserve premodern *concepts* like the Reformation's *solas* or Nicene Trinitarian categories of consubstantiality but not the premodern *hermeneutic* or *philosophical commitments* that went into the original articulation of such convictions. But we cannot expect to retain Reformational or Nicene *fruit* with an Enlightenment *root*.

This consideration of the Enlightenment is relevant for justifying a book like this in a time like the one in which it is written. In an age as unpredictable and unsettled as ours, it might seem inappropriate for Christian theologians to devote concentrated attention on anything other than the pressing social issues of our day. Gavin Ortlund summarizes the starkness of our situation well: "Athanasius stood *contra mundum*; Aquinas synthesized Aristotle; Luther strove with his conscience; Zwingli wielded an axe; but probably none of them ever dreamed of a world in which people could choose their gender. Secularizing late modernity is a strange, new animal."[12] Late modernity is a "strange, new animal" for other reasons as well. For example, Joseph Minich has recently demonstrated that in light of the insights gained by thinkers like Charles Taylor's reflections on "the immanent frame,"[13] late modernity is marked by a particular existential sense of divine absence.[14]

---

[11] Michael Allen and Scott R. Swain, *Reformed Catholicity: The Promise of Retrieval for Theology and Biblical Interpretation* (Grand Rapids, MI: Baker Academic, 2015), 70.
[12] Gavin Ortlund, *Theological Retrieval for Evangelicals: Why We Need Our Past to Have a Future* (Wheaton, IL: Crossway, 2019), 60.
[13] See Charles Taylor, *A Secular Age* (Cambridge, MA: Harvard University Press, 2018).
[14] See Joseph Minich, *Bulwarks of Unbelief: Atheism and Divine Absence in a Secular Age* (Bellingham, WA: Lexham Academic, 2023).

In the face of such a "strange, new animal," should not the theologians of Christ's church devote all their attention to answering questions surrounding personhood, gender, sexuality, and human nature? If (in *incredibly* broad and crude strokes) the fourth century was when the church was forced to articulate its convictions on the Trinity, the fifth century was when the church was forced to articulate its convictions on Christology, the medieval period was when the church was forced to articulate its metaphysics, and the sixteenth century was when the church was forced to articulate its convictions on revelation, Scripture, and soteriology, perhaps the twenty-first century is when the church will be forced to articulate its convictions on anthropology and sexuality. So, why write a book on retrieving the doctrine of the beatific vision when books on, say, anthropology and sexuality, for example, are sorely needed?

One answer—apart from simply granting that such treatments *are* necessary and should be commended as some theologians produce them—is that this is easier said than done. Christians in the twenty-first century, facing the perplexing concerns surrounding anthropology, differ in a serious way from Christians of earlier time periods who faced the doctrinal concerns of their respective eras. Prior theological commitments were hammered out in a context of self-conscious ecclesial and theological *heritage*. The fifth-century church fathers were able to work out their Christology precisely because they had not forgotten what the fourth century church fathers taught them about the Trinity. They were *building* on a foundation already laid. The same is true all the way down through the Reformation: the Reformers worked out their convictions on Scripture and justification within the inherited context of convictions about metaphysics, the Trinity, Christology, divine attributes, humanity, the relationship between the body and soul, and the like. What separates our crisis surrounding anthropology from the Reformers' crisis surrounding justification, in a way that is altogether unlike what separated their crisis surrounding justification from the fifth-century church fathers' crisis surrounding Christology, is a massive intellectual fissure we call the *Enlightenment*.

We cannot simply build on what we have inherited because what we have inherited has already been disregarded. In fact, we were *incentivized* to disregard this inheritance in the name of intellectual maturity. To grow up, we were told, we had to move out and start a name for ourselves. Our prodigal departure promised self-fulfillment and freedom. But now we find ourselves eating out of the pods with the pigs and wondering where we went wrong (cf. Lk 15:11-32). In other words, both fundamentalist biblicism *and* self-expressive individualism are the fruit of the Enlightenment,[15] and the best way to solve the problem of either is to subvert the chronological snobbery endemic to both. This is, in part, why retrieving a historic embrace of the beatific vision is not a waste of time in a radically confused age: the blessed hope is ever relevant. It touches a nerve within the soul; a nerve for which the post-Enlightenment imagination does not even have a category. The way we escape from the malaise of modernity is not by embracing individualistic biblicism, for individualistic biblicism is stuck in that very same malaise. The way forward is first the way backward. We must correct our course, and theological retrieval is the way to do this.

In this book, I develop a broad, historical account of the beatific vision. For readers who are altogether unfamiliar with the doctrine, I have tried to write in such a way that this book can function as something of a primer. Not only do I develop the biblical rationale for the doctrine, I also (1) establish its theological and philosophical foundations, (2) trace its reception in the thought of key theological voices throughout the centuries, (3) introduce and adjudicate some of the more contemporary articulations of the doctrine, and (4) elaborate on the beatific vision's bearing on the Christian life.

---

[15]For a helpful summary and description of the latter, see Carl R. Trueman, *The Rise and Triumph of the Modern Self: Cultural Amnesia, Expressive Individualism, and the Road to Sexual Revolution* (Wheaton, IL: Crossway, 2020).

As such, a major portion of the book, in terms of sheer size, is dedicated to historical considerations (chaps. 3 and 4). This is intentional. Some of the most important questions we may have when considering the doctrine biblically have been asked and answered in a number of ways by some of the great minds that Christ has given to his church down the ages—if we desire to have something useful to say about the doctrine today, we must become acquainted with the historical conversation, which began long before we arrived on the scene.[16]

Theological Foundations: Divine Blessedness

We cannot rightly understand the beatific vision until we reckon with God's own independent *beatitude*. In the beatific vision, we are begraced participants in a happiness that in no way depends on—or is even enriched by—us. We are, of course, referring to that glorious doctrine of *aseity*.[17] God is *a se*, or *of himself*. This doctrine can be stated both negatively and positively. Negatively, we get at this doctrine by stressing God's independence—he *needs* nothing. He depends on nothing. God plainly announces this independence in poetic fashion when he speaks through the psalmist:

---

[16] For readers who are somewhat familiar with the doctrine already, it may be useful for me to articulate, at the front end, what unique contributions I hope to make. The two most recent, and most adjacent works to this one are Michael Allen's *Grounded in Heaven* and Hans Boersma's *Seeing God*. See Michael Allen, *Grounded in Heaven: Recentering Christian Hope and Life on God* (Grand Rapids, MI: Eerdmans, 2018); Hans Boersma, *Seeing God: The Beatific Vision in Christian Tradition* (Grand Rapids, MI: Eerdmans, 2018). While I am indebted to both of these significant works, this present volume can be distinguished from theirs in a number of ways. In terms of focus, my project is broader than both of theirs. Whereas Boersma's book is largely historical, with brief theologically constructive portions, my book includes sections interacting with the biblical text (chap. 2) and developments of the philosophical and theological foundations of the doctrine (this chapter). I also include a dogmatic account of the doctrine in which I propose a positive constructive account from a Protestant and Reformed perspective (chap. 5), and a chapter on the doctrine's impact on various dimensions of the Christian life (chap. 6). Additionally, whereas Allen's book is concerned with retrieving the doctrine of the beatific vision and its ascetic implications for the Dutch Reformed tradition, mine is written with the more broadly evangelical world in mind. It also differs in other ways that will become apparent in future chapters.

[17] Much of this section is indebted to Steven J. Duby, *God in Himself: Scripture, Metaphysics, and the Task of Christian Theology* (Downers Grove, IL: IVP Academic, 2019).

> "Hear, O my people, and I will speak;
>   O Israel, I will testify against you.
>   I am God, your God.
> Not for your sacrifices do I rebuke you;
>   your burnt offerings are continually before me.
> I will not accept a bull from your house
>   or goats from your folds.
> For every beast of the forest is mine,
>   the cattle on a thousand hills.
> I know all the birds of the hills,
>   and all that moves in the field is mine.
> "If I were hungry, I would not tell you,
>   for the world and its fullness are mine." (Ps 50:7-12)

"God is absolute being," says Herman Bavinck, "the fullness of being, and therefore also eternally and absolutely independent in his existence, in his perfections, in all his works, the first and the last, the sole cause and final goal of all things."[18] This point of independence is incredibly important, since it is crucial for establishing a related doctrine, *divine simplicity*.[19] If God is independent, he *must* be simple; that is, he must not be a composite of any kind but rather *one*. At the most basic level, every Christian, regardless of his or her affinity with theology, affirms this doctrine. Every Christian knows that God is spirit and not body (cf. Jn 4:24) and therefore knows that God is not a composite of body and soul like humans are. But this doctrine implies much more.

If God is independent, he must not be a composite of *any* kind—not merely a composite of body and soul. This negation would include the composite of essence and accident (i.e., attributes that are essential to God's nature and those that are not), and even potentiality and actuality (i.e., God as he is and God as he might become). God

---

[18]Herman Bavinck, *Reformed Dogmatics*, 4 vols., ed. John Bolt, trans. John Vriend (Grand Rapids, MI: Baker Academic, 2003–2008), 2:152.

[19]Francis Turretin, *Institutes of Elenctic Theology*, 3 vols., ed. James T Dennison, trans. George Musgrave Giger (Phillipsburg, NJ: P&R, 1997), 1:191-94.

is not composed in any of those ways, otherwise he would not be *perfect*, nor would he be *independent*. If God could acquire accidental attributes and was therefore a composite of essential and accidental attributes, these accidental attributes would either enhance or deteriorate him. This would rule out his perfection, for if he could deteriorate, he would not be perfect (his perfection lacking both in the ability to deteriorate, and in the final state of deterioration), and if he could benefit, he would not be *essentially* perfect (perfection being that state only made possible after the accidental attribute is acquired). This kind of composition would *also* rule out God's independence, for if God could acquire accidental attributes, and if those attributes benefited him in any way, his final state of beatitude would *depend* on the accidental attribute acquired (and whatever "composer" joined his essential being to the accidental attribute in question).

As Herman Bavinck reasons, "If God is composed of parts, like a body, or composed of *genus* (class) and *differentiae* (attributes of differing species belonging to the same *genus*), substance and accidents, matter and form, potentiality and actuality, essence and existence, then his perfection, oneness, independence, and immutability cannot be maintained."[20] God's simplicity therefore demands that he is one. Nothing in God is accidental and nothing in God is potential. His essence is his existence, and his attributes are one.[21] He is *pure act*.[22] Richard Muller describes this affirmation of *actus purus* when he says that God is "the fully actualized being, the only being not in potency," and is therefore "absolutely perfect and the eternally perfect fulfillment of himself" and is "never *in potential*, in the state

---

[20] Bavinck, *RD*, 2:176.

[21] Obviously, there is much more we could say about the doctrine of divine simplicity. For more extended treatments on this doctrine, James E. Dolezal, *God Without Parts: Divine Simplicity and the Metaphysics of God's Absoluteness* (Eugene, OR: Pickwick, 2011); *All That Is in God: Evangelical Theology and the Challenge of Classical Christian Theism* (Grand Rapids, MI: Reformation Heritage, 2017); and Steven J. Duby, *Divine Simplicity: A Dogmatic Account* (New York: T&T Clark, 2015).

[22] Thomas Aquinas, *Summa Theologiae*, translated by The Fathers of the English Dominican Province (Westminster, UK: Christian Classics, 1983), I.3.3-8.

What Is the Beatific Vision?

of potency, or incomplete realization."[23] Here, Muller reminds us that God's *aseity* need not be expressed exclusively in negative terms—that is, we need not only conceptualize God's being of himself in terms of contrasting his independence from all creaturely contingency. We can take a step forward and define divine aseity positively as well. God needs nothing *because he is infinite fullness of life and blessedness*. God is plenitude, fullness, profusion. As Webster so powerfully puts it, "Aseity is not only the quality of being (in contrast to contingent reality) underived; it is the eternal lively plenitude of the Father who begets, the Son who is begotten, and the Spirit who proceeds from both."[24] Within the immanent life of God, there is no lack precisely because there is instead an infinite burning of abundance in the Father who communicates the divine essence eternally to the Son (Jn 5:26), and the Father and Son whose eternal life and love eternally proceed as the Spirit. This is precisely because these eternal modes of subsistence are, in fact, *eternal*. The notion that a divine person should exist in any way (volitionally, relationally, emotionally, etc.) independent from another is inconceivable.[25] The divine existence is a plenteous holy fire that ever burns as paternity, filiation, and procession. "Filiation is not a lack but a mode of God's eternal perfection, intrinsic to the wholly realized self-movement of God. Begetting—and likewise spiration—are the *form* of God's aseity, not its result or term, still less its contradiction."[26]

Tying the above themes together, we might say that the doctrine of aseity *negatively* stated accentuates our doctrine of divine simplicity, and aseity *positively* stated accentuates our doctrine of the Trinity. God is blessed. God eternally enjoys and delights in God.

---

[23] Richard A. Muller, *Dictionary of Latin and Greek Theological Terms: Drawn Principally from Protestant Scholastic Theology*, 2nd ed. (Grand Rapids, MI: Baker Academic, 2017), 11.
[24] Webster, "Life in and of Himself," in *God Without Measure*, 1:20.
[25] Turretin, in *Institutes*, 1:193, says, "Simplicity and triplicity are so mutually opposed that they cannot subsist at the same time (but not simplicity and Trinity because they are said in different respects): simplicity in respect to essence, but Trinity in respect to persons. In this sense, nothing hinders God (who is one essence) from being three persons."
[26] Webster, "Life in and of Himself," 1:21.

The triune God is the fullness of life and love and happiness in and of himself. Without this eternal divine beatitude—which in no way depends on or is answerable to another, and which is in no way enhanced or enriched by another—we would have no beatific vision for which to long. In the beatific vision we are entering into a happiness already occurring—a happiness that is not contributed to by our own enjoyment, not because our enjoyment does not matter, but because that divine happiness is already maximally actual. Though this does little for our petty conceits, it is *good* news for us. While this truth does not cater to our delusional sense of over-importance, it ought to be a great comfort to know that God is not indebted to or enriched by us, because this means that our blessed hope is one of utter and complete *generosity*.[27] The beatific vision is our enjoyment of a blessedness *gratuitously shared*.

The way we come to share in this blessedness concerns the topic of soteriology, which we will consider in due time. But before we can get there, we need to consider what kind of metaphysical vision is required for this kind of gratuitous enjoyment of God affirmed in the beatific vision to make sense. What vision of reality is necessary for us to properly conceptualize the beatific vision? The answer is what Hans Boersma calls a "sacramental ontology,"[28] what others have called a "participatory metaphysic,"[29] what some prefer to call "Christian Platonism,"[30] and what I will primarily refer to as "classical realism."

---

[27]This is the very foundation of the doctrine of *creatio ex nihilo*. See Webster, "'Love Is Also a Lover of Life': *Creatio Ex Nihilo* and Creaturely Goodness," in *God Without Measure*; "Trinity and Creation," in *God Without Measure*; and Matthew Levering, *Engaging the Doctrine of Creation: Cosmos, Creatures, and the Wise and Good Creator* (Grand Rapids, MI: Baker Academic, 2017).

[28]See especially Hans Boersma, *Heavenly Participation: The Weaving of a Sacramental Tapestry* (Grand Rapids, MI: Eerdmans, 2011).

[29]See especially Andrew Davison, *Participation in God: A Study of Christian Doctrine and Metaphysics* (New York: Cambridge University Press, 2019).

[30]See especially Craig Carter, *Interpreting the Scriptures with the Great Tradition: Recovering the Genius of Premodern Exegesis* (Grand Rapids, MI: Baker Academic, 2018); Craig A. Carter, *Contemplating God with the Great Tradition: Recovering Trinitarian Classical Theism* (Grand Rapids, MI: Baker Academic, 2021); Louis Markos, *From Plato to Christ* (Downers Grove, IL:

SETTING THE METAPHYSICAL STAGE[31]

In one of his lesser-known works, *The Discarded Image*,[32] C. S. Lewis paints a vivid picture of the medieval imagination. He does this, in part, by contrasting the medieval imagination with the modern one. Embodying these two radically different outlooks are two characters Lewis describes throughout the work: the medieval man and the nineteenth-century man. He imagines both men walking outside and looking up at a clear night sky. Their situation in this moment is, externally, identical in every way. They are standing on the same ground, feeling the same breeze, captivated by the same display of stars—like flecks of white paint on a black canvas. But where the nineteenth-century man imagines he is looking up at outer space, the medieval man imagines he is looking up into deep heaven. Nineteenth-century man views his world as full, and the sky as mostly empty. It is, essentially, nothing; its primary characteristic is absence. It is an unfathomable expanse of void. But where the nineteenth-century man conceptualizes his stargazing as looking out, medieval man imagines he is looking in. The blackness of the stars' backdrop, for him, does not bespeak a fundamental emptiness but rather instructs him on his own limitations. He does not assume that what he cannot see is not there; for him, the heavens are the province of a higher reality. They are not empty; they are full, teeming with life and activity that transcend his comprehension.

This description from Lewis helps us to illustrate the difference between the premodern enchanted cosmology and the modern disenchanted cosmology. Behind these two cosmological views are two opposing views of reality. This is what we mean when we talk about

---

InterVarsity Press, 2021); Paul Tyson, *Return to Reality* (Eugene, OR: Cascade, 2014); and Alexander J. B. Hapton and John Peter Kenny, eds., *Christian Platonism: A History* (New York: Cambridge University Press, 2021).

[31] The following section contains reworked and expanded material for a column I wrote for *Credo Magazine* titled, "Further Up and Further In: Appreciating the Platonic Tradition and the Reformed Conception of Union with Christ," vol. 12, Issue 1 (March 2022).

[32] C. S. Lewis, *The Discarded Image: An Introduction to Medieval and Renaissance Literature* (Cambridge: Cambridge University Press, 1964).

metaphysics. Metaphysics is concerned not merely with determining whether stars are burning balls of gas or angels (though, as Lewis points out, with the right metaphysic, even these two descriptions of "stars" are not mutually exclusive),[33] but rather with how to conceptualize reality as a whole. One metaphysic describes reality as a message; the other views it as an accident. The former produces thinkers like Jonathan Edwards, who doesn't simply observe roses or spiders or water or silkworms; he reads them. Roses mean more than they are; they mean "that true happiness, the crown of glory, is to be come at in no other way than by bearing Christ's cross by a life of mortification, self-denial and labor, and bearing all things for Christ. The rose, the chief of all flowers, is the last thing that comes out. The briery prickly bush grows before, but the end and crown of all is the beautiful and fragrant rose."[34] The latter metaphysic, the disenchanted one, produces thinkers like Richard Dawkins, who says, "The universe we observe has precisely the properties we should expect if there is, at bottom, no design, no purpose, no evil, no good, nothing but blind, pitiless indifference."[35]

As difficult as it is to imagine, the modern view of the universe is no forgone conclusion to Western thought. It was an accident. A mere decision to go left at a fork in a philosophical road where many great thinkers of the past went right. The proverbial fork is the choice between nominalism and realism. Nominalism is a very earthy outlook. It denies the existence of universals. For a nominalist, we are not saying anything definite or concrete or real when we talk about humanness or humanity. There is no such thing as humanness, since any expression of so-called humanity is necessarily individual and distinct from all other expressions. *Humanity* is simply the shorthand

---

[33]Recall the conversation between the Narnian star, Ramandu, and Eustace: "'In our world,' said Eustace, 'a star is a huge ball of flaming gas.' 'Even in your world, my son, that is not what a star is but only what it is made of.'" C. S. Lewis, *The Voyage of the Dawn Treader* (New York: HarperCollins, 1994), 115.
[34]Edwards, *WJEO*, 11:3.
[35]Richard Dawkins, *The Selfish Gene* (Oxford: Oxford University Press, 1978).

conventional term we use to group all these individual creatures together—it is an imaginary concept that is useful for intellectual sorting, but it has no metaphysical substance. So says the nominalist. How does this lead to the present state of disenchantment? Eventually, working out its own logical conclusion, it strips the natural world of transcendental meaning. Any transcendental meaning we intuit in the natural world is not really there but is rather an imposition of our own thought-life—it is our naming. While nominalism may not require something like Hume's skepticism and its subsequent fruit, the latter is not possible without the former.

The realist, on the other hand, insists on the reality of universals. The most significant realist in the ancient philosophical tradition is Plato (427–347 BC). He is so significant, in fact, that it is not uncommon to use *realism* and *Platonism* as interchangeable terms. For Plato, the individual expressions of reality in this world—the particulars—are individual participants in their true, transcendental "forms." These "forms" or "ideas" exist in an ethereal realm apart from the material world in which you and I inhabit, but the world you and I inhabit, according to Plato, participates derivatively in this world of "forms" or "ideas."[36] The essence of an individual human is humanness—and that essence is real, and is not exhausted by the individual human. I am truly human, but I do not exhaust the essence of humanity. Rather, I participate in the essence of humanity, which is real and would exist regardless of whether I was ever born. This insistence on the reality of universals—and the denial of nominalism—is an essential feature of the Platonic tradition. I intend to position myself within this intellectual tradition when I call myself a "classical realist."[37]

---

[36]For a very helpful and accessible introduction to this aspect of Plato's metaphysic, Markos, *From Plato to Christ*, chap. 2.

[37]There is obviously so much more we can say on this topic, but for the purpose of appropriate brevity, I content myself to commend the following resources to the interested reader: Tyson, *Return to Reality*; Lloyd P. Gerson, *From Plato to Platonism* (Ithaca, NY: Cornell University Press, 2013); Lloyd P. Gerson, *Platonism and Naturalism: The Possibility of Philosophy* (Ithaca, NY: Cornell University Press, 2020); Edward Feser, *Scholastic Metaphysics: A Contemporary*

Participating in God

Why do I make this appeal to classical realism? Simply this: such a metaphysic provides a rationale for what becomes incredibly an important point for our discussion on the beatific vision: creation's *participation* in God. To get at this topic, we seek the help of Thomas Aquinas. Aquinas famously makes use of Aristotle's four causes, formal causation (i.e., that which a thing is made into), efficient causation (i.e., that which acts upon a thing to make it what it is), material causation (i.e., that which a thing is made out of), and final causation (i.e., that for which a thing is made—its telos or end). According to Aquinas, God *is* three of these four causes in relation to creation, notably excluding material causation.[38] This exclusion capitalizes the Creator-creature distinction; were God to be creation's *material* cause, pantheism would be all but inevitable. But since God is creation's formal, efficient, and final cause—and is the *cause* of creation's material cause—creation participates in the gratuitous being of God asymmetrically. "All beings apart from God are not their own being," notes Aquinas, "but are beings by participation. Therefore it must be that all things which are diversified by the diverse participation of being, so as to be more or less perfect, are caused by one First Being, Who possess being most perfectly."[39]

Andrew Davison notes, "When it comes to creatures, the core of the idea of participation is that things are what they are by participation in God: they are what they are because they receive it from God."[40] This brings us necessarily into contact with the doctrine of *analogia entis*—the analogy of being, which is "the assumption of

---

Introduction (Heusenstamm: Editiones Scholasticae, 2014); Alexander J. B. Hapton and John Peter Kenny, eds., *Christian Platonism: A History* (New York: Cambridge University Press, 2021); Craig A. Carter, *Contemplating God with the Great Tradition: Recovering Trinitarian Classical Theism* (Grand Rapids, MI: Baker Academic, 2021); Craig A. Carter, *Interpreting Scripture with the Great Tradition: Recovering the Genius of Premodern Exegesis* (Grand Rapids, MI: Baker Academic, 2018); Boersma, *Heavenly Participation*; Sabastian Morello, *The World as God's Icon: Creator and Creation in the Platonic Thought of Thomas Aquinas* (New York: Anglico, 2020).

[38] Aquinas, *ST*, I.44.2-3.
[39] Aquinas, *ST*, I.44.1.
[40] Davison, *Participation in God*, 22.

an *analogia*, or likeness, between finite and infinite being, which lies at the basis of the a posteriori proofs for the existence of God."[41] Crucially, this doctrine stresses both similarity and dissimilarity between finite being and infinite being. The needle the *analogia entis* helps us thread is the avoidance of the dual error of assuming, on the one hand, that God and creation share nothing in common (equivocal being) and, on the other hand, that God and creation *share* in being (univocity of being). But God does not belong to a genus or species. He does not *participate* in a category of being broader than himself. By virtue of his simplicity, we must deny that his existence and being are distinct. God alone is his own existence. He, therefore, possesses his being by nature, while all that is creaturely has being by *reception*. Davison stresses the significance of this feature:

> A participatory approach to theology wishes to stress that God is prior to the world in every way. That underlines our problem when it comes to speaking about God, cautioning us to avoid idolatry. However, it also provides the key to understanding how human language, as used, for instance, in the Bible, can indeed apply to God after all. The legitimacy of that endeavor does not rest on God's being like the world but rather—as the trace-like way that we have encountered throughout this book—on the world imitating God.[42]

This means that the chief characteristic of all creaturely being is its indebtedness to divine beatitude. To say this much is to say far more than the simple statement that God made creation. We rather take a step forward and say that God made creation to share in his goodness after his likeness. The resounding announcement "it was good" in the creation narrative of Genesis's opening chapter can be fruitfully read in light of the *analogia entis*. Creation's Creator is *good*, and creation is good because it participates in and imitates the Creator. Infinite being is good, and finite being is good because

---
[41] Muller, *Dictionary*, 24.
[42] Davison, *Participation in God*, 172.

it participates in and imitates infinite being. This is how God is glorified in creation. He makes all that is creaturely to participate in and imitate that which is glorious. All things are from and through and to God (Rom 11:36; cf. Acts 17:24-27). And this means that God is also the *final* cause of everything that is creaturely. All that exists, exists *for God*.

Man is no exception to this creaturely rule, and indeed—as one who is made uniquely *in the image of God*—it is a punctuation thereof. And it is at this point that our metaphysical discussion above takes us directly into the fray of anthropological concerns and the beatific vision. God is the final cause of all creaturely being, including man. What does the final realization of that telos look like for man? *The beatific vision*. This is clear not only for Christians who fulfilled Plato's philosophy with doctrine he lacked but also, in some measure, to *Plato himself*. In his *Symposium*, Plato explains how the true philosopher is one who leaves the cave of shadows (the world of becoming) behind to ascend the ladder of philosophical contemplation to approach the world of forms (the world of being). This process begins "rather mundanely, with the love of physical beauty as it is manifested in one particular person. But the initiate does not stop here. Love of a single beloved must expand, in time, to include love for all forms of physical beauty."[43] "If he makes it this far up the runs of the ladder," notes Markos, "Plato promises . . . he will see, not only the Forms, but the Form of the Forms. He will see Beauty as it is in itself, a beauty that does not change or grow dim or die. Seeing that Beauty will mark the end of his journey (his *telos*), but the Beauty itself will be revealed to him as the *archē*, the origin or final cause of all his yearning."[44]

This journey of the philosopher that Plato envisions is the journey of the soul striving toward the beatific vision. What Plato saw as in a mirror dimly lit, God's saints, with the aid of regenerative grace

---

[43]Markos, *From Plato to Christ*, 73.
[44]Markos, *From Plato to Christ*, 74.

and special revelation, saw with clarity: the telos of the human soul was to "dwell in the house of the Lord" and to "gaze upon the beauty of the Lord"—*this* is the *one thing* to ask of the Lord (Ps 27:4).

Despite the differences that would develop among Aquinas and the post-Reformation theologians regarding a *donum superadditum* (Aquinas's view) vs. a *donum concreatum* (the post-Reformation view), both agreed with the conviction that the highest goal and final end of man was to *see God*.[45] For Aquinas, there is no stronger argument for this than the persistence of desire itself.[46] "There is pleasure in the intellect about knowing truth," says Aquinas, "but sadness results in the will about the known thing inasmuch as the thing's action causes harm, not inasmuch as it is known. But God is truth itself. Therefore, the intellect seeing God cannot fail to take pleasure in seeing him."[47] Davison observes how "Aquinas sees this desire for God, which is intrinsically also desire for one's own completion, as underlying all other desires. Anything we might worthily desire, for Aquinas, represents some step along the way to the attainment of God, just as the goodness of anything we might properly desire is there due to its participation in God."[48] As we shall see in chapters three and four, what Davison says about Aquinas here we can say about many other figures throughout the history of the church.

Rightful desire, in man, is the soul striving toward its telos, which it ultimately realizes in the beatific vision. All our longings for happiness are reflections of divine beatitude, beckoning us back to the efficient, formal, and *final cause* of all—the holy Trinity. In that sense, there is a kind of continuity between our desire on this side of our blessed hope, and our desire on the other side. The discontinuity is real and pronounced, but it is the difference between a

---

[45]These concerns will resurface in chaps. 4-5.
[46]Thomas Aquinas, *Compendium of Theology*, trans. Richard J. Regan (New York: Oxford University Press, 2009), 1.163-65.
[47]Aquinas, *CT*, 1.165.
[48]Davison, *Participation in God*, 118.

seed and its flower, not the difference between two kinds of seeds. "Through the participation that founds creation," notes Davison, "one apprehends God through creaturely things and concepts; in contrast, in the life of the world to come, the redeemed apprehend creaturely things in God, and through him."[49]

This, however, does not mean that in the beatific vision God is comprehended in a comprehensive sense. As the infinite one, God is *incomprehensible* to finite creatures. The infinite cannot be circumscribed by the finite. Creatures do not cease to be creatures in glory. In whatever sense a creature *sees* the essence of God, he sees him in a creaturely mode of knowing, which "always falls short of the knowability of God."[50] We ought not admit this fact reluctantly, as if it were a concession. It should not be a disappointment that a univocal vision of the essence of God is something we will never experience, as if we were missing out on something God would give us if he were more generous. All creaturely existence is a gift, *including* creaturely limitations. In that blessed vision, our comprehension and vision and delight, which are all *finite*, will be perpetually maximized. And as our capacity for comprehension and vision expands, so will our delight. In other words, the very limitations we are tempted to bemoan create the possibility of never-ending delight, where each level of enjoyment is topped by the next—forever. This upward spiral into deeper beatific communion with the Trinity will never be exhausted—because we are finite, and the object of our delight is infinite, our blessedness will increase forever. "In your presence there is fullness of joy; at your right hand are pleasures forevermore" (Ps 16:11).

All this means that the deeply human desire for transcendence does not occur in a vacuum. God did not make us with a desire that could not be satiated: he has "eternity" in our hearts (Eccles 3:11) so that our soulish thirst would be satisfied in this blessed hope, this

---

[49]Davison, *Participation in God*, 298.
[50]Davison, *Participation in God*, 299.

telos, this absolute end. The hopeless conclusion of nominalism's secular offspring is incorrect—the transcendent is not simply a projection. The sense of divine estrangement that has come to mark our disenchanted age is so devastating *because* it is so profoundly unhuman. Lewis was right, therefore, when he observed that "if I find in myself a desire which no experience in this world can satisfy, the most probable explanation is that I was made for another world."[51]

---

[51]C. S. Lewis, *Mere Christianity* (New York: HarperCollins, 2001), 136-37.

2

BIBLICAL FOUNDATIONS FOR THE BEATIFIC VISION

PART OF WHAT IT MEANS TO BE REFORMED and evangelical is that one affirms without any reservation the conviction of *sola Scriptura*. Such a conviction is the inheritance of the Protestant reformers, who recovered and codified this biblical and ancient allegiance to divine authority.[1] To affirm that our ultimate authority is Scripture alone is not to say that the only authority we recognize is Scripture. The Bible itself testifies to the legitimacy of other authorities, including the authority that parents exercise over their children (Eph 6:1-3), husbands over their wives (Eph 5:22-24), pastors over their flock (1 Tim 3:2-7; Heb 13:17), congregations over their wayward members (Matt 18:17), and governments over their subjects (Rom 13:1-2). Even the authority of tradition is recognized and legitimized within the Scriptures (2 Thess 2:15). In many an evangelical circle, this latter authority has been all but lost, and *sola Scriptura* has been misrepresented to signify a narrow biblicism that functionally amounts to an antipathy for tradition. In some cases, it can eventuate into gross and sinful hubris. In direct contradiction to biblical instruction, we can come to disobey the commands to "honor our fathers and mothers" (cf. Ex 20:12) and "remember our leaders" (Heb 13:7), and come to embrace a chronological snobbery in the

---

[1] I say "recover" because the Reformers did not *invent* this doctrine. See, for example, Mark D. Thompson, "Sola Scriptura," in *Reformation Theology: A Systematic Summary*, ed. Matthew Barrett (Wheaton, IL: Crossway, 2017).

stead of a humble disposition to gratefully receive the riches of God's gift of history. This is why our next two chapters unabashedly embrace our long Christian history. I believe we ought to have a deferential instinct toward tradition, and therefore part of my justification for retrieving the lost doctrine of the beatific vision is its historical pedigree. If we are to depart from such an ecumenical doctrine, we ought to have very good reasons, drawn faithfully from the Scriptures (and in this chapter, I intend to demonstrate that we do not).

Having said all of this, we would not help our current situation if we swung the pendulum too far in the other direction and concluded with a slavish subservience to tradition that functionally renders Scripture unable to speak for itself. The Scriptures' perspicuity and sufficiency are, after all, essential attributes that accompany the Reformation conviction of *sola Scriptura*. While *sola Scriptura* does not mean that every other relative authority ceases to exist, it does mean something. *Sola Scriptura* means that every authority bends the knee to God's authority exercised in the Scriptures. Our allegiance to the Bible is a direct reflection of our allegiance to God, since the Scriptures are his breathed-out, authoritative words (2 Tim 3:16). The great tradition is a derived authority—carrying a real authority because, and only insofar as, it faithfully transmits what the Bible grants as the "faith once for all delivered to the saints" (Jude 3). It is the whole counsel of God, including both that which is expressly taught and that which is binding by good and necessary consequence, that stands as the measuring stick for all other authorities.

I mention this conviction regarding biblical authority because while the historic witness of the beatific vision is significantly authoritative, it is authoritative only insofar as the doctrine has a biblical rationale. This chapter is dedicated to the biblical warrant for the beatific vision. I will here survey a handful of major biblical passages and themes that conspire together to give the great tradition (and us today) every justifiable reason for holding firm to this glorious doctrine.

OLD TESTAMENT DEVELOPMENTS[2]

We may categorize the Old Testament's teaching on the beatific vision in two broadly distinct categories: (1) passages about theophanic encounters with God, wherein the beatific vision is signaled to or longed for or partially glimpsed by individuals throughout the Old Testament, and (2) passages about eschatological promises of a consummate theophanic encounter with God. Several examples of each category are worth mentioning.

Old Testament theophanies. The first example of an Old Testament theophany we must mention is the first Old Testament theophany recorded: Genesis 3, which tells of how Yahweh himself would walk "in the garden in the cool of the day" (Gen 3:8). Here, in this unfallen state of innocence and original righteousness, Adam and Eve had unhindered access to the presence of Yahweh, and it was this access from which they were driven after their treachery with the forbidden fruit (Gen 3:22-24). Such a primeval experience should not properly be called *beatific*, since this whole episode bespeaks a future promise that Adam and Eve forfeit.[3] What they experienced was a theophanic encounter with Yahweh, which hinted at a fuller future fulfillment of beatitude associated with the tree of life (cf. Gen 2:9; 3:22-24; Rev 22:2). They never enjoyed this fuller experience, which explains the severe heartbreak of this episode. The tragedy lies not simply in what they *had* and lost but also what they *could have had* and forsook.

Despite Adam and Eve's treachery, theophanic encounters did not altogether cease at the fall. Throughout the Old Testament, Yahweh graciously grants partial glimpses of his glorious face, which often serve to awaken a desire within his saints for a greater beatific

---

[2] I am indebted to my colleague and friend Adam Brown for his crucial feedback on an early draft of this section, which served to strengthen it considerably.

[3] I am, of course, referring to the Covenant of Works, a defense and full explanation of which is beyond the scope of this present work. For more, see J. V. Fesko, *Adam and the Covenant of Works* (Ross-shire, UK: Mentor, 2021); J. V. Fesko, *Last Things First: Unlocking Genesis 1–3 with the Christ of Eschatology* (Ross-shire, UK: Mentor, 2007).

vision. These theophanic experiences are often portrayed as encounters with "the angel of the LORD." Some of these encounters may be properly described as "Christophanies"—that is, instances where the angel of the LORD is more specifically conceptualized as the pre-incarnate *Son* taking on a temporary *form* of a man—but not all.[4] Examples of "angel of the LORD theophanies" would include Genesis 16:7-16, when the angel of the LORD came to Hagar to promise the birth of Ishmael (note verse 13, when Hagar "called the name of the LORD *who spoke to her*"), or Genesis 32:22-32, when Jacob wrestles with the angel of the LORD and plainly declares, "I have seen God face to face, and yet my life is delivered" (Gen 32:30), or Joshua 5:13-15, when Joshua meets "the commander of the LORD's army" and is told to remove his sandals, since the ground on which he stands is made holy by the commander's presence (Josh 5:15; cf. Ex 3:5), or Judges 13:8-25, when the angel of the LORD comes to the wife of Manoah to promise the birth of Samson, which elicits the terrified exclamation of Manoah, "We shall surely die, for we have seen God" (Judg 13:23).

There are also examples throughout the Old Testament of theophanic encounters that do not directly involve the angel of the LORD, but rather describe God powerfully manifesting himself in glory in other ways. Such examples would include Genesis 28:1-22, when Jacob receives his dream of a ladder to heaven (cf. Gen 35:1-15), or Exodus 3–4, when Moses encounters the presence of God on Mount Horeb and is given his covenantal name for the first time: "I am who I am" (Ex 3:14). His second theophanic encounter with Yahweh on Mount Horeb in Exodus 33–34 (more on this episode below) could also be included; or Exodus 40:34-38, when the glory of the LORD fills the tabernacle upon its completion; or Isaiah 6, when Isaiah receives his vision of Yahweh enthroned in his heavenly

---

[4]For a helpful introductory overview of theophany and Christophany, see David H. Wenkel, *Shining like the Sun: A Biblical Theology of Meeting God Face to Face* (Bellingham, WA: Lexham, 2016), 6-7.

temple; or Ezekiel 1:4-28, when the prophet's vision includes his sight of "the likeness of the glory of the Lord" (Ezek 1:28).

In all these examples, theophanic encounters with the face or glory of Yahweh awakens fear and reverence from their participants. And yet, these episodes intrinsically maintain a hint of longing and intrigue. While Jacob, Moses, Joshua, Isaiah, and Ezekiel are terror-stricken by their theophanic encounters, we get no hint of *regret* or *resentment* for having experienced them. These figures get a taste of what Adam and Eve forfeit, which means there must have been, at some deep image-bearing level, a sense of gratification. And yet, they experienced this taste of Eden from a state of fallenness, which explains the sense of fear and humiliation (and in some cases, we might even say *terror*) that is characteristic in such episodes. These theophanies, therefore, rightly awaken within the careful reader a sense of expectation and hope for a full and unhindered consummate experience *without* the obstacle of sin. Before considering some Old Testament examples of eschatological promise, let us zoom in and consider at length a significant example of Old Testament theophany: Exodus 33–34.

What Moses experiences on Mount Horeb in this passage becomes paradigmatic for man's theophanic encounter throughout the Scriptures. In his book *Shining Like the Sun: A Biblical Theology of Meeting God Face to Face*, David H. Wenkel says that "in the book of Exodus Moses becomes the archetype of the one who meets with God and is physically changed."[5] From a purely literary point of view, this passage is picked up and quoted or alluded to all throughout the Scriptures, including in 1 Kings 19:9-18, when Elijah encounters God in his glory on the same mountain; Matthew 17:1-13, when Christ is transfigured; and crucially, 2 Corinthians 3:12-4:6, which we will return to with great interest. To enter fully into this passage is to be immersed in a profound mystery, whose

---

[5]Wenkel, *Shining like the Sun*, 30.

logic runs throughout the entire canon of Scripture: on the holy mountain, safe within the cleft of the rock, Moses glimpses the glory of God and is transformed by what he sees.

Chapter 33 of Exodus begins in a tragedy of sorts. After Israel's shameful episode with the golden calf at the foot of Sinai (Ex 32), God now instructs Moses to lead Israel away from Sinai, except this time, God informs him that he will not accompany them. Because they are a stiff-necked people, God's immanent presence with them poses an existential threat (Ex 33:3), and this grieves the people of Israel (Ex 33:4-6). In contrast to the rest of the children of Israel, Moses continued to meet with God regularly in the tent of meeting. God's presence *with Moses* was evidenced by the pillar of cloud that would stand at the entrance of the tent while Moses met with God inside, speaking with him "face to face" (or "mouth to mouth," according to Num 12:6-8), "as a man speaks to his friend" (Ex 33:10-11). Indeed, Moses had by now grown somewhat accustomed to experiencing intimate communion with God—something that began for him as early as Exodus 3, when Moses received his "call to ministry" before the bush that burned "and yet was not consumed" (Ex 3:2). It was here, on "Horeb, the mountain of God" (Ex 3:1), before the burning bush, that God introduces himself to Moses, naming himself as the *a se* covenant-making, covenant-keeping God of his ancestors: Yahweh, the one *who is*, is he who speaks with Moses (Ex 3:14). Now, in Exodus 33, we find Moses once again on Horeb, "the mountain of God," meeting with Yahweh.

Crucially, this entire episode must be kept in view of the *first* time Moses was instructed by Yahweh to ascend Sinai after Israel had been delivered (Ex 24:12). Just as then, here in Exodus 33, Moses went alone, having never withdrawn his instructions to the elders of Israel, "Wait here for us until we return to you" (Ex 24:14). The elders, in other words, were only permitted to remain at the base of the mountain, and never to ascend to the place where Moses went. This detail, though seemingly mundane, will be important to recall when considering our next passage in Isaiah 24–27.

Despite the fact that by Exodus 33, Moses had already encountered Yahweh's glory in unparalleled ways, he nevertheless expresses a deep yearning to transcend the "face to face," "mouth to mouth" experiences with which God had graced him. He begs, "Please show me your glory" (Ex 33:18). However significant his previous theophanic encounters were, they did not satiate the anticipatory desire that compelled Moses to make such an audacious request. "Whatever Moses saw in the fire," Wenkel argues, "was more diminutive than what he experienced as he was hidden in the cleft of the rock."[6]

The broad outlines of this event are clear enough. Moses requests to see God's glory (Ex 33:18), and God partially agrees to meet this request with the important qualifiers that (1) Moses is to receive his vision only from the confines of safety within the cleft of a rock and the protective hand of God himself, and (2) Moses is to only see God's *back* and not his *face* (Ex 33:19-23). God eventually fulfills this request, passing before Moses while proclaiming his name: "The LORD, the LORD, a God merciful and gracious, slow to anger, and abounding in steadfast love and faithfulness, keeping steadfast love for thousands, forgiving iniquity and transgression and sin, but who will by no means clear the guilty, visiting the iniquity of the fathers on the children and the children's children, to the third and fourth generation" (Ex 34:6-7). In response to this experience, Moses "quickly bowed his head toward the earth and worshiped" (Ex 34:8).

The full effects of this encounter are not yet known until Moses descends from the mountain to reunite with Israel. Here, we discover that Moses was transformed by his vision of God's glory. He discovers, because of their reaction, that "the skin of his face shone, because he had been talking to God" (Ex 34:29). Having beheld, in

---

[6]Wenkel, *Shining like the Sun*, 34.

some measure, the glory of God, Moses' face became glorious by consequence. Moses began to look a little like God. Fittingly, then, the people of Israel responded in fear; they required for the glory on his face to be hidden (Ex 34:30-35). Just as they were afraid to speak to God because of his glorious holiness (cf. Ex 20:18-21), so now they became afraid to speak to Moses directly on account of God's glorious holiness that lingered on Moses' face.

With a general outline of the passage before us, we can now focus in on several noteworthy characteristics of this biblical scene that should inform our conception of the beatific vision. First, there is a persistent note of *anticipation* throughout this entire scene. Not only is this clear from the fact that Moses feels compelled to ask for an experience of divine glory that he has not yet experienced, despite his speaking "face to face" and "mouth to mouth" with Yahweh in the tent of meeting, this note of anticipation persists even through and beyond this transcendent experience of Exodus 33-34. Moses' response is granted, but only in a qualified and partial sense. The question stubbornly remains: is there hope for fulfillment of this request to an even greater degree? Is there a scenario in which one can ache after the same vision that Moses longs for and receive what he seeks *without* the qualification—without the limitation of a *partial* fulfillment? Is there a scenario in which God will show his *face* and not merely his *back*? This question lingers and is not answered until later in redemptive history, but its persistence is itself informative for our doctrine of the beatific vision. Moses *wants* the beatific vision. At the very least, the desire for the sight of God's glory is good and biblical.

Second, this passage teaches us a great deal about the nature of the beatific vision. Namely, we learn from this passage that the beatific vision is a gracious accommodation, a gratuitous condescension. And in this way, it is a revelation of God's attributes. We should note, for example, what function as synonyms in this passage. Moses asks for God to show him divine "glory" (Ex 33:18), and God responds by assuring him that his "goodness" (Ex 33:19) shall pass before him as he proclaims his name. This vision will be a vision of his "back" (Ex 33:23), which will be a partial glimpse of what is found in God's "face" (Ex 33:20). Thus, God's "glory" will pass before Moses (Ex 33:22), a promise fulfilled when "the Lord passed before him" (Ex 34:4). Here, "glory," "goodness," "face," and even "back" are all, in an important sense, synonymous with *each other*, and a synecdoche for *Yahweh* himself. What Moses sees in part and obscurely (i.e., God's "back") is a glimpse of what he cannot see with his full gaze (i.e., God's "face"): God's "glory," his "goodness," his *self*. The beatific vision, therefore, is the sight of God himself. The beatific vision is God's incomprehensible and ineffable glory beheld directly. Again, Moses was not granted access to this beatific vision in full, but that is precisely what he was asking for.

Third, we learn from this passage that the sight of God's glory is transformative. Of course, Moses himself did not see God's *face* in this passage—he saw his "back." He never saw "the most intense and intimate display of God's glory."[7] And this fact of Moses' incomplete and partial experience actually drives home the point of theophanic transformation. "If Moses' face was shining from simply talking to God," reasons Wenkel, "how much more would he be changed if he could actually bear to come into his presence."[8] The transformative nature of the beatific vision is something we will return to throughout this book.

Fourth, this passage points beyond itself to a christological fulfillment. God's accommodation, by which he grants Moses' request, comes in the form of a mediation of sorts: Moses is hid in the cleft of the rock, covered over by the hand of God, prohibited from seeing God's face directly. The christological fulfillment of this passage practically preaches itself. We have explicit biblical warrant to identify the rock and its water in the wilderness with Christ and

---

[7] Wenkel, *Shining like the Sun*, 36.
[8] Wenkel, *Shining like the Sun*, 36.

Biblical Foundations for the Beatific Vision   31

his spiritual nourishment (cf. Ex 17:1-7; 1 Cor 10:4); is it not fitting to see *this* rock in which Moses hides too as a type of Christ?[9] Where else is an ultimate mediation to be found? From within the safety of the rock on Mount Horeb, Moses gets a glimpse of God's glory—but not his face—and from within the safety of Christ, God's glory is mediated. In him, and in his *face*, we see "the glory of God" (2 Cor 4:6). In order to see God's glory, God must accommodate our finitude and our weakness. He does this for Moses in the form of hiding him in the cleft of a Rock, and he does this for us by hiding us in the refuge of his Son (cf. Ps 2:12). God accommodates his glory by hiding Moses in the cleft of a Rock, we might say, "*who is Christ.*"

Old Testament eschatological promises of the beatific vision. In addition to theophanic encounters, the Old Testament also teaches on the beatific vision by way of eschatological promise. Job clings to such eschatological hope in Job 19:23-29 when he confesses, "After my skin has been thus destroyed, yet in my flesh *I shall see God*" (Job 19:26, emphasis added). Isaiah signals to this beatific vision throughout his prophecy, including Isaiah 24–27 (more on this below), 59–64, and 65:17–66:23. Such a beatific hope is at the heart of the great day of the LORD in its consummate and restorative form, promised in Joel 3:16-21, when "the mountains shall drip sweet wine, and the hills shall flow with milk, and the foundation shall come forth from the house of the LORD and water the Valley of Shittim" (Joel 3:18); Zephaniah 3:14-20, when "it shall be said to Jerusalem; 'Fear not, O Zion; let not your hands grow weak. The

---

[9]R. B. Jamieson and Tyler R. Wittman helpfully point out that while Gregory of Nazianzus and Gregory of Nyssa interpret the "rock" of Exodus 33 as Christ himself, while Augustine interprets it as Peter's being a stand-in for the entire church (see Augustine, *The Trinity* 2.30; Gregory of Nazianzus, *Oration* 28.3; and Gregory of Nyssa, *Life of Moses* 2.244). Jamieson rightly observe that the christological importance of this passage remains in either case: "Whether the rock is the teaching of Christ one finds in the church or Christ himself, God's glory now encounters us in the man Jesus Christ." R. B. Jamieson and Tyler R. Wittman, *Biblical Reasoning: Christological and Trinitarian Rules for Exegesis* (Grand Rapids, MI: Baker Academic, 2022), 8.

Lord your God is in your midst, a mighty one who will save; he will rejoice over you with gladness; he will quiet you by his love; he will exult over you with loud singing'" (Zeph 3:16-17); and Zechariah 14, when "the Lord will be king over all the earth" (Zech 14:9). Before we turn our attention to New Testament developments regarding this doctrine of the beatific vision, we might benefit from taking a closer look at one particular example of the eschatological promise of the beatific vision in the Old Testament: Isaiah's prophetic vision in Isaiah 24–27.

Isaiah 24–27 is certainly one of the high points of Isaiah's entire prophecy since its scope is universal and its promises unsurpassed. John N. Oswalt notes how these chapters have "often been called the Apocalypse of Isaiah, because their focus is upon the worldwide triumph of God," and it is properly called "eschatological" since "the overriding theme of the segment is the triumph of God, not only *over* his enemies but *for* his people."[10] These chapters tell of Yahweh's destruction of the earth in a display of perfect wrath (Is 24:1-20), his final triumph over death (Is 25:6-9), the resurrection of the dead (Is 26:19), the destruction of "Leviathan" (Is 27:1), the utter exaltation of Jerusalem (Is 27:12-13), and, central to our concerns, Israel's elder's enjoyment of the beatific vision (Is 24:23).

Adam Stewart Brown argues that Isaiah 24:1-20 "is the foundational text that is elaborated upon by the six sections in 24:21–27:13, each identified by the introductory ... 'it shall be' or ... 'in that day.'"[11] The sheer scope of these first twenty verses supports this claim: they describe "the day" that the rest of this apocalyptic poem refers to throughout. This is the day that Yahweh will "empty the earth and make it desolate" (Is 24:1). So thorough will be his judgment that no partiality will be discernible for those who

---
[10]John N. Oswalt, *The Book of Isaiah: Chapters 1–39* (Grand Rapids, MI: Eerdmans, 1986), 440, 443, emphasis original.

[11]Adam Stewart Brown, "The Isaiah Apocalypse: A New Form Critical Look at the Genre, Structure, Content, and Function of Isaiah 24–27," PhD diss., McMaster Divinity College, 2016, 117.

experience it. The priests will suffer with their people, the master with his slave, the mistress with her maid, the buyer with the seller, the lender with the borrower, the creditor with the debtor—all will feel the effect of this judgment (Is 24:3). Brown notes how "the allusions to Babel (especially Gen 11:4, 8, 9) and the Flood (Gen 6:11; 7:11; 9:1-7, 16) suggest that a universal judgment (akin to Babel) with cosmic, world-ending implications (akin to the Flood) are intended by the context."[12] Further, I would add that Isaiah 20:4-5 is strongly suggestive of an allusion to something even more primordial than the tower of Babel in Genesis 11 or the worldwide flood in Genesis 6: the fall of mankind in Genesis 3. Isaiah tells of how the earth in its entirety languishes as a result of the transgression of laws and the breaking of "the everlasting covenant" (cf. Rom 8:20-22). What Isaiah depicts in these verses, in other words, is the consummate repayment and resolution of sinful debt accrued not by individual sins here or there, but *sin itself*, beginning with that primeval sin in the Garden of Eden. It is therefore appropriate to see a parallel between the contrasting reaction of verses 14-16, and a similar contrast observable in Revelation 18:1–19:10. Just as how the fall of Babylon in Revelation 18–19 elicits praise in heaven (Rev 19:6-8) and mourning on earth (Rev 18:16-18), so too does Yahweh's judgment of the cosmos elicit praise from Israel's remnant who have escaped judgment (Is 24:14-16a), while Isaiah himself is left to take in the earthly horror of the scene (Is 24:16b). The same apocalyptic event calls forth praise and lamentation.

Importantly, included in this day of judgment is the final destruction of Satan himself. Interpreters argue over the precise identity of "Leviathan . . . the twisting serpent . . . the dragon that is in the sea" in Isaiah 27:1, whom Yahweh will "punish" and "slay" with his "hard and great and strong sword." Some emphasize that Yahweh's vanquishing of the serpent bespeaks his sovereign lordship

---

[12]Brown, "The Isaiah Apocalypse," 136-37.

over created things—including sea creatures and monsters that haunt the dreams of men—while others note how "it is possible to connect Leviathan with imperial powers."[13] Both of these realities are probably intended by Isaiah 27:1, but most fundamentally, Isaiah clearly has the ancient serpent Satan in view (cf. Gen 3:1; Rev 12:3-5, 17; 20:2, 7-10). Thus, "just as all imperial resistance to Yahweh shall fall, so also the root of human rebellion, the serpent itself, will be dealt a death blow once and for all. This climactic victory expunges the most basic and foundational source of rebellion in all creation."[14] This being the case, the events corresponding with Satan's destruction in Isaiah 24–27 match perfectly with the events corresponding to Satan's destruction in Revelation 21–22, namely, death being swallowed up forever (Is 24:7; cf. Rev 20:13), the resurrection of the dead (Is 26:19; cf. Rev 20:12), Yahweh wiping the tears from the eyes of his beloved saints (Is 25:8; cf. Rev 21:4), and Yahweh's glorious presence with his people, making all other sources of light completely obsolete (Is 24:23; cf. Rev 21:23-24; 22:3). In other words, here in this climactic high point described in Isaiah 24–27, we see not only the reversal of Israel's desolation brought about by her enemies but rather the complete reversal of sin and its many tragic effects.

The apex of this entire passage is found in the consummate reality of Isaiah 24:23, "Then the moon will be confounded and the sun ashamed, for the LORD of hosts reigns on Mount Zion and in Jerusalem and his glory will be before his elders." This detail of the elders' presence on the mountain and their access to the LORD's glory is noteworthy. Not only does it anticipate the presence of the "elders" before the throne of God in John's apocalypse (Rev 4:10-11; 5:6-14; 7:13-17), it also recalls Exodus 24:14, when the elders of Israel were disallowed from ascending the mountain of Yahweh with Moses. Here, in Isaiah 24:23, Yahweh delivers a promise of staggering proportions. Whereas Exodus 24:14 left the elders at the foot

---

[13]Brown, "The Isaiah Apocalypse," 191-92.
[14]Brown, "The Isaiah Apocalypse," 192.

of the mountain, unable to approach Yahweh to the degree granted to Moses, Isaiah 24:23 pictures them *on* the mountain, beholding the very glory Moses pined after—and was not *fully* given access to—in Exodus 33:18. In the end, when the last will be first and the first will be last, those who could not go as far as Moses will surpass him. What Moses longed for in Exodus 33:18, and what the elders are promised to receive in Isaiah 24:23, is none other than the blessed hope of the beatific vision. J. Alec Motyer makes this point well:

> Isaiah here looks back to Exodus 24:9-11. The Sinai covenant was consummated by a theophany, with the Lord among the elders of Israel. There, they saw but his feet; here, they will see his glory. Thus Isaiah sees the Zion-to-be as the fulfilment of all that the covenant implied. The adverbial translation *gloriously* is acceptable but Isaiah's Hebrew is exclamatory: "and before his elders, glory!" (cf. 4:5).[15]

Here, then, as in no other place in the Old Testament, the beatific vision is held out as a substantive and sure promise for the people of God, though exactly *how* Yahweh would accomplish this great feat without wiping out his people along with his righteous destruction of the wicked is not answered until Yahweh comes in the flesh to reveal as much.

New Testament Developments

As we approach the New Testament, the shape of this hope and vision comes into much sharper focus. The "vision of God" and the theophanic experience of seeing him "face to face" enters into a much higher and richer register with the redemptive-historical and literary entrance of Jesus Christ, the God-man. Christ, as the "yes and amen" to all of God's promises (2 Cor 1:20), is the embodied culmination of countless themes developed in the Old Testament, including this hope for the beatific vision. This is made explicit in

---

[15] J. Alec Motyer, *The Prophecy of Isaiah: An Introduction and Commentary* (Downers Grove, IL: IVP Academic, 1993), 206-7.

passages like 2 Corinthians 3:12–4:6, where believers of the new covenant are compared to Moses on Mount Horeb in Exodus 33–34. The new covenant is better than the old, Paul argues, in part because *all* who live within this new covenant community find themselves standing there with Moses, beholding the glory of God. However, unlike Moses, we feel no compulsion to veil what we have seen, since "we are not, like so many, peddlers of God's word, but as men of sincerity, as commissioned by God, in the sight of God we speak in Christ" (2 Cor 2:17; cf. 2 Cor 4:2). Speaking in Christ comes with a kind of sincerity and transparency; we *want* for others to see and hear our message, because "what we proclaim is not ourselves, but Jesus Christ as Lord, with ourselves as your servants for Jesus' sake" (2 Cor 4:5). We long for people to see the glory of God in our message because, unlike the terror-inspiring impact of Moses' glorious face, the glory that shines forth in the new covenant ministry *creates life* (2 Cor 4:6). This does not mean, of course, that the divine glory revealed to Moses was different from the divine glory believers behold in the face of Jesus Christ. God's glory does not change. The difference between this divine glory's *impact* has everything to do with the presence of Christ, our divine mediator.

What is more, we new covenant believers are not like Israel, asking for a veil to obscure our vision. We are rather like Moses, begging the Lord to show us his glory (2 Cor 3:18; cf. Ex 33:18). But God's "yes" to this request does not come with nearly as restrained a qualification as Moses received—we look straight on to the very same "light" that brought creation out of nothing (2 Cor 4:6), and as we look on, we, like Moses (but in a *better* way on account of our better promises enacted by a better covenant, per Heb 8), are transformed into what we behold.[16]

---

[16]For a thorough treatment of this theme of being transformed into what we behold, see G. K. Beale's magisterial work, *We Become What We Worship: A Biblical Theology of Idolatry* (Downers Grove, IL: IVP Academic, 2008). Also, for an extended treatment on this passage in 2 Corinthians in particular, see Parkison, *Irresistible Beauty: Beholding Triune Glory in the Face of Jesus Christ* (Ross-shire, UK: Mentor, 2022), chap. 5.

How is it possible for new covenant saints to see so much? Because what we look at by faith is "the glory of God in the face of Jesus Christ" (2 Cor 4:6). Christ, as the "image of the invisible God" (Col 1:15), the "radiance of the glory of God and the exact imprint of his nature" (Heb 1:3), and the eternal "Word" who was "with God" and "was God" (Jn 1:1), is the fullest revelation of God. The incarnation of God the Son is the absolute apex of all divine self-revelation, and the God-man is therefore the perfect and infallible exegete of the divine nature.[17] In Christ, the Trinity has done far more than temporarily place us within the cleft of a rock and shown us his back as he passed by—in Christ, God has "tabernacled" among us (cf. Jn 1:14). Because of this, those who encountered (and who *still* encounter by faith) the glory of Jesus experienced a theophany far more direct than any Old Testament figure without exception. The theophanic experience of beholding Christ's glory outshines Moses' encounter on Mount Horeb, and even Isaiah's heavenly vision (Is 6). To affirm this much is not to say that everyone who encounters Jesus' glory know themselves to be experiencing a theophanic encounter that dwarfs such Old Testament giants—indeed, there is an ironic "veiling" and "unveiling" dynamic to Jesus' ministry, wherein his glory is revealed *through* his weakness and suffering.[18] In fact, in John 12:36b-44, the beloved disciple explicitly states that the glory of Isaiah's heavenly vision in Isaiah 6 is the very same glory of the suffering servant described in Isaiah 53, which is manifested preeminently in the life and ministry of Christ. The glory of Isaiah 6 and Isaiah 53 is *Christ's* glory.[19] The inability to see Christ's glory truly is owing not to divine obscurity, but spiritual blindness (Jn 1:11).

Even still, there are moments in the life and ministry of Christ where those around him recognize the divine glory that confronts

---

[17]For more on this line of argumentation, see Parkison, *Irresistible Beauty*, chap. 3.
[18]See Jonathan King, *The Beauty of the Lord: Theology as Aesthetics* (Bellingham, WA: Lexham, 2018), 141-211.
[19]See Parkison, *Irresistible Beauty*, 119-22.

them—like Peter's Isaianic cry of despair, "Depart from me, for I am a sinful man" (Lk 5:8; cf. Is 6:5), or the disciples fearful worship of Christ on the boat after he calms the storm (Mt 8:23-27; Mk 4:35-41; Lk 8:22-25), or the transfiguration of Christ (Mt 17:1-13; Mk 9:2-13; Lk 9:28-36).

We will return to the transfiguration event momentarily, but the conspicuous absence of this episode in John's Gospel is worth mentioning. Why does John not write about Christ's transfiguration directly? We may begin to approach an answer when we consider how prominently John features the motif of "light" in his writings. The word "light" is used over thirty times in his corpus. "Whether we begin with John's Gospel or letters, we begin with a God who is light and life."[20] "Light" obviously features significantly in Jesus' transfiguration, and so it is not at all unfounded to suggest that the divine glory John beheld on the holy mountain that day is the effulgent radiance that enlightens *all* of his writings. In other words, there is a real sense in which John ascended the mountain with Christ and Peter and James, and *never came down*. All that John wrote was composed, as it were, within the light of Christ's transfigured glory.

First John 3:2.[21] Given John's preoccupation with the light of Christ's glory, it is not at all surprising that one of the most significant passages of the New Testament for our doctrine of the beatific vision comes from his writing. In his first epistle, John writes one of the most affective and pastorally tender passages in all the New Testament:

> See what kind of love the Father has given to us, that we should be called children of God; and so we are. The reason why the world does not know us is that it did not know him. Beloved, we are God's children

---

[20] Ike Miller, *Seeing by the Light: Illumination in Augustine's and Barth's Reading of John* (Downers Grove, IL: IVP Academic, 2020), 154.

[21] For a similar summary of 1 John 3:2 and 1 Corinthians 13:12, see Parkison, *Irresistible Beauty*, 209-13.

now, and what we will be has not yet appeared; but we know that when he appears we shall be like him, because we shall see him as he is. And everyone who thus hopes in him purifies himself and is pure. (1 Jn 3:1-3)

The affection-stirring impact of these verses is doubly punctuated when the context of 1 John is kept in view. This congregation was shaken by the horror of apostasy, and members who were thought to be faithful brothers and sisters in Christ had turned out to be antichrists (cf. 1 Jn 2:18-19). In addition to the painful experience of betrayal that accompanies such a church fracture, John's audience was in desperate need of assurance. One can imagine the self-doubt that can creep in if not only one, but *many* of your most trusted and mature fellow church members apostatize and depart from the faith. If such could happen to *them*, what assurance do any of us have that we are truly "in the faith?" This epistle is, in part, an answer to such a question. This means the confident confession of 1 John 3:1-3 is a *hard-won* confidence. Not lightly does John exclaim, "See what kind of love the Father has given to us, that we should be called children of God; and so we are" (1 Jn 3:1). With the full weight of such a thought settling on the minds of his audience, then, John naturally turns their gaze heavenward. Being called a child of God now comes with eschatological consequences: "Beloved, we are God's children now, and what we will be has not yet appeared" (1 Jn 3:2a). However, this ignorance of "what we shall be," for John, is not a reason to be discouraged or ambivalent about the future. Rather, such an ignorance intensifies the anticipatory nature of the hope.

John does not conclude his thoughts about "what we shall be" with his present ignorance, however. He goes on to say, positively, that "we know that when he appears we shall be like him, *because we shall see him as he is*" (1 Jn 3:2b). There are galaxies contained in that little word *hoti* ("because"). How should we understand the relationship between "being like him" and "seeing him as he is?" Thomas Andrew Bennet rightly answers that the "theological freight of the text as a whole pushes us to read the second clause as explanatory."[22] Which is to say, we shall be like him *because* we shall see him as he is. Thus, Bennet goes on to grant,

> The metaphysics of the idea must necessarily elude us, but the logic is quite familiar to human experience. Bearing witness to great beauty or great ugliness has transformative impact.... John imagines that this principle will apply in toto when we are confronted by the unvarnished beauty of Christ at his arrival. Seeing him "as he really is" indicates that up until that time, human eyes will not really have apprehended the full beauty and divinity of eternal life and that when they do, the sight will overwhelm and change them.[23]

Of course, this verse does not settle the difficult question of the relationship between the beatific vision and *theōsis* (or deification— the final and consummate union with God) in an *ultimate* or eschatologically initial sense (i.e., in glory, are we able to see God because we have been transformed into holy creatures by deification, or are we deified and sanctified because we see God? Does the beatific vision result from, or cause, *theōsis*?). We will return to this question again in chapter five. However, it is worth mentioning that 1 John 3:2 strongly suggests that however *theōsis* and the start of the beatific vision is initiated in the eschaton, the ongoing process of *theōsis* is at least in some sense furthered and intensified by *seeing* God. In other words, 1 John 3:2 seems to suggest that "being like him" is at least in some sense the result of "seeing him."

First Corinthians 13:12. Interestingly, engendering hope in the beatific vision is a pastoral concern shared by New Testament authors across differing contexts. This fact of contextual diversity hints toward the conclusion that the beatific vision is not the preoccupation of one or two biblical authors but exists as a kind of "north

---

[22]Thomas Andrew Bennett, *1–3 John: The Two Horizons New Testament Commentary* (Grand Rapids, MI: Eerdmans, 2021), 57.

[23]Bennett, *1–3 John*, 57. Smalley seems to concur with Bennett on this interpretation. See Stephen S. Smalley, *1, 2, and 3 John*, Word Biblical Commentary, rev. ed. (Grand Rapids, MI: Zondervan Academic, 2006), 139-40.

star" for all biblical authors. For example, Paul's concerns in his first epistle to the Corinthians are no less pastoral than John's for his audience in 1 John, but their contexts were incredibly different. "If John's audience was burdened with a crippling loss of confidence, marked by fear and timidity, Paul's audience was burdened with the opposite: a misplaced confidence in themselves."[24] And yet, even for the Corinthians, the hope of the beatific vision applies. John's audience needed the beatific vision to stir their hearts in confident hope in Christ, and Paul's audience needed the hope of the beatific vision to serve as a humbling corrector of sorts, reordering their values appropriately. The Corinthians pridefully boasted in the various manifestations of gifts in their body life (cf. 1 Cor 1:7), so much so that they prized the unruly exercise thereof (1 Cor 12-14) over the straightforward concerns of unity (1 Cor 1:10-17; 3:1-23; 11:17-34) and holiness (1 Cor 5:1-13; 6:12-20; 8:1-13; 10:1-22).

Right in the middle of instructions regarding right worship and the appropriate practice of spiritual gifts (1 Cor 12-14), Paul calibrates the attention of his audience with the heavenly permanence of love (1 Cor 13). In other words, in Paul's estimation, the Corinthian preoccupation with undisciplined exercise of spiritual gifts was evidence of an inappropriate this-worldly and vainglorious concern. He does not, however, calibrate their disordered priorities by disparaging the exercise of gifts. Indeed, Paul can even go so far as to encourage the Corinthians to "earnestly desire" the supernatural sign gifts (1 Cor 14:1), so long as those gifts are appropriately valued as a means to that which is more enduring and teleologically oriented: love (1 Cor 13:8-10). Love for Christ and his body is the end for which prophecy and tongues exist ultimately, which means love endures past this present age and into the eschaton, "when the perfect comes" (1 Cor 13:10). Tom Schreiner helpfully notes, "The gifts will become otiose and useless, not

---

[24]Parkison, *Irresistible Beauty*, 211.

because they are inherently bad, but because they are partial and incomplete . . . They are useful and edifying, but they are not the *summum bonum*."[25] The true *summum bonum*, the highest good, is not the practice of spiritual gifts, which serve as means to the end. The true end is none other than that for which Moses asked (Ex 33:18), what David asked of the Lord (Ps 27:4), and what John inspired his readers to confidently await (1 Jn 3:2): seeing God "face to face." "For now we see in a mirror dimly, but then face to face. Now I know in part; then I shall know fully, even as I have been fully known" (1 Cor 13:12). Amazingly, Paul calls our vision of Christ here and now a vision that is merely "in part" and as though through a "mirror dimly." This description is amazing because it almost appears to clash with what he has said elsewhere about how much we know and how much we see in this age. According to Paul, the natural world offers a perspicuous declaration of the divine nature and Godhead (Rom 1:20; cf. Ps 19:1-6). According to Paul, we see the image of the glory of God in the face of Jesus Christ, which is an image not unlike what Moses himself saw on Horeb (2 Cor 3:18–4:6). According to Paul, we have the Scriptures, which are the very breath of God himself (2 Tim 3:16). And yet, for all the glorious revelation we have in the book of creation and the book of the Scriptures, all our knowledge amounts to *dim* and *partial* insights compared with what we shall comprehend when we "see him as he is." Without diminishing the greatness of the revelation we have in this life, Paul magnifies the hope of our knowledge of God in the next. Calvin shows this point powerfully: "For we have in the word (in so far as is expedient for us) a naked and open revelation of God, and it has nothing intricate in it, to hold us in suspense, as wicked persons imagine; but how small a proportion does this bear to that vision, which we have in our eye! Hence it is only in a comparative sense, that it is

---

[25]Thomas R. Schreiner, *1 Corinthians: An Introduction and Commentary* (London: Inter-Varsity Press, 2018), 281.

termed obscure."[26] Similarly, Gregory of Nazianzus is instructive in his consideration of this verse in light of (1) God's incomprehensibility, and (2) *theōsis*. He writes,

> No one has yet discovered or ever shall discover what God is in his nature and essence. As for a discovery some time in the future, let those who have a mind to it research and speculate. The discovery will take place, so my reason tells me, when this God-like, divine thing, I mean our mind and reason, mingles with its kind, when the copy returns to the pattern it now longs after. This seems to me to be the meaning of that great dictum that we shall, in time to come, "know even as we are known."[27]

For Paul, any consideration of the supernatural sign gifts that are not eschatologically and teleologically oriented to this beatific vision of *love* for Christ is misguided. All other desires are subsumed under this one.

Second Peter 1:16-21. Another fascinating cluster of passages that instructs us regarding the beatific vision comes to us through 2 Peter 1:16-21. Peter wrote this letter toward the end of his life, as his "final word" to the church.[28] He clearly felt compelled to leave his readers with "reminders." In this way, he parallels Moses and the book of Deuteronomy, urging his readers to remain faithful and to

---

[26] John Calvin, *Commentary on the Epistles of Paul the Apostle to the Corinthians*, vol. 1, trans. John Pringle (Edinburgh, UK: Calvin Translation Society, 1848), 431.

[27] Gregory of Nazianzus, *Oration* 28.17.

[28] I am taking Petrine scholarship for granted here, in part because exhaustively *arguing for it* is beyond the scope of this work, and also because none of the arguments *against* Petrine authorship are all that convincing, since (1) they are predicated questions of dating that often assume what they are trying to prove; (2) they take for granted that the real Peter could not have possibly been influenced by the real Jude, and vice versa; and (3) they unnecessarily assume that the extreme stylistic difference between 1 and 2 Peter precludes that the author could be the same (imagine arguing that either the author of the Narnian books or the author of *The Discarded Image* had to be pseudepigraphal by the same logic). The best argument of Petrine authorship for a biblical inerrantist like myself is found in 2 Peter 1:1: "Simeon Peter, a servant and apostle of Jesus Christ." I rest my case there. For similar and more robust defenses, see Peter J. Leithart, *The Promise of His Appearing: An Exposition of Second Peter* (Moscow, ID: Canon, 2004); Thomas R. Schreiner, *1 & 2 Peter and Jude* (Nashville: B&H Academic, 2003); and D. A. Carson and Douglas J. Moo, *An Introduction to the New Testament*, 2nd ed. (Grand Rapids, MI: Zondervan Academic, 1992), 659-63.

"enter into the heavenly Promised Land," so to speak. This parallel is why "remembering" is such a central theme of this letter (2 Pet 1:9, 12, 13, 15; 3:1). Peter desires not only for his readers to hear one more parting word from him before he finishes his pilgrimage, he also desires for his readers to pick up the mantle and continue to run the race of faith to the end in light of the impending "day of the Lord" (cf. 2 Pet 3:1-13). So, the occasion for 2 Peter is twofold: first, the end of Peter's *life* is at hand, and second, the end of *history* is approaching. As Peter finishes his pilgrimage on this earth, leaving followers and students behind, he wants them to stay faithful to the end, with their hope set on the resurrection of the dead. The new heavens and the new earth, and endless communion with Christ: this is the Promised Land they must not shrink back from.

Crucial for understanding 2 Peter is the recognition that Peter's audience was *mocked* for holding on to the promise of the future arrival of Christ and a future kingdom (cf. 2 Pet 3:4). Because of this, a perennial temptation for them would be to forsake a heavenly hope in otherworldly blessings and instead embrace this-worldly indulgences (cf. 2 Pet 2:14-16). Why should they continue to suffer for some future promise that looks less and less real, when the promise of sensual gratification is immanent?

Peter meets this challenge head on. It is as if Peter says with this final letter, "I'm not going to be with you much longer, so before I leave, let me remind you to keep your eye on the prize—keep your hope secure in Christ and keep steadfast in your pursuit of godliness until you cross over the Jordan River into the Promised Land." Second Peter 1:16-21 in particular includes one angle of this motivation for faithfulness: Peter *entices* his readers with *the majesty of Christ*. He showcases how beautiful and awesome and glorious Christ is, and thus shows how faithfulness to him dwarfs anything the scoffers could ever conjure up:

> For we did not follow cleverly devised myths when we made known to you the power and coming of our Lord Jesus Christ, but were

eyewitnesses of his majesty. For when he received honor and glory from God the Father, and the voice was borne to him by the Majestic Glory, "This is my beloved Son, with whom I am well pleased," we ourselves heard this very voice born from heaven, for we were with him on the holy mountain. (2 Pet 1:16-18)

Peter reminds his readers that the gospel he shared with them, and the hope of heaven that he called them to, was not the invention of some overactive imagination. They received this message from someone who walked and talked with the Lord Jesus. Not only that, Peter himself—the one who "made known to [them] the power and coming of our Lord Jesus Christ"—*saw* the majesty of Christ with his own two eyes. Peter impresses upon his readers the value and bona fide assurance of what is offered them in Christ, as if to say, "The kind of blessing you are looking forward to in the second coming is no pipe-dream: *I saw it myself, and it was glorious.*" Of course, Peter thus refers to the transfiguration of Christ (cf. Mt 17:1-13; Mk 9:2-13; Lk 9:28-36). While it does not often receive very much attention from evangelicals, this sacred event is an important development in the life and ministry of Christ, and indeed, in the whole Bible.[29] In this event, Jesus takes Peter, James, and John up on what Peter calls "the holy mountain." In doing so, these three disciples follow the path of many Old Testament figures, including (most relevantly), *Moses* and *Elijah*.

In order to fully grasp the weight of what Peter is doing with this reference to "the holy mountain," it is worth reflecting on the experiences of divine glory which Moses and Elijah similarly had on their own "holy mountain." For Moses, as we saw before, the "holy mountain" experience is described in Exodus 33–34. On Mount Horeb, Moses asks to see God's glory, and God graciously accommodates his glory to partially grant his request. The nineteenth

---

[29] Many thanks to Patrick Schreiner, who let me peek at an early draft of *The Transfiguration of Christ: An Exegetical and Theological Exploration* (Grand Rapids, MI: Baker Academic, 2024) while I wrote this chapter.

chapter of 1 Kings recounts Elijah expressing a similar request. After his famous standoff with the priests of Baal (1 Kings 18:20-38), he, like Moses, goes up to Mount Horeb (1 Kings 19:8) and hides himself in a cave (1 Kings 19:9). Even if Elijah did not enter the same cave (or "rock") as Moses, the literary parallels are suggestive of, at the very least, *conceptual* proximity between Elijah's cave and Moses' rock. In the narrative, Elijah flees to this place in distress: he thought that he alone was the only faithful one left in Israel (1 Kings 19:10), so he went to this spot in order to receive a glimpse of God. Like with Moses, the Lord passes by Elijah. However, God did not pass by in the wind, the earthquake, or the fire, but rather in a low whisper (1 Kings 19:11-12). Elijah's coming to this location was a request to experience God's glory, and like with Moses, God graciously grants him this request. In response, Elijah veils his face—he "wrapped his face in a cloak" (1 Kings 19:12).

These are striking parallels: both these men went up on the very same mountain to (possibly) the very same spot in order to experience the glory of God. *Both* of them were graciously met with an experience of divine glory—both wanted to *see* and both *heard* the glory of God (Moses in Yahweh's declaration of his divine name in Exodus 34:6-8, and Elijah in the whisper of Yahweh's voice in 1 Kings 19:12). *Both* of them were transformed by the experience—Moses had a shining face (Ex 34:29-35), and Elijah was transformed from a fearful and cowering fugitive into a courageous and obedient prophet (1 Kings 19:19-21). And *both* of them covered their face in response (Ex 34:29-35; 1 Kings 19:12).

That these similarities of mountain experiences should exist between these two figures who stand with Jesus in his moment of transfiguration is very unlikely to be a coincidence. Of all the figures that could be standing with Jesus on the holy mountain as James, John, and Peter look on, it is Moses and Elijah—both of whom requested and experienced divine glory on the "mountain of God"—who are present. The christological and trinitarian implications that result from this passage are significant. Moses' and Elijah's being on the mountain when Christ was transfigured is not merely pointing to the fact that the Law and the Prophets are fulfilled in Christ (with the Law being represented by Moses and the Prophets being represented by Elijah). This may very well be the case (indeed, there are probably many other dimensions to their being on the mountain with Christ beyond this potential symbolism).[30] But their presence surely also testifies to the divine glory of Christ. Both of these men requested to see the glory of God on the mountain, and here they are, talking *with Christ on the holy mountain*. It is as if their request is being granted all over again.

Thus, by seeing and hearing the glory of Jesus on that mountain, Peter, James, and John saw and heard the glory of the holy Trinity. Descending from heaven, the Holy Spirit manifests himself as a bright cloud. And it is from this glory cloud that the Father speaks and testifies to the identity and trustworthiness and biblical fulfillment of his Son (Mt 17:5; Mk 9:7; Lk 9:34). So the Spirit—who proceeds eternally from, and is eternally breathed out by, the Father and the Son[31]—with his bright presence gives voice to the Father's speech, and the testimony from this trinitarian mountaintop experience is clear: divine glory is revealed preeminently in none other than Jesus Christ. "He is God from God," as the Nicene Creed says, "Light from Light, very God from very God." To behold the glory of Christ is to behold the glory of *God*—the same glory Moses saw and heard, Elijah heard, and Isaiah saw (Is 6:1-7; 53; cf. Jn 12:36-43) is the glory James, John, and Peter saw and heard on the holy mountain.

Returning to 2 Peter, the connection between the transfiguration and the beatific vision should become clear. Peter reminds his

---

[30]For an exploration of how to interpret the Old Testament prophets' presence with Jesus on the mountain, see Schreiner, *The Transfiguration of Christ*, chap. 2.

[31]See Schreiner, *The Transfiguration of Christ*, chap. 2. Cf. Matthew Barrett, *Simply Trinity: The Unmanipulated Father, Son, and Spirit* (Grand Rapids, MI: Baker Books, 2021), chap. 9; Scott R. Swain, *The Trinity: An Introduction* (Wheaton, IL: Crossway, 2020), chap. 6; and Thomas Joseph White, *The Trinity: On the Nature and Mystery of the One God* (Washington, DC: The Catholic University of America Press, 2022), chap. 27.

readers of this crucial event to confirm his authority, and he does so within the context of his final letter to them. Everything he writes in this letter is self-consciously written within the shadow of God's heavenly mountain. In other words, this story is recounted in service to his exhortation to stay faithful as they look forward to their hope of heaven (see the end of verse 19: "until the day dawns and the morning star rises in your hearts"). Is it not interesting that as Peter's days on earth come to a close, he finds his mind returning to this moment of his life, when he saw Christ transfigured on the holy mountain? Is this not because he saw, on that mountain, a preview of coming attractions? He received a foretaste of heaven there on that mountain a foretaste of *the beatific vision*—that happy sight of God.

Of course, the relevance for Peter's own personal experience on the lives of his readers is not immediately apparent. How does *his* personal experience benefit them? If this were all Peter had to offer his readers, it would not be immediately obvious how they would benefit from remembering that Peter experienced such a vision on the holy mountain (apart from confirming Peter's authority, which is no small point, to be fair). Peter, however, goes on in this same passage to assure his readers that they are *not* left emptyhanded. In fact, this moment of transfiguration on the holy mountain actually serves to confirm more fully something else:

> And we have the prophetic word more fully confirmed, to which you will do well to pay attention as to a lamp shining in a dark place, until the day dawns and the morning star rises in your hearts, knowing this first of all, that no prophecy of Scripture comes from someone's own interpretation. For no prophecy was ever produced by the will of man, but men spoke from God as they were carried along by the Holy Spirit. (2 Pet 1:19-21)

Peter's argument does not reach its climax with the transfiguration of Jesus but rather with the *Scriptures* that Jesus' transfiguration confirm. If Peter's readers wish to see the light of Christ's glory—the very same light that he saw on the holy mountain—he assures them that they can. In fact, they are charged to *carry* this light with them on their pilgrimage through this dark world—this light is found, Peter assures his readers, in the Scriptures. And this point parallels the theology of 2 Corinthians 3:12–4:6 as well. The "light of the glory of God in the face of Jesus Christ" (2 Cor 4:6), according to Paul, *objectively* emanates from the Old Testament (or "Moses" per 2 Cor 3:15). Those who are blinded by the satanic veil that remains over their hearts do not see Christ's glory there (2 Cor 3:13-15; 4:4), but this does not change the fact that Christ's glory shines there. The same creative light that shone forth at the creation of the cosmos—and that *will* shine forth at the re-creation of the cosmos—shines forth in the hearts of individuals when Christ is preached (2 Cor 4:6). Here, in the faithful proclamation of the Word, the beatifical glory of God in the face of Christ—the glory that Peter saw in part on the holy mountain, and which we shall all see in full in glory—is accessible for the eyes of faith.[32]

Revelation 22:3-5. An inescapable conviction for all Christians is that human history is marching on toward a conclusion in the eschaton. History has a telos. All who confess the Nicene Creed express the yearning: "I look for the resurrection of the dead and the life of the world to come. Amen." The consummate place in all of Scripture wherein this telos is described is in the Bible's capstone: the book of Revelation, and particularly Revelation 21–22. These final chapters come on the heels of war and struggle and violent, just, *judgment*. Believers seem to never tire over disputing the nature of the millennium in Revelation 20:1-6 and the subsequent judgment of Satan and all unbelievers in 20:7-14, but for all the diversity of interpretations for Revelation 20, no one can deny the clear contrast that erupts in the book with the arrival of chapters 21 and 22. With the final defeat of Satan, sin, and death, and the final

---

[32] For a much more in-depth look at this passage and theme, see Parkison, *Irresistible Beauty*, chap. 5.

exclusion of all signs of sin and its consequences behind, the final chapters of Revelation look forward to nothing but light and holiness and satisfaction and bliss. The accumulation of descriptions, mysterious and awe-inspiring, are nearly too much for the careful and immersed reader.

Revelation 21:1-8 describes the scene in sweeping and general terms. Here, at last, Christ's bride—the church—is "adorned for her husband" (Rev 21:1-2). Here, at last, "the dwelling place of God is with man. He will dwell with them, and they will be his people, and God himself will be with them as their God" (Rev 21:3). What all the Scriptures anticipate and long for is realized in this passage. No more does God's dwelling with man elicit fear or dread, because here at the close of redemptive history, every vestige of sin (and therefore, every vestige of reason for fearing the presence of holiness) is already excluded (Rev 21:8; cf. Rev 21:27). God's presence, now, does not mean the undoing of his people (cf. Is 6:5), for he comes to "wipe away every tear from their eyes," for "death will be no more, neither shall there be mourning, nor crying, nor pain anymore, for the former things have passed away" (Rev 21:4).

John then goes on to describe the New Jerusalem in vocative terms, deploying a multitude of images that overwhelm the senses. The "holy city Jerusalem" is said to have "the glory of God, its radiance like the most rare jewel, like a jasper, clear as crystal" (Rev 21:10-11). In this new Jerusalem, the walls are built of jasper, the city is made of pure gold—"like clear glass"—the wall's foundations are "adorned with every kind of jewel": jasper, sapphire, agate, emerald, onyx, carnelian, chrysolite, beryl, topaz, chrysoprase, jacinth, and amethyst (Rev 21:18-20). The gates of this new Jerusalem are made "of a single pearl, and the street of the city" is also made of pure gold (Rev 21:21). Such a description of earthly royal adornments is surely suggestive of even greater spiritual realities we cannot fathom, yet even the analogous imagery of these familiar earthly riches stretches the imagination. The brightness and majesty of such a mental picture can scarcely be painted by the most imaginative among us. Yet, lest we be tempted even for a moment to make the eschaton about material possessions, John explicitly states the heart of what makes the holy city so richly beautiful. These adornments befit and express and reflect the eternal beatitude—the gratuitous and enriching presence—of the eternally rich and majestic triune God. "And the city has no need of sun or moon to shine on it, for the glory of God gives it light, and its lamp *is the Lamb*. By its light will the nations walk" (Rev 21:23-24, emphasis added). Here, the theologically pregnant statement of David in Psalm 36:9 is manifested in eschatological glory: "For with you is the fountain of life; in your light do we see light." Christ, according to John, is God's light within this new Jerusalem. In *his Light*—who is Christ—we shall see light. This city is described as so overwhelmingly rich, in other words, because he who is life and light *himself*—the King and his Lamb and the Spirit of the bride who says "come" (Rev 22:17, emphasis added)—is there. What makes heaven *heaven* is the enlightening and enlivening presence of God himself. Andrew Davison is right, therefore, to note that "through the participation that founds creation, one apprehends God through creaturely things and concepts; in contrast, in the life of the world to come, the redeemed apprehend creaturely things in God, and through him."[33]

So, John uses such a rich array of images to describe this heavenly city because only such language befits a description of what impact God's presence has. If this much were not clear enough from Revelation 21, John goes on to punctuate the point of God's beatific presence in the first verses of chapter 22. The "river of life" that nourishes the "tree of life" whose leaves are "for the healing of the nations," *flows from the throne of God and of the Lamb* (Rev 22:1-2). All that heals and feeds and nourishes and grants life overflows

---

[33]Davison, *Participation in God: A Study of Christian Doctrine and Metaphysics* (New York: Cambridge University Press, 2019), 298.

from the triune God himself, which is why his saints are described the way they are in the very next verses: "No longer will there be anything accursed, but the throne of God and of the Lamb will be in it, and his servants will worship. They will see his face, and his name will be on their foreheads. And night will be no more. They will need no light of lamp or sun, for the Lord God will be their light, and they will reign forever and ever" (Rev 22:3-5).

If the book of Revelation is the Bible's capstone, and chapters 21–22 are Revelation's capstone, we could scarcely exaggerate the importance of the saints' worship in these verses. Herein do we find the telos of all who are called to be sons of God: the worshipful gaze of God on his throne and his Lamb. Brian Tabb notes how the phrase, "They will see his face," "signals a new level of intimate knowledge and access to God not previously experienced by his people."[34] Tabb goes on to demonstrate that Revelation 22:4 is the culmination and realization of all that the saints long for throughout the Scriptures. The promise of Revelation 22:4 is what Moses asked for (Ex 33:18), what the Old Testament priests hopefully and faithfully pronounced over Israel as a promised benediction (Num 6:25-27), and what the faithful throughout the Psalter beseeched God for (Ps 31:16; 67:1; 80:3, 7, 19; 119:135). "Finally," says Tabb, "in the holy city 'the upright will see his face' (Ps 11:7), gaze upon his beauty (Ps 27:4) and be transformed by his glorious sight (Rev 22:4; cf. Matt 5:8; 1 John 3:2; *4 Ezra* 7.89; *T. Zeb.* 9.8)."[35] If John does *not* intend for his readers to latch onto this blessed vision as their hope of hopes—as heir consummate fulfillment of *all* their longings for God—then he was hopelessly obscure about what kind of hope he *was* intending to encourage his readers with. The beatific vision as the Christian's telos is overwhelmingly communicated with Revelation 22:4.

---

[34]Brian J. Tabb, *All Things New: Revelation as Canonical Capstone* (Downers Grove, IL: IVP Academic, 2019), 197.
[35]Tabb, *All Things New,* 197.

Conclusion

This chapter has scratched the surface of biblical support for the doctrine of the beatific vision. Thus far, I have not even mentioned the hope of Christ's *appearing* described throughout the pastoral epistles (cf. 1 Tim 6:14; 2 Tim 4:1-2; 4:8; Titus 2:12).[36] Further, the hope of the beatific vision is expressed in many ways throughout the Scriptures that do not speak explicitly about *seeing* but rather employ other analogies, such as the absence of evil, final justice, light and glory, treasure, eternal Sabbath rest, the new Jerusalem, and the like.[37] If this is true, then in addition to the passages listed above in making our biblical case for the beatific vision, it would be appropriate to elicit support from a plethora of other passages (e.g., Is 7:17, 7; 25:8; 32:17; 49:10; 65:16, 19; Mt 8:11; 22:1-10; Lk 14:16-24; 2 Cor 5:1; Eph 1:14; 5:27; Col 1:12; 1 Pet 1:4). While we will have time to explore some of these other metaphors in the coming pages, even the modest examination of the handful of passages I have examined in this chapter provides some very useful observations regarding the beatific vision. Simply in light of what lies on the surface of the texts explored above, we conclude with the following five observations.

First, *the desire for the beatific vision is good and godly*. One of the most incredible features of Moses' experience on Mount Horeb is that he was not rebuked as being audaciously presumptuous for requesting to see God's glory (Ex 33:18). Instead, God condescends and partially grants his request, insofar as Moses is able to have this request granted (given his location from a redemptive-historical and eschatological perspective). At the very least, this reveals that Moses was not *wrong* to want to see God's glory. Which is to say, it is not as if Moses is indulging in craven and ungodly curiosity here,

---

[36] For a brief discussion on these passages, see Parkison, *Irresistible Beauty*, 209.
[37] See Francis Turretin, *Institutes of Elenctic Theology*, 3 vols., ed. James T. Dennison, trans. George Musgrave Giger (Phillipsburg, NJ: P&R, 1997), 20.8.18; and Jaimeson and Wittman, *Biblical Reasoning*, 6.

longing to look into something that does not in the least concern him. Indeed, there seems to be the subtext of a moral pronouncement when Moses' glowing face is contrasted with Israel's fearful demand for a veil. Israel's unwillingness to see Moses without his veil parallels their unwillingness to be addressed by Yahweh directly, and God's (and Moses') concession in both these examples communicates that they did, in fact, have a point. They are right, in other words, to be uneasy, and so they are not *entirely* wrong for wanting Moses to mediate their relationship with God (and for wanting the veil to mediate their relationship with Moses' face). But this concession is in light of their *sinfulness*. Contained in the concession, in other words, is a rebuke: it would be better if *all* Israel shared with Moses the desire to see Yahweh's glory. This suggestion is further reinforced by David's "one thing" desired in Psalm 27:4. By inspiring and placing such a prayer in the Psalter, God the Spirit endorses this desire as good and godly. It is right, in other words, for we who read David's prayer to say along with him: "One thing have I asked of the Lord, that will I seek after: that I may dwell in the house of the Lord all the days of my life, to gaze upon the beauty of the Lord and to inquire in his temple." And the final confirmation that this desire is good and godly comes when we see this desire met in glory, when the saints worship before the throne of God, *seeing him* (Rev 22:4). While we will return again to the theme of "desire" and its place in the beatific vision, it is fitting for us to conclude with C. S. Lewis that this desire for the beatific vision is deeply human, and organically connected with *all* human desire:

> If I find in myself a desire which no experience in this world can satisfy, the most probable explanation is that I was made for another world. If none of my earthly pleasures satisfy it, that does not prove that the universe is a fraud. Probably earthly pleasures were never meant to satisfy it, but only to arouse it, to suggest the real thing. If that is so, I must take care, on the one hand, never to despise, or be unthankful for, these earthly blessings, and on the other, never to mistake them for

something else of which they are only a kind of copy, or echo, or mirage.[38]

Second, *the beatific vision entails a paradox of somehow "seeing" the invisible.* Some theologians, particularly of the (Dutch) Reformed of evangelical variety, have tended, in the past couple hundred years or so, to minimize the significance of the doctrine of the beatific vision. Even a towering figure like Herman Bavinck cannot seem to discuss the doctrine without stating far more explicitly what he *does not* believe about it than what he does.[39] So, while Bavinck does not formally criticize or deny the doctrine, he is very critical of how it has been received throughout the great tradition, and some have said he ends up "sidelining it as the ultimate human telos."[40] There are any number of reasons for this minimization of the beatific vision (and we will explore them in greater detail in chap. 4),[41] but one of the reasons worth mentioning here is the very clear biblical affirmation of God's *invisibility* and *incomprehensibility*. Some would dismiss the doctrine as nonsensical simply because, as God told Moses, "no one can look at [him] and live" (Ex 33:20). God is he who is "the King of the ages, immortal, invisible" (1 Tim 1:17). God is he who "alone has immortality, who dwells in unapproachable light, whom no one has ever seen or can see" (1 Tim 6:16). God is he whom "no one has ever seen" (1 Jn 4:12). "No one has ever seen God" (Jn 1:18), says the Beloved Apostle. Certainly, God *is* incomprehensible, and his

---

[38]C. S. Lewis, *Mere Christianity* (New York: HarperCollins, 2001), 137, emphasis added.

[39]See, e.g., Hermann Bavinck, *Reformed Dogmatics*, 4 vols. ed. John Bolt, trans. John Vriend (Grand Rapids, MI: Baker Academic, 2003–2008), 2:188-91; 2:542-48; 4:720-30.

[40]Hans Boersma, *Seeing God: The Beatific Vision in the Christian Tradition* (Grand Rapids, MI: Eerdmans, 2018), 40. For Boersma's interaction with Bavinck, see *Seeing God*, 33-40. It should be acknowledged that Boersma's assessment has not gone unchallenged. In response to his reflections in *Seeing God*, both Cory Brock and Nathaniel Gray Sutanto have responded at length. See Cory Brock, "Revisiting Bavinck and the Beatific Vision," *Journal of Biblical and Theological Studies* 6, no. 2 (2021), 367-82; Nathaniel Gray Sutanto, "Herman Bavinck on the Beatific Vision," *International Journal of Systematic Theology*, August (2022), https://doi.org/10.1111/ijst.12610. For more on this discussion, see chap. 5.

[41]See also Michael Allen, *Grounded in Heaven: Recentering Christian Hope and Life on God* (Grand Rapids, MI: Eerdmans, 2018), chap. 1.

incomprehensibility for creatures is not a result of creaturely *sin* but rather creaturely *nature*. The infinite cannot be circumscribed by the finite, and so the creature cannot comprehend the Creator.

But the seemingly paradoxical relationship between God's invisibility and the beatific vision is simply none other than the paradoxical relationship between God's incomprehensibility and any divine self-revelation at all. In fact, virtually every passage that affirms God's invisibility paradoxically includes, within the same or nearby context, an affirmation of God's self-revelation. While "no one has ever seen God," John says in the same breath that "God, who is at the Father's side, he has made him known" (Jn 1:18). God is an "invisible God," says Paul, and yet "Christ is the image of the invisible God" (Col 1:15). Moses could not see God directly because "no one can look upon [him] and live," and yet, the author of Hebrews affirms Moses saw "him who is invisible" (Heb 11:27). The mystery of revelation is that the unknowable God makes himself known to creatures in a mode that befits their creatureliness. Similarly, the mystery of the beatific vision is that the invisible God is *beheld* in a mode that befits the creatureliness of the ones who will see him.

While there is certainly more to say about the relationship between God's invisibility and the beatific vision, we can content ourselves with the assurance that the seeming paradoxical nature of the dilemma is no reason for rejecting the doctrine. The Scriptures affirm that God is invisible, they also affirm that the saints in glory will *see him*; however we are to take these affirmations, we believe that they cannot be contradictory, and that they thus cohere at some mysteriously glorious level. In fact, the incomprehensibility of God, rightly conceived, actually serves to reinforce and amplify the bliss of the beatific vision. Man cannot know God *comprehensively*, but he can know him *truly*. Our finitude—in light of the infinite nature of his object—means that knowledge of God will increase in perpetuity *forever*. Likewise, man cannot *see* God's essence comprehensively, but the texts we have examined require for us to say that we can nevertheless see him truly at some level. And like with our knowledge of revelation in general, the finitude of our *seeing*, in light of the ineffable infinitude of our object, means that our happy vision will increase in depth and breadth and intensity forever. God's incomprehensibility and invisibility, in other words, need not contradict the beatific vision, but can in fact make it more glorious.

Third, *the beatific vision in the life to come entails some level of continuity with faith in the present time*. Both 2 Corinthians 3:12–4:6 and 2 Peter 1:16-21 are concerned primarily with seeing Christ's glory *by faith* now, not with seeing his glory in the beatific vision in the age to come. Nevertheless, in light of the eschatological context we have seen from our examination of these passages, they both imply that there is some continuity between what believers behold by faith now, and what they will behold by sight in glory. This is a point that John Owen brings up particularly well when he says that "no man shall ever behold the glory of Christ by *sight* hereafter, who doth not in some measure behold it by *faith* here in this world."[42] If Owen is right about how to understand the relationship between sight by faith in this life, and sight by beatific vision in the next, this affirmation makes sense of the observations listed above regarding *desire*. Does it not make sense for the object of all our love in this life to become sweeter and more desirable on our pilgrimage as we draw nearer to the Promised Land? Is it not right for our faith in Christ to increase in warmth and depth throughout this life? How fitting is it, then, for all the anticipation in this life to reach its zenith in the next, with the consummate realization of all we rightly longed for given in infinitely and ever-increasing measure?

Fourth, *the beatific vision and the transformation of the saint go hand in hand*. This affirmation is a direct continuation from the last.

---

[42]John Owen, *The Works of John Owen*, 16 vols., trans. William H. Goold (Edinburgh: The Banner of Truth Trust, 1968), 1:288, emphasis original.

If our "sight by faith" in the present life retains some kind of conceptual continuity with our beatific vision in the next, then there should persist a continuity with what our faith by sight effects in us now and what the beatific vision effects in us in glory. Like Moses in the cleft of the rock, when we behold the glory of God in the face of Jesus Christ, we are *transformed* "from one degree of glory to another" (2 Cor 3:18). Fitting, then, is John's description that in glory, we shall be like him, because we shall see him as he is (1 Jn 3:2). Seeing God more clearly transforms us into God more accurately; this is true for us now in this life, and it will be true for us later in the next as well. However, there is a "chicken and egg" conundrum that accompanies this clear transformative relationship between "seeing" and "becoming." This is because other passages seem to indicate that transformation is *prerequisite* for seeing God (cf. Mt 5:8). Revelation 22:4 says that the saints will see God, but before this happens, they will have already been vindicated in Christ and spared from divine judgment (Rev 20:11-15), and all that is ungodly and unbecoming of God's holy presence will have been banished (Rev 21:4; 8, 27; 22:3). This is to say, what we have seen at present does not definitively yield an answer to the question of which causes which in an *ultimate* sense: the beatific vision or the total transformation of the saint in glory. On the other hand, however we answer this question in an ultimate sense, we must at least say that ongoing transformation occurs *because* of the vision of God. Vision and transformation go hand in hand.

Fifth, *while believers in the intermediate state experience a kind of beatific vision, the consummation thereof is a resurrection reality.* The biblical account offers rich assurances to the believer who is "absent from the body." Such saints are "present with the Lord" (2 Cor 5:8), and this state of absence from bodily existence, Paul says, is something we should "rather" have. In other words, the intermediate state is *better* than the present state of dwelling in a fallen world with a body still burdened with the weight of "the flesh" (redeemed though we may be). The superiority of the intermediate state is owing not only to the fact of sinless perfection but more directly to the fact that such a state is marked by being *present with the Lord*. Such a prospect renders Paul "hard pressed" with what he would prefer between longevity of life in this world or death and intimate communion with Christ in the intermediate state: "Yet which I choose I cannot tell. I am hard pressed between the two. My desire is to depart and be with Christ, *for that is far better*. But to remain in the flesh is more necessary on your account" (Phil 1:22-23, emphasis added). I agree, then, with the Westminster Confession of Faith when it affirms that after death, "the souls of the righteous, being made perfect in holiness, are received into the highest heavens, *where they behold the face of God*, in light and glory, waiting for the full redemption of their bodies."[43] Thus, this "beholding the face of God" can, in some sense, be described as a "beatific vision." It is not *partial* in the sense we experience now—that is, in the way that our sight by faith is seeing "dimly" in this life (1 Cor 13:12)—and in that sense, there is nothing higher the departed saint can hope for in terms of the object of his sinless and perfect contemplation. Such a sight is beatific indeed.

However, our contemplation of God is not meant to be abstracted from bodily existence in a teleological sense. As human beings, we are created as body-soul components, and so while we cannot point to any reason for *discontentment* in the intermediate experience of beatific vision, we cannot point to such a state as consummate or teleologically fulfilled. The end for which we are made is not in any sense a bodyless state—even a *glorious* bodyless state, like the one into which departed saints enter. The consummation of the beatific vision, then, is the sight of God in the *resurrection*—after the glorified soul reunites with the glorified body. We say, with Job, "after my skin has been thus destroyed, yet *in my flesh* I shall see God"

---

[43] *The Westminster Confession of Faith*, 3rd ed. (Lawrenceville, GA: Committee for Christian Education and Publications, 1990), 32.1, emphasis added.

(Job 19:26, emphasis added). The final enjoyment of the beatific vision, therefore, cannot be when the souls of saints in the intermediate state "come alive" to "cry out with a loud voice, 'O Sovereign Lord, holy and true, how long before you will judge and avenge our blood on those who dwell on the earth?'" (Rev 6:9)—that is, when they "come alive" to "reign with Christ for a thousand years" (Rev 20:4)—but rather when in resurrected bodies, they stand before "the throne of God and of the Lamb" to "worship him," when "they will see his face, and his name will be on their foreheads" (Rev 22:3-4). Our theological reflections here are modest. After our historical survey, we will have recourse to more in-depth conclusions, as resolutions to the various quandaries raised over the centuries present themselves. Still, even this very brief list of theological conclusions reveals there is *much* to work with in the biblical data.

3

A CLOUD OF WITNESSES, PART ONE

Pre-Reformation Historical Witness

LEARNING FROM OUR OLDER BROTHERS and sisters of the faith is good stewardship. We have been given an embarrassment of riches in the inheritance of the great tradition. It does not honor our Father to ignore or disregard the gifts he has given us. We honor him, rather, by gratefully receiving the witness of the great tradition with an eagerness to learn. Doing so is to act in direct obedience to the sacred Scriptures (Heb 13:7). In his ascetic work, *On Virginity*, Gregory of Nyssa (AD 335–394) counsels his readers in much the same vein as Hebrews 13:7 ("Consider the outcome of their way of life, and imitate their faith."). "If you see a man so standing between death and life," says Gregory, "as to select from each helps for the contemplative course, never letting death's stupor paralyze his zeal to keep all the commandments, nor yet placing both feet in the world of the living, since he has weened himself from secular ambitions . . . imitate his youth and his gray hairs."[1] Gregory did not seem to have the same craving for originality so common among theologians today. For Gregory, far more important than seeing some new truth or concept that no one else had formerly seen was *seeing God*; he would accept the aid of anyone who could help him in that endeavor. "Look on him who has succeeded," he says, "and

---

[1]Gregory of Nyssa, *On Virginity*, 24.370.

boldly launch upon the voyage with confidence that it will be prosperous, and sail on under the breeze of the Holy Spirit with Christ your pilot and with the oarage of good cheer."[2]

What Gregory says here of the hypothetical saint, I wish to say in this and the following chapter about Gregory himself—along with Augustine (354–430), Anselm of Canterbury (1033–1109), Thomas Aquinas (1224–1274), Dante Alighieri (1285–1321), Gregory Palamas (1296–1359), John Calvin (1509–1564), Johann Gerhard (1582–1637), John Owen (1616–1683), Francis Turretin (1623–1687), and Jonathan Edwards (1703–1758). In the spirit of self-conscious and humble reception, we will survey how these figures understood and articulated the doctrine of the beatific vision. In doing so, I should stress the modesty of my purposes here. This sampling is not intended to offer the conclusive and definitive rendering of the beatific vision as it has been received throughout the tradition.[3] Rather, I wish to show by surveying figures that span the spectrums of time, geography, and theological convictions that *some notion* of the beatific vision (however differently it is described and understood) persists as something of a universal hope for all Christians.[4] The one, holy, catholic, and apostolic church has, since its birth, groaned to see the face of God. We ought to listen to those groanings,

---

[2]Gregory of Nyssa, *On Virginity*, 24.370.
[3]On the "Westward leaning" character of this list of theologians, I offer two defenses. First, while the Eastern tradition is by no means unanimous, it appears to me as though Gregory Palamas is heralded by virtually all Eastern Orthodox theologians *today* as the best articulator and defender of the Eastern Orthodox conception of the beatific vision and all concepts related thereunto. Differences seem to arise on the question of how to interpret Palamas, but not on whether his prominence is fitting. Giving Palamas his own section will allow me to address not only Palamas himself but also some of the variances surrounding how Palamas is interpreted. Second, while my tradition shares much with the Eastern Orthodox tradition—including the same heritage of the early church fathers—I myself am not Eastern Orthodox, and Eastern Orthodoxy is not the audience I *primarily* address in this volume. I write as a Reformed Baptist—an evangelical Protestant, which is a retrieval movement that began in the bosom of the medieval Catholic church, so the figures that will be *most* relevant for this work are those within that same historic stream.
[4]That is, "a universal hope for all Christians *until* very recently," as we will discuss in chap. 5.

therefore, in a spirit of anticipation, letting our own desire for the vision of God spring up in our hearts as a result.

Gregory of Nyssa

Any honest treatment of Gregory of Nyssa's doctrine of the beatific vision must reckon with what he describes as God's drastic *incomprehensibility*. In his writings against the Eunomians, Gregory makes this point clear: "The uncreated Nature alone," Gregory insists, "which we acknowledge in the Father, and in the Son, and in the Holy Spirit, surpasses all significance of names."[5] Gregory takes for granted that "the Divine Essence is ineffable and incomprehensible," and considers it axiomatic that human nature cannot "be taught the essence of God."[6] For Gregory, prerequisite for any knowledge of God is the embrace of a thoroughgoing *apophaticism*. We have not even *begun* to discuss the topic of the divine if we imagine our topic is something within our grasp of comprehension. "The fact that the Divine greatness has no limit is proclaimed by the prophecy," says Gregory, "which declares expressly that of His splendour, His glory, His holiness, 'there is no end': and if His surroundings have no limit, much more is He Himself in His essence, whatever it may be, comprehended by no limitation in any way."[7]

And yet, we would be mistaken to conclude that Gregory's doctrine of incomprehensibility leads him to agnostic despair. He does in fact affirm that there is a real and genuine kind of knowledge that we can have of God, even while he completely rules out the possibility of that knowledge being comprehensive. God's incomprehensibility, according to Gregory, is itself revelatory and worship-inducing: "Now we know the loftiness of the glory of Him Whom we worship, by the very fact that we are not able by reasoning to comprehend in our thoughts the incomparable character of His

---

[5]Gregory of Nyssa, *Against Eunomius*, 2.3.
[6]Gregory of Nyssa, *Against Eunomius*, 2.3.
[7]Gregory of Nyssa, *Against Eunomius*, 3.5.

greatness."[8] Thus, for Gregory, a litmus test for whether or not someone conceives of God rightly is *praise* and *wonder*. Patristic scholar Khald Anitolios is helpful in this matter: "The distinctive character of Gregory's epistemology, therefore, lies not so much in delimiting the extent of information that can be gleaned by the mind (he insists there is no limit) as in locating the act of knowledge radically within the movement of receptive wonder."[9] In other words, Gregory is less concerned with denying a certain amount of knowledge to the creature with his *apophaticism*, and is far more concerned with describing the inexhaustible and never-ending upward ascent of knowledge; and the nature of that ascent is one of perpetual *wonder*.

Gregory *does* speak positively of the beatific vision. Contrary to what some might insist, I do not tend to think Gregory's resolution to the tension between beatific vision and God's incomprehensibility is achieved with an appeal to the essence-energies distinction. This language certainly shows up in Gregory's writing, but I remain unconvinced that it was central to his conception of the beatific vision, and indeed, to his theology as a whole.[10] Rather, Gregory resolves the tension by paradoxically turning the *telos* into a *journey*: the beatific vision is not a punctiliar event; it is the upward ascent into union with Christ and contemplation of the divine forever.[11] Jaroslav Pelikan is right, I think, to emphasize that "without retracting

---

[8]Gregory of Nyssa, *Against Eunomius*, 3.5.
[9]Khald Anitolios, *Retrieving Nicaea: The Development and Meaning of Trinitarian Doctrine* (Grand Rapids, MI: Baker Academic, 2011), 164. Anitolios goes on to say, "Those who fail to appreciate this distinction can misunderstand Gregory's notion of not knowing the essence as a quantitative statement. Rather, it is a qualitative statement about the nature of knowing as such and how knowing relates to the inexhaustibility of being. . . . In a word, the kind of knowing that Gregory of Nyssa considers appropriate to an integral relation between the human mind and being is that which is permeated by wonder" (164).
[10]Here I concur with Hans Boersma's analysis in *Seeing God: The Beatific Vision in the Christian Tradition* (Grand Rapids, MI: Eerdmans, 2018), 94-95.
[11]Boersma is helpful here: "Gregory recognizes the correspondence between divine infinity and the insatiability of human desire, so that a proper Christian spirituality holds out the hope of a vision that does not culminate in a static point but ever continues and increases in relation to the ultimate object of this vision." Boersma, *Seeing God*, 94.

anything they had said about *apophasis,* the Cappadocians thus found it possible to speak in 'ontological terms' about 'seeing God in reality [*ontōs*].'"[12] Thus, Pelikan concludes, "their teleology was summed up in the vision of God, which was end and goal and ceaseless attraction."[13] This is why Gregory can hold both of these realities together (i.e., the soul-defining, teleological desire to see God and the inability to see him comprehensively) in the same context: "no consideration will be given to anything enclosing infinite nature. It is not the nature of what is unenclosed to be grasped. But every desire for the Good which is attracted to that ascent constantly expands as one progresses in pressing on to the Good."[14]

To portray how Gregory's teleology makes sense of both the beatific vision and his thoroughgoing apophaticism more clearly, it may be helpful to briefly consider broadly the teleology of the Cappadocians in Gregory's day. Gregory, along with his brother Basil of Caesarea (AD 330–379) and their friend Gregory of Nazianzus (AD 329–390), articulated their conception of *telos* in contrast to both *tychē* (chance or fortune) and *anankē* (determinism or fate).[15] Both of these rival views in the classical world were partially true in their response to the other. Over and against the meaninglessness of *tychē,* the *anankē* of the astrologers was committed to heeding the order of the cosmos. The movement of the stars and their corresponding events played out in history were not *random,* and with this conviction, the Cappadocians could agree. On the other hand, the true nature of creaturely reality and the ripple effects of real choice and human freedom would not allow the Cappadocians to

---

[12]Jaroslav Pelikan, *Christianity and Classical Culture: The Metamorphosis of Natural Theology in the Christian Encounter with Hellenism* (New Haven, CT: Yale University Press, 1993), 165.

[13]Pelikan, *Christianity and Classical Culture,* 165.

[14]Gregory of Nyssa, *The Life of Moses,* trans. Abraham J. Malherbe and Everett Ferguson (New York: HarperCollins, 2006), 106.

[15]"Gregory of Nazianzus . . . clearly saw the classical views of a random *tyche* on the one hand, and the deterministic *ananke* of fate and the stars on the other hand, as the principal rivals to the Christian doctrine of God and to the teleology of divine providence." Pelikan, *Christianity and Classical Culture,* 154.

affirm the lifeless, mechanistic determinism of *ananke*. With the classical notion of *tyche*, the Cappadocians pushed against such determinism. Humans, as image bearers of a free God, were genuinely *free* in the minds of the Cappadocians. "Yet," Pelikan is quick to remind us, "their opposition to philosophies of *tyche* and chance was no less thoroughgoing than was their rejection of deterministic necessity."[16] How then did the Cappadocians thread the needle between *tyche* and *ananke*? They did so with their providential understanding of "the correlation between *arche* and *telos*, between beginning and ending, which yielded a teleology that could be inferred from the structure of the world as cosmos."[17] Such a correlation made it possible for the Cappadocians to embrace a sort of *fixed dynamism*. From the beginning, God's purpose for creation (*arche*) was union with him (*telos*). And "because the *telos* was not merely the end but the goal and the consummation, it comprehended the *arche* in a complete schema, which was 'coextensive with the development of humanity' across all of human history."[18] Because God is infinite and all that has a *telos* is final, and since the *telos* of humanity is union with him, its consummation is perpetual. Summing up this point about the Cappadocians, Pelikan writes, "This 'ceaseless attraction' made the *telos* not only a goal but a lure, and not at all an 'end' in the sense that nothing would come after it. As a lure, the transcendence of God evoked a yearning that was insatiable either in time or eternity."[19] Everything we consider regarding Gregory's doctrine of the beatific vision should be read in the context of this overarching teleology, which was shared by Basil and the other Gregory as well.

Consider Gregory's fifth homily on the Song of Songs. In this sermon, Gregory spends considerable time on the second half of

---

[16]Pelikan, *Christianity and Classical Culture*, 160.
[17]Pelikan, *Christianity and Classical Culture*, 161-62.
[18]Pelikan, *Christianity and Classical Culture*, 163.
[19]Pelikan, *Christianity and Classical Culture*, 164.

2:13, "Arise, my love, my beautiful one, and come away." Gregory takes this invitation to be spoken by the bridegroom to his bride, whom he interprets allegorically as Christ and the saint's soul respectively. Essential to Gregory's reading is the basic affirmation that in Christ, the divine and human natures are hypostatically united in the person of the Son, so that coming to Christ may look like approaching the man Christ Jesus, but in coming to the man, one is also approaching *the divine nature*. Of this nature, wherefrom Christ beckons to the soul, Gregory affirms that "the simple and pure and uniform and unalterable Nature, being always so stands unlimited in its goodness and is never alienated from itself because it is not open to participation in evil. It sees no limit of itself, because it sees none of its contraries in itself."[20] To approach the bridegroom is to approach the unbounded well of the divine nature—a nature that is not limited and therefore does not abide evil (since the presence of evil would imply limitations of Goodness). What does this then mean for the creature who is, in some way, mingled with the imperfection of evil? Gregory answers:

> As, therefore, [this Nature] draws human nature to participation in itself, it always surpasses that which participates in it to the same degree, in conformity with its superabundance of goodness. For the soul is always becoming better than itself on account of its participation in the transcendent. It does not stop growing, but the Good that is participated remains in unaltered degree as it is, since the being that ever more and more participates in it discovers that it is always surpassed to the same extent.[21]

For Gregory, the creature, in approaching the beloved, is ever purified to see and adore more of him. The soul is made ever fitter, from one degree to another—without exhaustion—to be in the presence of the beloved. In this way, the invitation that Christ offers

---

[20]Gregory of Nyssa, *Homilies on the Song of Songs*, trans. Richard A. Norris Jr. (Atlanta: Society of Biblical Literature, 2012), 5.171.
[21]Gregory of Nyssa, *Homilies*, 5.171.

to the souls of the saints is forever heeded and forever extended: he continues to say, "Come!" and the soul continues to say, "I will!" "For to one who has risen up in this manner there will never be wanting and up-rising without end," says Gregory, "nor for one who runs to the Lord will opportunity for the divine race be used up. For it is always necessary to rise up, and it is never right for those who are drawing near by their running to halt."[22]

This sentiment is repeated and elevated throughout Gregory's homilies on the *Song of Songs*. Building on everything he describes in Homily 5, for example, he emphasizes the soul's continual upward climb in Homily 6, when he describes the bride's longing for her bridegroom in Song of Solomon 3:1-8. "After all this," says Gregory, "it seems that the soul has been blessed with ascent to the heights and has attained the highest of her desires. For what greater blessing can be conceived than that of seeing God?"[23] Or again, in Homily 11, Gregory affirms that

> the person who looks toward that divine and infinite Beauty glimpses something that is always being discovered as more novel and more surprising than what has already been grasped, and for that reason she marvels at that which is always being manifested, but she never comes to a halt in her desire to see, since what she looks forward to is in every possible way more splendid and more divine than what she has seen.[24]

What Gregory describes here in his homilies on the Song of Songs is echoed in his book *The Life of Moses*. We should not miss the fact that the context of this brief work is an inquiry regarding the Christian life: *The Life of Moses* is Gregory's response to the request for a treatise on how Christians should live (which is to say, it is not primarily a book dealing with eschatology). However, many of Gregory's most profound statements on the beatific vision come

---

[22]Gregory of Nyssa, *Homilies*, 5.171.
[23]Gregory of Nyssa, *Homilies*, 6.191.
[24]Gregory of Nyssa, *Homilies*, 11.339.

from this little treatment, which highlights the fact that for Gregory, there is a fundamental continuity between beholding the face of God by faith in this life and beholding the face of God by glorified vision in the next.

Gregory portrays the entire story of Moses' life, spanning from the beginning of Exodus to Israel's wandering in the wilderness and Moses' death in Numbers and Deuteronomy, as a type for the Christian life. The pursuit of virtue, for Gregory, was one and the same with the pursuit of enjoyment of God in the beatific vision. When Gregory arrives at the events of Moses' life described in Exodus 33, for example, he emphasizes the same feature of Moses' *desire* that we noted in the previous chapter. "Made to desire and not to abandon the transcendent height by the things already attained," says Gregory, the soul "makes its way upward without ceasing, ever through its prior accomplishments renewing its intensity for the flight."[25] Gregory goes on to list the virtuous accomplishments of Moses to that point, and the experiences of the divine he had gone through, and stresses that "although lifted up through such lofty experiences, he is still unsatisfied in his desire for more. He still thirsts for that with which he constantly filled himself to capacity, and he asks to attain as if he had never partaken, beseeching God to appear to him, not according to his capacity to partake, but according to God's true being."[26] Every desire met to experience the glory of God creates a new desire for more. And so, according to Gregory, "the true sight of God consists in this, that the one who looks up to God never ceases in that desire."[27]

Whereas other figures we will consider below speculate on the mechanics of the beatific vision (i.e., what is the nature of "seeing?" Is it an ocular or intellectual vision? Do we see the divine essence

---

[25]Gregory of Nyssa, *The Life of Moses*, 103.
[26]Gregory of Nyssa, *The Life of Moses*, 104.
[27]Gregory of Nyssa, *The Life of Moses*, 104-5.

or the divine energies? Do we see Christ in his human nature or the divine nature directly?), Gregory will not be weighed down by any of those questions. Rather, he is far more concerned with the perpetual nature of the beatific vision than its form or manner. The never-ending ascent is what captures his imagination. Thus, Gregory can even go so far as to define the vision as this upward process: "This truly is the vision of God: never to be satisfied in the desire to see him. But one must always, by looking at what he can see, rekindle his desire to see more."[28] The beatific vision is a thirst that is perpetually satiated and exacerbated. And crucially, for Gregory, this vision is christocentric. "For," says Gregory, "since Christ is understood by Paul as the rock, all hope of good things is believed to be in Christ, in whom we have learned all the treasures of good things to be. *He who finds any good finds it in Christ, who contains all good.*"[29] Thus, as Hans Boersma concludes his own reflections on Gregory's doctrine of the beatific vision, "What makes the beatific vision so glorious is that the soul revels with increasing intensity and intimacy in the infinite, ever-greater gift-giving of the invisible God who in Christ has made himself visible."[30] This means that Gregory's doctrine of God's incomprehensibility and his affirmation of the beatific vision are not *truly* in tension with each other at all. Man, as a finite creature, cannot have a telos that is ever actualized in a final sense, since such a state would imply that he ceases to be mutable. To be creaturely is to be finite, and to be finite is to change. If man's chief end, as a finite and temporal being, is oriented toward the infinite and inexhaustible being, his final state—the *realization* of his telos—*is* a state of perpetuity, wherein he always increasingly *becomes* more than what he is as he grows into "a deeper union with Christ."[31]

---

[28]Gregory of Nyssa, *The Life of Moses*, 106.
[29]Gregory of Nyssa, *The Life of Moses*, 109, emphasis mine.
[30]Boersma, *Seeing God*, 94.
[31]Boersma, *Seeing God*, 95. For a fuller analysis on Gregory's doctrine of the beatific vision than what I have included here, see Boersma, *Seeing God*, 76-95.

Augustine

In the first volume of his seminal five-volume work on the history of the development of doctrine in the Christian tradition, Jaroslav Pelikan introduces Augustine of Hippo with these lofty words: "In any history of philosophy [Augustine] must figure prominently; no history of postclassical Latin literature would be complete without a chapter on him; and there is probably no Christian theologian—Eastern or Western, ancient or medieval or modern, heretical or orthodox—whose historical influence can match his."[32]

Augustine was a mountain of a man. In the face of such a mountain, knowing where to begin can be daunting.[33] This includes his conception of human nature and the relationship between nature and grace, as well as Augustine's conception of the relationship between sign (*signum*) and reality (*res*). For my purposes, I will simply take for granted that Augustine's metaphysic was a thoroughly participatory one, embodying the Christian-Platonic synthesis of classical realism in a truly definitional way. I agree with Hans Boersma that "Augustine's view is sacramental," by virtue of the fact that "Augustine argued that the divine substance is omnipresent, and his participatory metaphysic would be incompatible with a strict separation between sign and reality."[34]

Therefore, rather than bringing the full weight of Augustine's entire system (and the scores of secondary literature wherein it is debated) to our consideration of his doctrine of the beatific vision, I will briefly examine two places from his corpus where he addresses the doctrine directly and poignantly: *The City of God*, and Homily IV in his *Homilies on the First Epistle of John*. The former treatment provides us with a suitable example of the nature of the

---

[32] Jaroslav Pelikan, *The Christian Tradition: A History of the Development of Doctrine*, vol. 1, *The Emergence of the Catholic Tradition (100–600)* (Chicago: The University of Chicago Press, 1971), 292.

[33] At the risk of overly hedging, therefore, I want to acknowledge this section will gloss over a great deal of hotly contested interpretive discussions regarding Augustine's thought.

[34] Boersma, *Seeing God*, 108-9.

beatific vision in Augustine's speculative theology—showcasing his contribution in what we might call the "mechanics of the beatific vision"—and the latter provides us with how the doctrine functions in Augustine's personal piety and pastoral care.

Unlike Gregory, who was content to keep his contemplation of the beatific vision out of the speculative realm of asking *how* the vision is a "vision," and what it has to do with the physicality of the resurrected body, Augustine launches into such a discussion in the concluding chapters of *The City of God*. After decisively distancing himself from those who imagine the beatific vision requires the detachment of the body, and after cogently arguing for the necessity of the resurrection in a properly Christian eschatology,[35] Augustine concludes his work with an extended reflection on the beatific vision.[36] "And now let us consider," says Augustine, "how the saints shall be employed when they are clothed in immortal and spiritual bodies, and when the flesh shall live no longer in a fleshly but a spiritual fashion."[37] However, lest we think Augustine is a fool who rushes in where Gregory fears to tread, Augustine acknowledges the shadow of mystery that covers this whole discussion: "to tell the truth, I am at a loss to understand the nature of that employment, or, shall I rather say, repose and ease, for it has never come within the range of my bodily senses."[38] With this caution and admission in place, Augustine begins by stressing that whatever the beatific vision is, it is in some way similar to "the vision of the holy angels."[39] As they are in the presence of God, beholding him truly, so will we be.

What, then, is the object of our vision? We shall see the "face of God." But, Augustine stresses, "by 'the face' of God we are to understand His manifestation, and not a part of the body similar to that

---

[35] Augustine, *City of God*, 22.11-28.
[36] Augustine, *City of God*, 22.29-30.
[37] Augustine, *City of God*, 22.29.507.
[38] Augustine, *City of God*, 22.29.507.
[39] Augustine, *City of God*, 22.29.507.

which in our bodies we call by that name."[40] Thus, the beatific vision is not the ocular vision of a physical face of God. This, however, does not mean that for Augustine the ocular aspect is altogether absent. Augustine insists that the saints will "in the body see God; but whether they shall see Him by means of the body, as now we see the sun, moon, stars, sea, earth, and all that is in it, that is a difficult question."[41] The distinction between seeing "in the body" and "by means of the body" is important, and gets at the key difference between mediate knowledge and immediate knowledge. Mediate knowledge is knowledge gained by process of reason, but immediate knowledge is knowledge present in an a priori way. I see the redness of an apple and *know* that it is red not by process of syllogistic reason. At present, we see God in creation (cf. Ps 19:1-6; Rom 1:20) but not in this *immediate* way. To recognize God in all things, it is incumbent upon us to reason from creation to its Creator in an a posteriori manner. While it is not immediately obvious to all people, Augustine stresses the Christian conviction that God truly is omnipresent, and therefore can be mediately known by all things: "He is all in heaven and all on earth, not at alternate intervals of time, but both at once, as no bodily nature can be."[42] He is truly there, even if we cannot see him. But, Augustine speculates, what if a feature of the glorified resurrected spiritual bodies was the ability to see the incorporeal reality of God's presence everywhere in the same way that I immediately see the redness of an apple? "Wherefor it may very well be," Augustine says,

> and it is thoroughly credible, that we shall in the future world see the material forms of the new heavens and the new earth in such a way that we shall most distinctly recognize God everywhere present and governing all things, material as well as spiritual, and shall see Him, not as now we understand the invisible things of God by the things that are

---

[40] Augustine, *City of God*, 22.29.507.
[41] Augustine, *City of God*, 22.29.507.
[42] Augustine, *City of God*, 22.29.508.

made, and see Him darkly, as in a mirror, and in part, and rather by faith than by bodily vision of material appearances, but by means of the bodies we shall wear and which we shall see wherever we turn our eyes.[43]

Does it not make perfect sense, reasons Augustine, that in our resurrected spiritual bodies we should not just know by faith that God is everywhere, but that we should *see* God and *immediately know* him to be everywhere? For his own part, Augustine views this less as some "quality" in the glorified eyes themselves but rather a new kind of state of the creature's conscious relation to God where "God will be so known by us, and shall be so much before us, that we shall see Him by the spirit in ourselves, in one another, in Himself, in the new heavens and the new earth, in every created thing which shall then exist; and also by the body we shall see Him in every body which the keen vision of the eye of the spiritual body shall reach."[44]

Satisfied with this account of what this vision will entail as it relates to the eyes and knowledge, Augustine spends his final chapter reveling in "how great shall be the felicity, which shall be tainted with no evil, which shall lack no good, and which shall afford leisure for the praises of God, who shall be all in all!"[45] Augustine explores the relationship between work and rest, friendship and degrees of blessedness, and the freedom of the will as it all relates to the beatific vision in this final chapter of *The City of God*. For Augustine, the work of praise and the rest of blessedness will be one and the same in this blessed vision, when "He shall be the end of our desires who shall be seen without end, loved without cloy, praised without weariness."[46] And while there will certainly be degrees of honor among the saints, this lack of egalitarian uniformity will itself be a blessing, since "in that blessed city . . . no inferior shall envy any superior . . . because no one will wish to be

---

[43] Augustine, *City of God*, 22.29.509.
[44] Augustine, *City of God*, 22.29.509.
[45] Augustine, *City of God*, 22.30.509.
[46] Augustine, *City of God*, 22.30.510.

what he has not received, though bound in strictest concord with him who has received; as in the body the finger does not seek to be the eye, though both members are harmoniously included in the complete structure of the body."[47] Augustine concludes his reflections with a meditation on the eternal sabbath of the beatific vision. "There," says Augustine, "we shall rest and see, and see and love, and love and praise. This is what shall be in the end without end. For what other end do we propose to ourselves than to attain to the kingdom of which there is no end?"[48]

Given that Augustine could not help but conclude his sophisticated philosophical treatment on the beatific vision in *The City of God* with doxological revelry, it is not at all surprising that this note of doxology takes center stage in his pastoral and homiletical considerations on the same topic. In his fourth homily on 1 John—which covers 1 John 2:27–3:8—Augustine is as affective as we would expect. Notwithstanding the valid argument Hans Boersma makes that Augustine did in fact have a category for ecstatic experiences of seeing God in this life,[49] it is difficult to deny that Augustine draws a clear contrast between faith in this life and sight in the next.[50] "For us then, what are we?" asks Augustine. "Already we are begotten of Him, but because we are such in hope, he saith, 'Beloved, now are we sons of God.' Now already? Then what is it we look for, if already we are sons of God?"[51] This is a reasonable question. If so great an inheritance is ours already in this life, to what exactly are we to look forward? Part of John's answer, of course, is paradoxically no answer at all, but rather a negation ("and what

---

[47] Augustine, *City of God*, 22.30.510.
[48] Augustine, *City of God*, 22.30.511.
[49] See Boersma, *Seeing God*, 112–125. The implication, of course, is that "the difference between East and West may not be quite as stark or obvious as it is sometimes thought to be" (99).
[50] "And we believe on Him whom we have not seen, and we look for Him to come. Whoso look for Him by faith, shall rejoice when He cometh: those who are without faith, when that which now they see not is come, shall be ashamed." Augustine, *Ten Homilies on the First Epistle to John*, 4.2.482.
[51] Augustine, *Homilies on the First Epistle to John*, 4.5.484.

we will be has not yet appeared"; 1 Jn 3:2). Whatever we are to be, John notes, we will be as a consequence of *seeing God* "as he is." "Therefore," says Augustine,

> we are to see a certain vision, my brethren, "which neither eye hath seen, nor ear hath heard, nor hath entered into the heart of man": a certain vision, a vision surpassing all earthly beautifulness, of gold, of silver, of groves and fields; the beautifulness of sea and air, the beautifulness of sun and moon, the beautifulness of the stars, the beautifulness of angels: surpassing all things: because from it are all things beautiful.[52]

Notice how here, as in his reflection in *The City of God*, Augustine connects the beatific vision with the vision of earthly beauty. The most obvious relation between the two in the passage quoted above is made by way of contrast: the "certain vision" we shall behold "surpasses all earthly beautifulness." But the final clause of this passage stresses that something deeper resides in the relation between earthly beauty and the object of the beatific vision who is God: "because from it [God himself, the object of this "certain vision"], are *all things beautiful*." The beauty of creation that beckons its beholder to itself and beyond itself is none other than the beauty that will occupy the glad-hearted adoring gaze of the saints in the beatific vision. This connection between the beatific vision and earthly beauty makes sense of the subsequent pastoral charges Augustine offers to his listeners. Like any good preacher, Augustine recognizes his need to impress the Word proclaimed onto the lives of his hearers, so he charges them: "because ye cannot at present see, let your part and duty be in desire. The whole life of a good Christian is a holy desire."[53]

At this point, Augustine begins to sound remarkably like Gregory. There is an ache that accompanies the desiring saint that Augustine considers altogether fitting in light of the beatific vision. By longing, says Augustine, "thou art made capable, so that when that is come

---
[52] Augustine, *Homilies on the First Epistle to John*, 4.5.484.
[53] Augustine, *Homilies on the First Epistle to John*, 4.6.484.

which thou mayest see, thou shalt be filled . . . by stretching thou makest it capable of holding more: so God by deferring our hope, stretches our desire; by the desiring, stretches the mind; by stretching, makes it more capacious. Let us desire therefore, my brethren, for we shall be filled."[54] Unlike any other desire in this life, Augustine insists that longing for the mystery of "what we shall be" when we "see him as he is" cannot possibly lead to disappointment. No hopes on this vision can be set too high. Further, Augustine argues that part of faith in this life consists in longing for vision in the next, and this longing is itself a sanctifying agent by which God *fits* us for vision in glory. Thus, "holy longing exercises us just so much as we prune off our longings from the love of the world."[55]

For Augustine, even when we cautiously speculate about the mechanics of the beatific vision, a great deal of mystery prevents us from going too far or saying too much. But where mystery stops speculation from venturing too far, mystery inspires and stirs up desire. Desire rushes into the mystery where speculation fears to tread! For all the discontinuities that may exist between our experience of God in this life by faith, and our experience of God in the next life by vision, *desire* is one of the ties that bind both dispensations together.

Anselm of Canterbury

In many ways, the whole of Anselm's life, that great archbishop of Canterbury in the eleventh century, was an ascent toward the beatific vision. In his *History of the Christian Church*, historian Philip Schaff recounts the oft-told story of Anselm's boyhood vision of God. "In his childish imagination," says Schaff, "Anselm conceived God Almighty as seated on a throne at the top of the Alps, and in a dream, he climbed up the mountain to meet him."[56] In this "dream,"

---

[54] Augustine, *Homilies on the First Epistle to John*, 4.6.485.
[55] Augustine, *Homilies on the First Epistle to John*, 4.6.485.
[56] Philip Schaff, *History of the Christian Church*, vol. 5, *The Middle Ages: From Gregory VII, 1049, to Boniface VIII, 1294* (Grand Rapids, MI: Eerdmans, 1907), 598-99. Although, it is only fair

Anselm is interrupted in his trek by the sight of negligent maidens shirking their work. Determined to report their slothfulness to their king, the young Anselm is welcomed to dine at the king's table. So full was his joy at the king's table that he forgot all about his mission to climb the mountain in search for God. "Then," concludes Schaff, "refreshed with the whitest of bread, he descended again to the valley. The following day he firmly believed he had actually been in heaven and eaten at the Lord's table."[57] In a very real way, Anselm spent the rest of his life trying to get back to that table. Once ascending the mountain to dine with the King of kings, his imagination never really left that place. This much is true of all Anselm's writing, but it is particularly true of his profoundly dense little book, *Proslogion*, "the most basic aim" of which, according to Gavin Ortlund, is "Anselm's pursuit of the soul's heavenly vision of God."[58]

The Godward tone of *Proslogion* is set with its very first chapter. The only two parties addressed in the book are himself and the God after whom he longs. "Come now," he says to himself, "insignificant man, fly for a moment from your affairs, escape for a little while from the tumult of your thoughts.... Abandon yourself for a little to God and rest for a little in Him."[59] Having addressed himself, he turns his attention to God in direct prayer, and maintains this mode of address for the majority of the work: "Come then, Lord my God, teach my heart where and how to seek You, where and how to find You."[60] Anselm's desperation for a sight of God is made clear when he begs,

> Teach me to seek You, and reveal Yourself to me as I seek, because I can neither seek You if You do not teach me how, nor find You unless You reveal Yourself. Let me seek You in desiring You; let me desire You in

---

to mention that whether Anselm's Godward journey in the Alps was a "memory of a dream" or simply a "memory" has been disputed down through the ages.
[57]Schaff, *HCC*, 5:599.
[58]Gavin Ortlund, *Anselm's Pursuit of Joy: A Commentary on the* Proslogion (Washington, DC: The Catholic University of America Press, 2020), 8-9.
[59]Anselm, *Proslogion*, in *Anselm of Canterbury: The Major Works,* ed. Brian Davies and G. R. Evans (New York: Oxford University Press, 1998), 1.84.
[60]Anselm, *Proslogion*, 1.84-85.

seeking You; let me find You in loving You; let me love You in finding You.... For I do not seek to understand so that I may believe; but I believe so that I may understand.[61]

Often, the *Proslogion* is cited in philosophical discussions regarding his innovative (and oft-derided) ontological argument for the existence of God, and this is fitting, insofar as it goes. He more or less says that this argument lies behind the book's origin in his own preface. But we would be sorely mistaken to take this as the sum and substance of the meditation, a fact that becomes clear by Anselm's pause in his argument at chapter fourteen. According to Ortlund, Anselm's self-interpretation of his work here in *Proslogion*'s fourteenth chapter "provides a kind of hermeneutical window into the first half of the book."[62] At this point in the *Proslogion*, Anselm has already developed the meat of his ontological proof for God's existence, and yet he asks, "Have you found, O my soul, what you were seeking?"[63] Were his sole purpose for writing the need to flesh out this ontological proof, he could simply answer his question with "yes," in which case this short book would be even shorter. However, Anselm is not yet finished. After summarizing what he has thus far discovered, he is left pining: "Why, O Lord God, does my soul not experience you if it has found you?"[64] Evidently, Anselm has not yet accomplished what he set out to accomplish at the book's genesis, which is why he continues to beseech God: "Lord my God, You who have formed and reformed me, tell my desiring soul what You are besides what it has seen so that it may see clearly that which it desires."[65] This whole chapter conveys Anselm's strong "sense of exile from the *visio Dei*."[66] He thus marches on, showing that his deepest and most central aim is not merely to

---

[61] Anselm, *Proslogion*, 1.86-87.
[62] Ortlund, *Anselm's Pursuit of Joy*, 150.
[63] Anselm, *Proslogion*, 14.95.
[64] Anselm, *Proslogion*, 14.95.
[65] Anselm, *Proslogion*, 14.95.
[66] Ortlund, *Anselm's Pursuit of Joy*, 154.

develop a proof for God's existence but to contemplate God in his soul.

Anselm continues to ascend the spiral staircase heavenward when he presses into the inexpressible nature of the light within which God dwells. Like the other figures we have thus far explored, divine incomprehensibility is not, for Anselm, a doctrine that prevents ascent toward beatific vision. Divine incomprehensibility brings Anselm not further from but closer to the beatific vision. "It is striking," Ortlund observes, "that Anselm begins with God's more visible qualities and then moves onto his more hidden qualities, rather than the other way around. One might expect God's hiddenness to be reduced, not increased, as Anselm comes to understand God more accurately."[67] The more Anselm understands the divine nature, however, the greater the transcendent gap between Creator and creature is felt. Yet this does not cause Anselm to despair of searching and finding; quite the opposite. Ortlund is right to observe how "in the very bewilderment that Anselm continually falls back upon, he is moving forward toward joy and certainty."[68]

As Anselm continues in his beatific pilgrimage toward God, he reaches a climax in chapters twenty-three to twenty-six. At the conclusion of chapter twenty-three, Anselm says, "This is, moreover, that one thing necessary in which is every good, or rather, which is wholly and uniquely and completely and solely good."[69] In alluding to Jesus' commendation of Mary, sitting at the feet of Christ in Luke 10:42, Anselm draws on an illustrative tradition of reflections on Mary sitting at the feet of Christ. Ortlund demonstrates how Anselm's appropriation of this Lukan phrase has a long historical pedigree, with strong representation in Augustine, Bede, and a litany of other medieval figures.[70]

---

[67] Ortlund, *Anselm's Pursuit of Joy*, 158.
[68] Ortlund, *Anselm's Pursuit of Joy*, 158.
[69] Anselm, *Proslogion*, 23.100.
[70] Ortlund, *Anselm's Pursuit of Joy*, 194-98.

Having thus discovered the "one thing necessary," he addresses himself for the final time in chapter twenty-four ("Now, my soul, rouse and lift up your whole understand and think as much as you can on what kind and how great this good is"),[71] except, importantly, Anselm's self-address here "continues on in one long, sustained *soliloquium* through the end of *Proslogion* 25, the climax of the book."[72] Here at this climax, Anselm identifies God not merely as the chief and highest happiness, but as the source and substance of all true happiness in this life. For Anselm, as with Augustine and Gregory of Nyssa before him, all roads of desire in this life lead most naturally and truly to the God who will dwell with his saints in heaven *as* their heaven. Anselm positively charges his own soul: "Love the one good in which all good things are, and that is sufficient. Desire the simple good which contains every good, and that is enough. For what do you love, O my flesh, what do you desire, O my soul? There it is, there it is, whatever you love, whatever you desire."[73]

Anselm goes on to reflect on the individual's delight in heaven with a meditation on fourteen "heavenly beatitudes,"[74] which eventually gives way to one of his most unique and noteworthy contributions to Christianity's conception of the beatific vision: heavenly friendship. Once "in heaven," so to speak, Anselm turns his contemplating gaze around to consider how his blessedness impacts those surrounding him. Though this pilgrimage is in the isolation of his own mind, he cannot now help but look outward: "But surely if someone else whom you loved in every respect as yourself possessed that same blessedness, your joy would be doubled for you would rejoice as much as for him as for yourself."[75] Anselm envisions how

---

[71] Anselm, *Proslogion*, 24.101.
[72] Ortlund, *Anselm's Pursuit of Joy*, 200.
[73] Anselm, *Proslogion*, 25.101.
[74] Anselm, *Proslogion*, 25.101-2. These beatitudes are beauty, strength, freedom, life, abundance, drunkenness (intoxication with God), music, pure pleasure, wisdom, friendship, unity, power, honor and wealth, and security. For an examination of these beatitudes, see Ortlund, *Anselm's Pursuit of Joy*, 207-12.
[75] Anselm, *Proslogion*, 25.102.

the heavenly ability to perfectly fulfill the law of love ("You shall love the Lord your God with all your heart and with all your soul and with all your mind . . . and you shall love your neighbor as yourself"; Mt 22:37-40) will multiply the joy of the individual. The love of neighbor as love of self will not, in that day, be an ideal but a true reality. So, when I gaze upon the face of God, my joy will be maximized. Every individual saint and angel experiences their *own* climax of delight in God, which is topped by the next without exhaustion on account of God's infinitude. But when I become aware of my neighbor's maximized joy in God on account of *his* experience of the beatific vision, my joy will be quite literally doubled—one hundred percent of his maximal joy will be *my* maximal joy, because I love him perfectly as I love myself. Anselm says, "If, then, two or three or many more possessed it you would rejoice just as much for each one as for yourself, if you loved each one as you loved yourself."[76] By consequence, one's capacity for more joy and more delight will, according to Anselm, grow with the multiplication of innumerable saints and angels. The love of God and love of neighbor will, in that day, encompass a single and ever-expansive movement *further up and further in* the happiness of heaven: "But if they love God with their whole heart, their whole mind, their whole soul, while yet their whole heart, their whole mind, their whole soul, is not equal to the grandeur of this love, they will assuredly so rejoice with their whole heart, their whole mind, and their whole soul, that their whole heart, their whole mind, and their whole soul will not be equal to the fullness of their joy."[77]

I agree with Ortlund that Anselm's *Proslogion* climaxes with a doctrine of heaven in which there is no greater joy than that of contemplating God. From this high point, Anselm settles into a calmer prayer to conclude the *Proslogion*. Surprisingly, however, Anselm does not conclude his work with a contented

---

[76]Anselm, *Proslogion*, 25.102.
[77]Anselm, *Proslogion*, 25.103.

resolution—as if his heavenward contemplation has reached his completion. Though chapter twenty-six can most assuredly be read as a prayer of *thanksgiving* for what Anselm had discovered, it is in an even deeper way a repetition of the prayer of *petition* with which he began his treatise: "God of truth, I ask that I may receive so that my joy may be complete. Until then let my mind meditate on it, let my tongue speak of it, let my heart love it, let my mouth preach it. Let my soul hunger for it, let my flesh thirst for it, my whole being desire it, until I enter into the "joy of the Lord" [Mt 25:21] who is God, Three in One, blessed forever. Amen."[78]

Anselm will not be ultimately satisfied with anything short of the beatific vision itself. Faith-precursors of the vision, for Anselm, serve the purpose of driving him ever onward toward his pilgrimage's end in heaven. "For all the progress Anselm has made in the *Proslogion*," Ortlund rightly observes, "this discovery has not resulted in a relaxation of those impulses that led him to initiate his search for God, but—if anything—has only further aggravated them."[79] Therefore Anselm stands in essential continuity with figures like Gregory of Nyssa and Augustine when he concludes that the beatific vision is not punctiliar or static, but is rather dynamic and perpetual, expanding and growing in delight with the expanse and growth in the capacity for delight.

Thomas Aquinas

"In the history of 'theology' understood as systematic theology, the thirteenth was undeniably one of the most important of all centuries."[80] So says Jaroslav Pelikan, who is correct thanks almost single-handedly to that tower of a figure, the Dumb Ox and Angelic Doctor, Thomas Aquinas. With the arrival of Aquinas, and his

---

[78] Anselm, *Proslogion*, 26.104.
[79] Ortlund, *Anselm's Pursuit of Joy*, 221.
[80] Jaroslav Pelikan, *The Christian Tradition: A History of the Development of Doctrine*, vol. 3, *The Growth of Medieval Theology (600-1300)* (Chicago, IL: University of Chicago Press, 1978), 268.

incomplete *magnum opus,* the *Summa Theologia,* the doctrine of the beatific vision takes a quantum leap in terms of theological and philosophical precision.

Aquinas deals with the beatific vision at length in two particular sections of his *Summa Theologia*: part 1, question 12, and part 3, question 92. In both of these sections, Aquinas dives headlong into the tension we have already identified several times: how can we claim to behold the essence of God in glory if God is incomprehensible? The first objection Aquinas lists puts the matter succinctly: "It seems that no created intellect can see the essence of God."[81] This objection takes on many forms and occupies not a little attention for Aquinas, both in his comments here and toward the end of his *Summa*. As is often the case, Aquinas's resolution to the conundrum is consistent with much of the great tradition before him, but with a striking degree of added precision. Like in the case of Gregory and Augustine and Anselm, described above, Aquinas also resolves the tension by appealing to the idea of perpetuity—God's incomprehensibility does not mean he cannot be known at all, but rather that what can be known of God is inexhaustible. Succinctly and memorably, Aquinas gets at this idea by describing God as *infinitely knowable.*

> But God, whose being is infinite . . . is infinitely knowable. Now no created intellect can know God infinitely. For the created intellect knows the divine essence more or less perfectly in proportion as it receives a greater or lesser light of glory. Since therefore the created light of glory received into any created intellect cannot be infinite, it is clearly impossible for any created intellect to know God in an infinite degree.[82]

God is incomprehensible not because there is nothing to know, but because he is endlessly *knowable*. "Hence," says Aquinas, "it does not follow that He cannot be known at all, but that He exceeds every kind of knowledge; which means that He is not comprehended."[83]

---

[81] Aquinas, *ST*, I.12.1.
[82] Aquinas, *ST*, I.12.7.
[83] Aquinas, *ST*, I.12.1.

Aquinas goes on to echo Augustine by reasoning that the beatific vision of God's essence is a sure outcome simply by reason of *desire*. Beholding the essence of God is, according to Aquinas, "ultimate beatitude," for "there resides in every man a natural desire to know the cause of any effect which he sees; and thence arises wonder in men. But if the intellect of the rational creature could not reach so far as to the first cause of things, the natural desire would remain void."[84] This, for Aquinas, is as unthinkable a prospect as suggesting that a creature can exist without a telos. Indeed, to suggest that man's highest desire is a desire that is absolutely foreign to his nature *is* tantamount to suggesting that he is made without a telos: if the absolute end for which he most naturally longs is an impossibility, he *has* no ultimate telos. This emphasis on natural telos, however, does not lead Aquinas to conclude that the power to behold God in the beatific vision lies naturally in man, unaided by grace. What man longs for as his ultimate telos is a telos that "exceeds" his nature. Thus, Aquinas insists that "since the natural power of the created intellect does not avail to enable it to see the essence of God . . . it is necessary that the power of understanding should be added by divine grace."[85] Aquinas's contribution of this concept, the *donum superadditum*, will be the occasion of no small amount of discussion among the post-Reformation tradition, but this need not distract us at present.[86] For now, it is worth simply acknowledging that for Aquinas, nature is perfected by grace. Additionally, Aquinas makes three other unique contributions to the doctrine of the beatific vision to which we should give recognition.

First, as Gavin Ortlund puts it, Aquinas distinguishes "between our vision of God's essence and God's vision of his own essence."[87] Aquinas says that "the vision whereby we shall see God in His

---

[84] Aquinas, *ST*, I.12.1; cf. III.92.1.
[85] Aquinas, *ST*, I.12.5.
[86] We will pick up on this idea in chap. 5.
[87] Gavin Ortlund, "Will We See God's Essence? A Defence of a Thomistic Account of the Beatific Vision," in *Scottish Journal of Theology*, issue 1070 (2021): 74, 325.

essence is the same whereby God sees Himself, as regards that whereby He is seen, because as He sees Himself in His essence, so shall we also see Him."[88] Yet, this does not eradicate the distinction between seeing God's essence and comprehending God's essence, which we just observed from Aquinas, since our vision of God's essence will be suitable to our nature: "in that vision we shall see the same thing that God sees, namely His essence, but not so effectively."[89]

Second, Aquinas agrees with Augustine that God will be seen immediately, but Aquinas makes the unique and fascinating observation that this immediate sight is a sight that shares in *God's mode* of being seen, "not according to the saints' and angels' mode of seeing."[90] There, in that vision, God will not be "known by the images of other things, as He is known now, for which reason we are said to see now in a glass," but rather our knowledge will be "united to that uncreated substance in the aforementioned manner. Yet this medium [of God's mode of being seen] will not cause that knowledge to be mediate, because it does not come in between the knower and the thing known, but is that which gives the knower the power to know."[91]

Third, Aquinas emphasizes that this vision will be spiritual and not strictly ocular—the beatific vision is not, for Aquinas, a merely physical vision, but a spiritual vision we will experience in glorified bodies. According to Aquinas, "It will be impossible for [the body] to see the Divine essence as an object of direct vision."[92] This should not be taken, however, as a gnostic minimization of the body in glory, since Aquinas immediately goes on to say that the body will see the Divine essence as

---

[88] Aquinas, *ST*, III.92.1.
[89] Aquinas, *ST*, III.92.1.
[90] Ortlund, "Will We See God's Essence?," 326.
[91] Aquinas, *ST*, III.92.1.
[92] Aquinas, *ST*, III.92.2

an object of indirect vision, because on the one hand the bodily sight will see so great a glory of God in bodies, especially in the glorified bodies and most of all in the body of Christ, and, on the other hand, the intellect will see God so clearly, that God will be perceived in things seen with the eye of the body, even as life is perceived in speech. For although our intellect will not then see God from seeing His creatures, yet it will see God in His creatures seen corporeally.[93]

The idea is that our glorified bodily eyes will not see a thing called "the Divine essence"; they will behold the divine essence in everything they behold, preeminently in the glorified body of Christ. Since in God's light we will see light (cf. Ps 36:9), the divine essence will be so immediately and immensely present that the beatific vision will be *everywhere* in glory—"most of all in the body of Christ." In that world, the vision of *everything* is beatific—all vision is subsumed by the beatific vision, because the God who fills (the new) heaven and earth will be seen in his filling. Thus, the often-expressed notion that Aquinas's view of the beatific vision makes the resurrected body superfluous fails to do justice to his articulations. Yes, the beatific vision is an intellectual vision, but this does not make it indifferent to the body, because the soul was never made to function in isolation from the body. As Robert Llizo notes, "It is in its wholeness that body and soul benefit from the beatific vision: the soul through its direct apprehension, and the body indirectly by seeing and experiencing its effects."[94]

Yet, we can be even more emphatic here regarding how Christology functions in Aquinas's beatific vision. It is not merely the case that the body of Christ will "most of all" be a glorified object wherein we will see the glory of God in the beatific vision. Even more fundamentally, Thomas believes that the believer's beatific vision is causally dependent on Christ's glorification—we experience the

---

[93] Aquinas, *ST*, III.92.2.
[94] Robert Llizo, "The Vision of God: St. Thomas Aquinas on the Beatific Vision and Resurrected Bodies," *Perichoresis* 17, no. 2 (2019): 25.

beatific vision that in our union with him on account of *his* beatific vision. "Now man is in potentiality to the knowledge of the blessed," says Aquinas, "which consists in the vision of God.... Now men are brought to this end of beatitude by the humanity of Christ."[95] How are they brought to this end by the humanity of Christ? Aquinas answers: "it was necessary that the beatific knowledge, which consists in the vision of God, should belong to Christ preeminently, since the cause ought always to be more efficacious than the effect."[96]

Here, in Christ, and nowhere else, can man truly be united with "uncreated beatitude"—which simply *is* the beatific vision—because here, in Christ, and nowhere else, is the uncreated and created hypostatically united. This is the christological logic of Aquinas, who points out that "the soul of Christ, which is a part of human nature, through a light participated from the Divine Nature, is perfected with the beatific knowledge whereby it sees God in essence."[97] In other words, for Christ to take humanity to its telos—beatific union with the divine—he had to experience this telos in his human nature, this is the "beatitude, whereby His soul was established in the last end of human nature."[98] Not only is the body of Christ included in what we see in the beatific vision as the *object* of our delight, he is also the cause of our beatific vision. Christ experiences the beatific vision foremost as the God-man, and in him, we see what he sees: in Christ, we see God.

DANTE ALIGHIERI[99]

To say that Dante Alighieri's (1265–1321) entire *Divine Comedy* builds up to the central hope of the beatific vision is no

---

[95] Aquinas, *ST*, III.9.2.
[96] Aquinas, *ST*, III.9.2.
[97] Aquinas, *ST*, III.9.2.
[98] Aquinas, *ST*, III.9.2.
[99] Some of these reflections on Dante are repeated in my article, "Staring at the Sun: The Theologian's Pursuit of Holiness and His Obligation to the Church," *Journal of Classical Theology* 1 (2022): 83-105.

exaggeration. The second book of this *Comedy*, *The Purgatorio*, documents Dante's preparation for heaven.

> "Next: 'Holy Souls, you cannot advance
> if the fire does not sting you first.
> Enter into them and be not deaf to the singing there.'"[100]

These are the words Dante reports hearing toward the close of his *Purgatorio*. Having traveled through the nine circles of hell and up the mountain of purgatory, led by his guide, Virgil, Dante finds himself coming to the precipice of heaven. The climb up the mountain has been arduous but rewarding: he has experienced the painful and joyful process of sanctification, losing in succession the vices of pride, envy, wrath, sloth, avarice, and gluttony. He desires to leave earth's mountain behind in his ascent to heavenly beatitude among the starry host, but before he can enter Paradise, he must walk through Purgatory's wall of fire, where the seventh and final vice, lust, will melt away. Before entering the realm of heaven, Dante must be made to be fit for heaven. Once he does, the prospect of concluding *The Purgatorio* and beginning *The Paradisio* thrills his soul:

> I returned from the holy wave,
> remade as new plants that are
> renewed with new fronds,
> pure and prepared to rise to the stars.[101]

The Paradisio takes the reader to dizzying heights. His guide through heaven, now, is Beatrice, and she takes Dante where Virgil never could. As Dante gains wisdom from each saint in heaven, anticipation builds steadily as the narrative focuses increasingly on

---

[100]"Poscia «Più non si va, se pria non morde, / anime sante, il foco: intrate in esso, / e al cantar di là non siate sorde»," di Dante Alighieri, *La Divina Commedia, Cantica II, Purgatorio*, Canto 27.10-12. I am greatly indebted to John R. Gilhooly, who provided most of the original translations of Dante for this book.

[101]"Io ritornai da la santissima onda / rifatto sì come piante novelle / rinovellate di novella fronda, / puro e disposto a salire a le stelle." Dante, *Purgatorio*, Canto 33.142-46.

the center of heaven—the light that enlightens all else: the triune God. In this poem, God is portrayed as a pure light encircled by angels, the size of a pinprick, radiantly enlightening all of heaven. As Dante's eyes adjust to this dazzling subject of heaven's praises, what he makes out he can only describe by paradox:

> In the deep and clear essence
> Of that lofty light three circles appeared
> In three colors but the same dimensions
> And one and the other—Iris by Iris–
> Seemed reflected by the other
> And the third was like fire breathed equally by them both
> O how short my speech is, how weak, when compared to my thoughts!
> And this—to what I saw–
> it is not enough to call my words too little.[102]

Dante expresses here, in poetic fashion, Nicene trinitarianism. To express God's incomprehensibility, he employs paradoxical language: God is a depthless "deep" whose "essence" is nevertheless "clear." To approach God is to approach an endless abyss, but where "deep" typically conjures ideas of darkness and obscurity, here in this beatific heavenly enjoyment, Dante calls God a "deep of lofty *light.*" In this abyss of light, "three circles appeared—in three colors," emphasizing the distinct personal modes of subsistence, "but the same dimensions" (or, you might say, *one in circumference*), emphasizing their single, simple divine essence.

The Nicene articulation of the Son as "God of God" is portrayed by Dante here as "Iris by Iris." Some might find it odd that Dante would make reference to a mythological Greek goddess in reference to the doctrine of eternal generation, but we must remember

---

[102]"Ne la profonda e chiara sussistenza / de l'alto lume parvermi tre giri / di tre colori e d'una contenenza; / e l'un da l'altro come iri da iri / parea reflesso, e 'l terzo parea foco / che quinci e quindi igualmente si spiri. / Oh quanto è corto il dire e come fioco / al mio concetto! e questo, a quel ch'i' vidi, / è tanto, che non basta a dicer 'poco.'" Dante, *Cantica III: Paradiso*, Canto 33.115-23.

that Iris was the goddess of the rainbow. This, then, is Dante's way of saying that the Son is "God of God, *Light of Light*." In other words, Dante says that the Son is "rainbow from rainbow." The Spirit's procession from the Father and Son, likewise, is portrayed as "fire breathed equally by" the Father and Son. *This* triune God is the central object of Dante's beatific vision. At this point, however, without moving away from *the Trinity* as the object of the beatific vision, Dante almost seems to anticipate the need for a robust christological account of the beatific vision when he goes on to say:

> O Eternal Light, that alone indwells yourself
> you alone are understood and understand yourself
> self-knowing and self-known, you love and smile upon yourself!
> That circle, so conceived
> Was, in you, as a Light reflected—
> Or so it seemed to my eyes—
> within itself, of its very own color,
> seemed to me to be painted with our effigy:
> and my sight was utterly transfixed by what I saw.[103]

As Dante continues to focus on the "three circles—three in color but the same dimension"—as he continues to stare at this sight of the Father (the Self-knowing, the divine Understander), the Son (the Self-known, the divine Understood) and the Spirit (the Self-loved and divine Self-smiled-upon)—he finds his attention being drawn particularly to the Son: "that circle" who is eternally generated from God, "as a Light reflected"—or, in biblical dictum, the "image of the invisible God" (Col. 1:15). It seems to Dante as if the Son's "coloration" which is "painted with our effigy"—or, the image of man—is more tolerable for Dante's fixed attention. The Son's accommodation in the incarnation invites Dante to behold him. But

---

[103]"O luce etterna che sola in te sidi, / sola t'intendi, e da te intelletta / e intendente te ami e arridi! / Quella circulazion che sì Concetta / pareva in te come lume reflesso, / da li occhi miei alquanto circunspetta, / dentro da sé, del suo colore stesso, / mi parve pinta de la nostra effige: / per che 'l mio viso in lei tutto era messo." Dante, *Paradiso*, Canto 33.124-32, author's translation.

"invitation" might be too mild, for Dante is "transfixed" by the sight of God the Son incarnate, glorified in beatific delight. So, he rests content to fix his eyes on Christ alone "in rapturous contemplation."[104]

Gregory Palamas

From the historical survey we have explored thus far, I could forgive the reader for assuming that the only theological tradition that had anything to say about the beatific vision was the Western one. This assumption, however, would be a mistake. For while Western thought on the beatific vision was developing through Augustine and Anselm, reaching a high point in the work of Aquinas, an Eastern tradition had been developing through figures like Maximus the Confessor (580–662), John of Damascus (675–749), and Symeon the New Theologian (949–1022), reaching a high point in the work of Gregory Palamas (1296–1359). With the arrival of Gregory, the Eastern Orthodox theological tradition hits a significant stride. Crucial for understanding Gregory's contribution to the notion of the beatific vision is his theological system as a whole, and crucial for understanding his theological system as a whole is getting a grasp on his magisterial *Triads* (or *For the Defense of Those Who Practice Sacred Quietude*).

The occasion for this work was the antagonism by a philosopher by the name of Barlaam of Calabria (1290–1348), who won a name for himself by criticizing a group to which Gregory belonged: the *hesychasts*. The *hesychia* movement was a monastic liturgical movement that focused on quiet breathing and repetitious and contemplative practices of piety. These methods were intended to facilitate a state of spiritual communion with God—and, if possible, the experience of "taboric light" (Mount Tabor is the location in Israel where it is traditionally believed that Christ was transfigured). Barlaam condemned such practices, and so Gregory wrote his

---

[104]Dante Alighieri, *The Divine Comedy: The Inferno, The Purgatorio, The Paradiso,* trans. John Ciardi (New York: New American Library, 2003), *Paradiso,* Canto 33.132.

Triads as a polemic response to Barlaam. It is here, in his *Triads*, that Gregory articulates what would become essential and absolutely definitional for Eastern Orthodox theology: the distinction between divine essence and divine energies. This defense of experiential theology is therefore the context of Gregory's primary theological contributions, a fact we ought not lightly dismiss. One of Gregory's most significant insistences regarding the beatific vision is that it is possible in a real way to attain now in this life, and it is not *strictly* reserved for the eschaton. Gregory's polemical context is therefore significant: Gregory does not merely defend the hypothetical as an intellectual exercise, but he rather seeks to defend and legitimize the claim that he and other hesychasts had in fact experienced this beatific vision—this "taboric light."

Gregory has three primary theological concerns in the *Triads* that provide him with the occasion for describing divine essence and energies (i.e., the theological context in which his conception of the beatific vision must be understood). First, Gregory is concerned with avoiding an overly intellectualized theology. For Gregory, knowledge of God cannot be reduced to mere intellectual ascent, in part because of God's absolute transcendence and incomprehensibility. Knowledge of God must be experiential. Gregory begins to emphasize this point by highlighting the limitations of philosophy. While not rejecting the pursuit of philosophy wholesale ("if you put to good use that part of the profane wisdom which has been well excised, no harm can result, for it will naturally become an instrument for good"),[105] Gregory stresses the point that "it cannot in the strict sense be called a gift of God and a spiritual thing, for it pertains to the order of nature and is not sent from on high."[106] For true knowledge of God, that which *can* "in the strict sense be called a gift of God," one must be plunged into the

---

[105] Gregory Palamas, *The Triads*, ed. John Meyendorff, trans. Nicholas Gendle (Mahwah, NJ: Paulist Press, 1983), 29.
[106] Palamas, *Triads*, 29.

"dazzling darkness" wherein "the divine things are given to the saints."[107] "Thus," summarizes Gregory,

> the perfect contemplation of God and divine things is not simply an abstraction; but beyond this abstraction, there is a participation in divine things, a gift and possession rather than just a process of negation. But these possessions and gifts are ineffable: If one speaks of them, one must have recourse to images and analogies—not because that is the way in which these things are seen, but because one cannot adumbrate what one has seen in any other way.[108]

Such an ineffable experience, according to Gregory, cannot be circumscribed by the analogies given to describe them. However, this emphasis on transcendence does not keep the affective and even bodily experiences at beat. The transcendent experience Gregory imagines in divine contemplation transcends even the limitations we would ordinarily place on reserving such experiences to the psychological realm. For Gregory, appeal to bodily experience in these hesychastic spiritual experiences was not a counterbalance to his emphasis on transcendence, but a further articulation thereof.[109]

Second, Gregory is concerned with upholding the absolute incomprehensibility of the divine essence. According to Gregory, "The essence of God transcends the fact of being inaccessible to the senses, since God is not only above all created things, but is even beyond the Godhead."[110] While such a statement may strike the reader as mere esoteric sophistry, Gregory's insistence that "God" is beyond "Godhead" makes sense within the context of his distinction between divine essence and energies. At present, it is worth emphasizing that this "beyondness" is Gregory's way of emphasizing divine

---

[107] Palamas, *Triads*, 36.
[108] Palamas, *Triads*, 36.
[109] "There are indeed blessed passions and common activities of body and soul, which, far from nailing the spirit to the flesh, serve to draw the flesh to a dignity close to that of the spirit, and persuade it too to tend towards what is above." Palamas, *Triads*, 51.
[110] Palamas, *Triads*, 57.

incomprehensibility in no uncertain terms: "The excellence of Him Who surpasses all things is not only beyond all affirmation, but also beyond all negation; it exceeds all excellence that is attainable by the mind."[111] Whatever picture of the beatific vision Gregory will allow, he simply will not abide any notion that claims to grasp God's essence in himself. Thus, while the divine light one beholds in hesychastic ecstasy "is not an angel, for it bears the marks of the Master," it also "is not the essence of God, for that is inaccessible and incommunicable."[112] This incomprehensibility, however, does not lead to utter agnosticism. We should understand Gregory's apophaticism not as a denial of any real knowledge of God but as the denial that true deifying knowledge of God can come "through concepts"; it is rather "contemplative." As Vladimir Lossky puts it, deification, in Gregory's conception, raises "the mind to those realities which pass all understanding. This is why dogmas of the Church often present themselves to the human reason as antinomies, the more difficult to resolve the more sublime the mystery which they express."[113]

Third, Gregory is concerned with insisting that it is possible to experience the eschatological heavenly vision of God in this life, before the resurrection. For Gregory, the beatific vision is the vision of the deifying light of God in Christ. According to Gregory, "on the Last Day, [this light] will deify in a *manifest* fashion 'the sons of the Resurrection,' who will rejoice in eternity and in glory in communion with Him Who has endowed our nature with a glory and splendor that is divine."[114] Chief among the biblical themes Gregory meditates on in this regard is Christ's transfiguration. For Gregory, what Peter, James, and John saw on the holy mountain was not a created light of a creature, but the preexistent light of the divine. "Thus," says Gregory, "he was divine before, but He bestowed at the

---

[111] Palamas, *Triads*, 57.
[112] Palamas, *Triads*, 57.
[113] Vladimir Lossky, *The Mystical Theology of the Eastern Church* (Crestwood, NY: St. Vladimir's Seminary Press, 1957), 43.
[114] Palamas, *Triads*, 57.

time of His Transfiguration a divine power upon the eyes of the apostles and enabled them to look up and see for themselves. This light, then, was not a hallucination but will remain for eternity, and has existed from the beginning."[115]

Or, more pithily stated, "The Savior did not ascend Tabor, accompanied by the chosen disciples, in order to show them that He was a man."[116] So, Gregory believes that what the disciples saw on the holy mountain was that vision the saints will enjoy in the age to come in the beatific vision. Yet, Gregory is quite insistent (and indeed, *animated* in his *Triads* by this insistence) that this eschatological vision is not reserved exclusively for the eschaton. Thus, while Gregory can say with one breath, "Such is the vision of God which in the Age which is without end will be seen only by those judged worthy of such a blessed fulfillment," he can say with the next, "This same vision was seen in the present age by the chosen among the apostles on Tabor, by Stephen when he was being stoned, and by Anthony in his battle for inner stillness—indeed by the saints, that is, the pure in heart."[117] Similarly, Lossky, very much in the same vein as Gregory, says, "Perfect vision of the deity, perceptible in its uncreated light, is 'the mystery of the eighth day'; it belongs to the age to come. But those who are worthy attain to this vision of 'the Kingdom of God come with power' even in this life, a vision such as the three apostles saw on Mount Tabor."[118]

Thus, Gregory inherits the same tension that every other theologian we have covered in this survey inherited (and indeed, the tension impressed upon every careful reader of Scripture): how can we maintain God's incomprehensibility while also holding fast to the biblical hope of seeing God? Except, for Gregory, the tension receives the added stress of his *hesychasm*. Not only will this tension

---

[115] Palamas, *Triads*, 76.
[116] Palamas, *Triads*, 78.
[117] Palamas, *Triads*, 67-68. Cf. *Triads*, 32-33.
[118] Lossky, *Mystical Theology*, 220.

have to be resolved for how we conceptualize the saint's experience in the eschaton, Gregory has to resolve it for the hesychast's experience in contemplative prayer and taboric light! Divine "essence and energies" are, in part, Gregory's resolution to the tension. Lossky essentially insists as much: "These distinctions in God which are made by the theology of the Eastern Church do not in any way contradict its apophatic attitude in regard to revealed truth. On the contrary, these antinomical distinctions are dictated by a concern for safeguarding the mystery, while yet expressing the data of revelation in dogma."[119]

So, what is the distinction between divine essence and divine energies? For as central as this concept is for Eastern theology, the answer is not as straightforward as one may hope.[120] At times, the distinction seems to indicate little more than the distinction between *theologia* and *oikonomia* (God in himself and God's works), as when Gregory says, "Since God is entirely present in each of the divine energies, we name Him from each of them, although it is clear that He transcends all of them . . . how could each provide Him with a name and manifest Him entirely, thanks to indivisible and supernatural simplicity, if He did not transcend all these energies?"[121] At other times, however, he prohibits us from concluding that the essence and energies amounts to the distinction between *theologia* and *oikonomia*. "It is clear," says Gregory, "that these unoriginated and endless rays are other than the imparticipable essence of God, and different (albeit inseparable) from the essence."[122] Divine energies are therefore a kind of mediatorial

---

[119]Lossky, *Mystical Theology*, 87.
[120]This is a point even David Bradshaw readily acknowledges: "The eastern tradition as we have presented it so far is rich but polyphonic. One finds terms as fundamental as energeia and 'the things around God' being used differently by different authors, and concepts such as ceaseless prayer and the uncreated light achieving great importance without any attempt to incorporate them into a dogmatic synthesis." David Bradshaw, *Aristotle East and West: Metaphysics and the Division of Christendom* (New York: Cambridge University Press, 2004), 221.
[121]Palamas, *Triads*, 96.
[122]Palamas, *Triads*, 99.

effulgence of the divine essence. They are unoriginated expressions of God, wherein God dwells entirely but not exhaustively. These divine energies are not the divine essence of God, nor are they personal modes of subsistence or divine missions. By participating in the divine energies, creatures really are participating in God, but not in his ineffable divine essence. Thus, Lossky summarizes:

> The doctrine of the energies, ineffably distinct from the essence, is the dogmatic basis of the real character of all mystical experience. God, who is inaccessible in His essence, is present in His energies. . . . Wholly unknowable in His essence, God wholly reveals Himself in His energies, which yet in no way divide His nature into two parts—knowable and unknowable—but signify two different modes of the divine existence, in the essence and outside of the essence.[123]

Adonis Vidu insightfully points out, "It is precisely the 'real distinction' that enables the concept of uncreated energies to do its dogmatic work. The energies mediate between the world and God, while preserving the distinction between the two and the divine transcendence."[124] Thus, for Eastern theology in general, and Gregory in particular, "God is not identical with his energies, which nevertheless naturally flow from him. These energies nevertheless permeate creation, ultimately deifying it, allegedly without compromising divine transcendence."[125] As it relates to the beatific vision, this distinction allows for Eastern Orthodox theologians to affirm the reality that believers will behold God in the life to come (and in some instances, the present age), while, in their estimation, adequately safeguarding divine transcendence.

Before concluding this chapter, it is worth briefly responding to Gregory's proposal. While I have refrained from doing so with the other figures described in this chapter, interacting with Gregory's

---

[123] Lossky, *Mystical Theology*, 86.
[124] Adonis Vidu, "Triune Agency, East and West: Uncreated Energies or Created Effects?," *Perichoresis* 18.1 (2020): 61.
[125] Vidu, "Triune Agency," 61.

thought critically here is appropriate for at least two reasons. First, this is the most natural place for me to interact briefly with the Eastern tradition in general, and Palamas in particular. Because I write from within the Western theological tradition, the figures I will explore in the following chapter will not build on the work of Gregory in any significant manner, and the synthetic proposal I offer in chapter 5 will primarily interact with the Reformers and their reception of the theology of Aquinas, Anselm, and Augustine. Therefore, there will not be another natural occasion for our study to return to Gregory. Second, and related, the exclusion of Gregory and the Eastern tradition throughout the rest of this volume should receive some explanation. My decision to stay within the Western tradition on this matter is a critical decision based both on the strengths of the Western tradition and the weaknesses, in my estimation, of the Eastern tradition. This is as good a place as any to offer some justification for my ongoing selectiveness. So, while I am grateful for some of the peripheral contributions of Gregory's system—which will receive some brief attention in the subsequent chapters of this book—and while common Western caricatures of Eastern theology should be stridently avoided,[126] I consider Gregory's theology problematic and less preferable to the Western tradition of Aquinas for the following reasons.

First, returning back to the occasion for the *Triads*, Gregory seems to explicitly endorse what Paul seems to (at least) implicitly discourage as the norm of Christian piety. Remember, the context for writing *Triads* was a defense of hesychasm and the spiritual ecstatic experiences that arise from its practices. But I am not confident such practices *should* receive a defense. On the surface, at the very least, they strike a concerning resemblance to the kind of thing

---

[126] This would include the notion that the Eastern Orthodox conception of "deification" flattens the Creator-creature distinction, or that the Eastern Orthodox tradition is oblivious to the challenge of maintaining divine simplicity in the face of the distinction between divine essence and energies, both of which are sorely mistaken.

Paul strictly forbade the Colossians from dabbling in (Col 2:8-15). Repeatedly, Gregory appeals to Paul's heavenly vision in 2 Corinthians 12:2-6 in order to justify the kind of formula that positions one to experience contemplative communion with God in ecstatic rapture.[127] On the one hand, this appeal should not be lightly dismissed. Moses, after all, seemed to request the very thing Paul experienced—or, at the very least, something very much like it—and, as we saw in the previous chapter, he was not rebuked for his request. Furthermore, Paul *did* experience this transportive vision. This experience must be conceptualized *somehow*. On the other hand, taking Paul's example in 2 Corinthians 12:2-6 as an invitation to seek after a similar experience seems to get the logic of the text almost entirely backward. Paul resorts to the revelation of this experience as a final effort to illustrate for the Corinthians how inappropriate their craven lust for leaders with exotic spiritual experiences was. The entire thrust of 2 Corinthians 11:1-12:10 is satirical. He intends to hold up a mirror to the Corinthians as they fawn after their "super apostles" to show them the vanity of their criteria (cf. 2 Cor 12:11-13). Paul's description of his experience in the third heaven was not intended to inspire Corinthian aspiration to achieve similar spiritual heights (the Corinthian sensibility was in no way lacking such aspirations—this is the very spirit Paul attempted to exorcise!), but rather to put such vain judgments of greatness to bed once and for all. It would seem, in other words, that a careful reading of Paul's description of his experience in 2 Corinthians 12:2-6 would put one, in part, on the side of Barlaam and not Gregory.[128]

Second, I do not believe Gregory adequately punctuates the clear qualitative difference between sanctification in this life and deification in the next. Instead, Gregory seems to flatten these two

---

[127] E.g., Palamas, *Triads*, 38.
[128] My conclusions here should come as no surprise, since even Bradshaw portrays Barlaam as "the unwitting representative of the West" who "imbibed certain elements of Augustine's thought." Bradshaw, *Aristotle East and West*, 230. What Bradshaw means to serve as a criticism against Barlaam I am inclined to chalk up as a compliment.

realities out as one experience. This temptation to "flatten" is a kind of occupational hazard for Gregory in his polemical response to Barlaam: his whole purpose is to defend the practices of the hesychasts, and one of his arguments is that they legitimately experience a kind of pre-eschatological experience of the beatific vision in tandem with their practices. While there are some possible noteworthy examples here and there,[129] the tradition of the West seems to capture to a greater degree that the sight of divine glory in this life is a sight by *faith*, while the sight of divine glory in the next life is a sight of glorified *vision*. The line that distinguishes the two kinds of sight is the line that divides death and resurrection—fallen creation under the curse of sin on one side, and the new heavens and the new earth on the other. In an effort to defend his fellow *hesychasts*, Gregory seems to inappropriately blur this line.

Third, I remain unconvinced that the distinction between divine essence and energies resolves the theological complications its proponents seem to think it does. While Gregory (along with Lossky after him) insists that the inaccessible nature of the divine essence and its distinction from divine energies does not conclude with agnosticism of the divine essence, some kind of agnosticism seems unavoidable. What, in the Eastern Orthodox conception, do the divine energies truly reveal about God's essence? Simply insisting that energies are "inseparable" from the divine essence does not really say much. Inseparable *how*? In what way? In truth, it seems that rather than resolving the tension between God's incomprehensibility and the creature's vision of God with his notion of divine energies, Gregory simply pushes the problem back one step further and puts God's essence even further out of reach. I agree with Vidu's assessment when he says:

---

[129]Consider Boersma's reflections on Augustine in *Seeing God*, 117-26. Though even the example of Augustine is noteworthy because of its uniqueness, Augustine's custom was to stress the *discontinuity* between faith and vision. Nowhere did he positively *encourage* his readers to attempt at a vision of "taboric light"—or anything like it—on this side of the resurrection.

The key question has to do with the *joint* between the tri-personal essence of God and his energies. The insistence that his energies change, yet without his essence changing raises the question of the manner of the derivation of the energies from the essence. Either the energies are grounded in some way in the essence, or they are not. Since the second option is utterly unacceptable . . . the question is, in what way are they grounded in the essence? Whatever the energies are grounded in, whether the divine will (to highlight the divine freedom), or in something else, there must be some sort of correlate to the economic change in the immanent Trinity. The typical suggestion . . . is to say the divine will. But does a change in the energies also entail a change in the divine will? If so, can simplicity still be claimed to obtain at the level of the essence, if there is a correlate to an energetic change?[130]

In other words, the Eastern Orthodox distinction between divine essence and energies appears to be caught on the horns of a dilemma. Either the divine energies do not correspond in any truly meaningful way to the divine essence, and therefore cannot thereby truly *reveal* anything of God, or they *are* grounded in the divine essence and therefore seem to imply change in the divine essence, which would compromise the doctrine of divine simplicity. In sum, despite his clear insistence to the contrary, Gregory's conception of divine essence and energies seems to pose a legitimate problem for the doctrine of divine simplicity.[131] For these reasons, I will favor the Western tradition in my reflections on the great tradition's

---

[130] Vidu, "Triune Agency," 70.

[131] This observation obviously thrusts us into a debate regarding how to conceptualize simplicity. After all, Bradshaw argues that it is Aquinas's view of God, not Gregory's, that compromises divine simplicity, since it appears to be "inconsistent with his position on divine free choice." Bradshaw, *Aristotle East and West*, 257. Further, he argues that Aquinas's "account of the participation in God—through the sharing of all creatures in *esse* and the sharing of rational creatures in grace—relies too heavily on the category of efficient causality, thereby leaving the relationship between God and creatures merely extrinsic" (257). It would appear as though Eastern criticisms of the West and Western criticisms of the East mirror each other, and depend entirely on *how* one conceptualizes the doctrine of divine simplicity. Adjudicating this ancient debate is beyond the scope of this project. Suffice it to say, I believe the Western formulation of simplicity is preferable to the Eastern version, and that the challenges of the East against the Western notion of pure actuality can be adequately answered, as Vidu demonstrates in "Triune Agency," 71-74.

reception of this doctrine throughout the rest of this historical survey and beyond.[132]

Conclusion

This modest survey shows that the beatific vision occupied the imagination of pre-Reformation theologians—across the board—in no small or insignificant way. In the next chapter, we will conclude our historical survey by examining a selection of Reformation and post-Reformation theologians, who stood in basic continuity with the figures discussed in this chapter. Without jettisoning the tradition, these Reformed and post-Reformation theologians enriched the tradition with their own unique meditations on the blessed hope of the saints throughout the ages.

---

[132] I should acknowledge it does seem possible to formulate the Palamite essence-energies distinction in such a way as to harmonize with a Thomistic doctrine of God. James Rooney has made a valiant effort to do just this in his chapter, "Classical Theists Are Committed to the Palamite Essence-Energies Distinction (Or, How to Make Sense of the Fact That God Does Not Intrinsically Differ Even Though He Can Do Otherwise)," in *Classical Theism: New Essays on the Metaphysics of God*, ed. Jonathan Fuqua and Robert C. Koons (New York: Routledge, 2023). Though Rooney even seems to admit the idiosyncratic character of his presentation when he says, "Because it seems to me that there are as many versions of the Palamite distinction as interpreters, and I aim at analyzing the systematic issues of whether the distinction is coherent and truly said of God, I will use merely two short texts of Palamas as a starting point" (319). For my own part, I remain unconvinced that Rooney's portrayal is accurate, since he essentially reduces the essence-energies distinction to a matter of linguistic predication, while I believe Gregory intends for the distinction to carry more metaphysical freight. Though, admittedly, this puts me in a sea of interpreters who have their own ideas about what Gregory might have meant. It may be that a "proper" definition of Gregory's distinction is beyond the ability of anyone but Gregory himself.

4

A CLOUD OF WITNESSES, PART TWO

Reformation and Post-Reformation Historical Witness

CONTRARY TO POPULAR BELIEF, the Reformers of the sixteenth century were not schismatic radicals, jockeying for theological independence and attempting to start a new tradition outside of the catholic tradition. Rather, they perceived themselves as pushing for a renewal movement from *within* the "one, holy, catholic, and apostolic Church."[1] True, there was significant theological divergence between the Reformers and the status quo of the high medieval church, but they believed that they had catholicity on *their* side. Indeed, Calvin positively insists that he and his fellow Reformers were more catholic than his papist counterparts.[2] They never intended to start a new theological tradition, and there is a real sense in which they never left the catholic church. It was not until the Council of Trent, when the staple doctrines of the Reformers

---

[1] For a recent and thorough defense of this thesis, see Matthew Barrett, *Reformation as Renewal: Retrieving the One, Holy, Catholic, and Apostolic Church—An Intellectual History* (Grand Rapids, MI: Zondervan Academic, 2023).

[2] See Calvin's perforator letter to the *Institutes,* addressed to King Francis I (1515–1547), in which he wrote, "It is equally unfair of [the Papists] to set the ancient Fathers against us—that is, those who wrote in the early years of the church—as if they sided with them in their godlessness. If the Father's authority could be invoked to settle the dispute between us, victory would very largely go with us." John Calvin, *Institutes of the Christian Religion: Translated from the First French Edition of 1541,* trans. Robert White (Edinburgh: The Banner of Truth Trust, 2014), xxv.

were anathematized, that Roman Catholicism as such existed in contradistinction from the other Western theologians we now identify as Protestants. The Protestant church, as such, was created not by the Reformers but their Roman contemporaries. Luther and Calvin and Vermigli and Melancthon and Bucer, in this sense, never left the catholic church—rather, the Roman church left them.

We should be careful not to exaggerate this point, however, important though it is. The Reformation, though it was a *renewal* movement within the catholic church, was a radical renewal movement that left no sacred cow unscathed. So many doctrines that had become essential to the Western tradition—from penance and indulgences to the papacy, from transubstantiation and the Latin mass to the celibacy of clergy—were directly challenged. In that way, the Reformers took liberty to treat tradition as a relative and authoritative, yet fallible, guide. Scripture alone was *absolutely* and *unquestionably* authoritative. If barnacles and accretions had grown around the great ship of Christ's church, the Reformers did not hesitate to put some elbow-grease into scraping them off with extreme prejudice.[3]

Judging from the state of their theological progeny today, particularly Reformed and evangelical churches, we might expect that the Reformers dispensed with the beatific vision in this overdue maintenance of the ship. This would be a mistake, however. The Reformers did not reject the beatific vision as one of the many unwelcome distractions and errors that Rome had picked up in the Middle Ages. No, this doctrine was, for the Reformers, an essential feature of the catholic church to which they proudly belonged. As I will show in this chapter, the tradition that would develop out of the Reformation *would* offer unique contributions to the doctrine, but its contributions are those offered in essential continuity with what we saw in the previous chapter.

---

[3] I first heard this analogy from Gavin Ortlund, who uses it frequently to describe the Reformation on his YouTube channel, "Truth Unites."

John Calvin

Two equal and opposite temptations persistently threaten any fruitful discussion on Calvin's doctrine of the beatific vision. The first is to take his lack of explicit language or extended discussion on the topic to mean that he did not have a category for the doctrine altogether.[4] The second is to overcorrect the first error and insist that the doctrine was the animating gravitational center of Calvin's theology. In point of fact, Calvin's relationship to the doctrine of the beatific vision is far more complicated than either of these oversimplifications imply. On the one hand, the beatific vision played a very important role in Calvin's ethic more broadly, and his theology of the Christian life in particular.[5] On the other hand, Calvin has markedly less to say about the doctrine, in speculative terms, than the pre-Reformation figures discussed in the previous chapter (or many of the figures who will come after him in the Reformed tradition, for that matter).[6] The reason for Calvin's modesty, on his own terms, has everything to do with his high view of the Scriptures and the commitment to avoid going "beyond what is written" (cf. 1 Cor 4:6). While recent work on the Reformation has convincingly demonstrated that Calvin and the other Reformers conceptualized themselves as standing in organic continuity with the entire great tradition, and specifically the church fathers, we should not exaggerate this point and fail to recognize that

---

[4] Hans Boersma names and takes issue with this view when he notes, "So far, most Calvin scholarship has argued that Calvin simply abandoned the traditional doctrine of the beatific vision." Boersma, *Seeing God: The Beatific Vision in the Christian Tradition,* (Grand Rapids, MI: Eerdmans, 2018), 258. Strikingly, Suzanne McDonald can go so far as to state, almost axiomatically, "Calvin has nothing directly to say about it in the *Institutes*" ("Beholding the Glory of God in the Face of Jesus Christ: John Owen and the 'Reforming' of the Beatific Vision," in *The Ashgate Research Companion to John Owen's Theology*, ed. Kelly M. Kapic and Mark Jones [Burlington, VT: Ashgate, 2012], 141n1).

[5] See Carsten Card-Hyatt, "Christ Our Light: The Expectation of Seeing God in Calvin's Theology of the Christian Life," *Perichoresis* 18, no. 1 (2020): 25-40.

[6] Boersma is right to note, "Nowhere in his writings does John Calvin provide any kind of extended discussion of the doctrine of the beatific vision. Unlike many in the earlier tradition, Calvin did not devote a treatise to the topic. Nor did he write the kind of devotional theology, common in the Middle Ages and revived in the later Puritan thought, that dissected the spiritual steps leading up to the beatific vision." Boersma, *Seeing God*, 257.

Calvin was not afraid to disagree with his theological heroes. On such occasions, Calvin reserved his sharpest criticisms for what he considered an unbecoming curiosity among the fathers to go beyond the revelation of the Scriptures. For example, on 1 John 3:2, while Calvin offers insightful reflections, as we saw in chapter 2, he nevertheless opts to "pass by ... refined questions," such as those pondered by Augustine, whom Calvin faults for unnecessarily "tormenting himself with these."[7]

Another example we could point to in order to establish Calvin's chastened hermeneutical instincts is an interpretive divergence between myself and Calvin on a significant passage for our discussion: Exodus 33:18. Recall from chapter two, I argued that Moses' desire to see God's glory was itself good and proper, despite the necessary impossibility of full satiation in this age. Moses, I argued, was *not* stepping beyond his proper boundary to ask for that which he could not experience in full until glory. Calvin, by contrast, insists that Moses was doing exactly that! Moses' "desire itself was improper," says Calvin, even if "its object was correct."[8] Indeed, according to Calvin, Exodus 33:18 shows how Moses is "carried beyond due bounds, and longs for more than is lawful or expedient."[9] For Calvin, what Moses receives as a *word*, in the declaration of Yahweh's name, is "more excellent" than the accommodation of his vision in showing Moses his back, since by receiving his name, "Moses may know Him more by His voice than by His face; for speechless visions would be cold and altogether evanescent, did they not borrow efficacy from words."[10] On this point, I concur with Carsten Card-Hyatt who suggests that Calvin is "overcorrecting" here.[11]

---

[7] John Calvin, *Commentaries on the Catholic Epistles,* trans. John Owen (Edinburgh: Calvin Translation Society, 1855), 181.

[8] John Calvin, *Harmony of the Evangelists, Matthew, Mark, and Luke,* vol. 2, trans. William Pringle (Edinburgh: Calvin Translation Society, 1848), 387.

[9] Calvin, *Harmony of the Evangelists,* 387.

[10] John Calvin, *Harmony of the Law,* vol. 3, trans. Charles William Bingham (Edinburgh: Calvin Translation Society, 1852), 387.

[11] Card-Hyatt, "Christ Our Light," 30.

Before elaborating, though, it is important to recognize the value of Calvin's correction: even if it is excessive, what is the error he seeks to avoid? The answer is a conflation of faith and vision—the kind of thing I briefly objected to in the writing of Gregory Palamas in the previous chapter. Calvin is against "a false continuity between the way faith knows God now and the way it will be fulfilled after the resurrection."[12] This is a legitimate concern—one that can arguably distinguish the Western Christian tradition from the Eastern Christian tradition, broadly speaking. Nevertheless, while attempting to avoid a genuine error, Calvin overcorrects when he places Moses' request in Exodus 33 in such a category. Scripture nowhere indicates that Moses' request was inappropriate, and indeed, his "audacity" is tacitly commended when his bold request is rewarded with a kind of qualified acceptance. Thankfully, this overcorrection does not have the final word on Calvin's view of the beatific vision, since the danger he risks here (i.e., the danger of "leaving the promised beatific vision without content, without force for life in the present")[13] is avoided elsewhere in his corpus. I concur with Boersma that "although the beatific vision only had a small place in Calvin's *Institutes*, he was nonetheless convinced that only God himself constitutes our final end, so that only our vision of him yields true happiness."[14]

Calvin's most explicit section on the beatific vision in his *Institutes* is also perhaps his most chastened and modest. In book 3, chapter 25, section 10, Calvin is concerned with the saint's "everlasting blessedness." "For though we very truly hear that the Kingdom of God will be filled with splendor, joy, happiness, and glory," says Calvin, "yet when these things are spoken of, they remain utterly remote from our perception, and, as it were, wrapped in obscurities, until that day comes when he will reveal to us his

---

[12]Card-Hyatt, "Christ Our Light," 30.
[13]Card-Hyatt, "Christ Our Light," 30.
[14]Boersma, *Seeing God*, 259.

glory, that we may behold it face to face."[15] The caution described in his commentaries above is felt particularly in this section of the *Institutes*, when Calvin reminds his readers how "we must . . . keep sobriety, lest forgetful of our limitations we should soar aloft with the greater boldness, and be overcome by the brightness of the heavenly glory. We also feel how we are titillated by our immoderate desire to know more than is lawful."[16] Nevertheless, such caution should not at all be interpreted as Calvin's unwillingness to put the weight of significance on such an eschatological vision. Indeed, Calvin surprises the reader when he puts such a vision as the load-bearing telos of *every single* good, *every single* happiness for which creatures long in this life. On this concept, Calvin sounds dangerously like a Christian-Platonist:

> If God contains the fullness of all good things in himself like an inexhaustible fountain, nothing beyond him is to be sought by those who strive after the highest good and all the elements of happiness, as we are taught in many passages. . . . If the Lord will share his glory, power, and righteousness with the elect—nay, will give himself to be enjoyed by them and, what is more excellent, will somehow make them to become one with himself, let us remember that every sort of happiness is included under this benefit.[17]

As in the case with Aquinas and Anselm and Augustine, Calvin sees this heavenly blessedness—which is summed up as "seeing him face to face"—as the telos of every good in this life. Calvin can therefore conclude this section by stating that "as Christ begins the glory of his body in this world with manifold diversity of gifts, and increases it by degrees, so also he will perfect it in heaven."[18] Thus, the beatific vision, while shrouded in a cloud of mystery (one that Calvin strongly felt like he did not have permission to

---

[15] John Calvin, *Institutes of the Christian Religion*, 2 vols., ed. John T. McNeill, trans. Ford Lewis Battles (Louisville, KY: Westminster John Knox, 1960), 3.25.10.
[16] Calvin, *Institutes*, 3.25.10.
[17] Calvin, *Institutes*, 3.25.10.
[18] Calvin, *Institutes*, 3.25.10.

attempt to penetrate in this life), was still all-important from a teleological perspective.

If this much were all Calvin had to say on the beatific vision, his contribution would not be all that interesting. But fascinatingly, Calvin elsewhere breaks his own rule on speculation and ventures into uncharted territory when he writes about the role of Christ's mediation in the final state of glory: "When as partakers in heavenly glory we shall see God as he is, Christ, having then discharged the office of Mediator, will cease to be the ambassador of his Father, and will be satisfied with that glory which he enjoyed before the creation of the world."[19] While such a statement may strike some as jarring—and indeed, I will argue there are good reasons for us to disagree with Calvin here—we should nevertheless acknowledge the biblical rationale behind this kind of statement. Jesus' words in John 17:5 ("And now, Father, glorify me in your own presence with the glory that I had with you before the world existed") have to be explained *somehow*, and Calvin puts forth one possible proposal: this refers to a post-resurrection state whereby his mediatorial role is completed and knowledge of God through the Son is no longer necessary. Commenting on 1 Corinthians 15:27-28, which describes the culmination of Christ's second-Adamic ministry, when the Son will subject all things to the Father so that "God may be all in all," Calvin insists that the "veil being then removed, we shall openly behold God reigning in his majesty and Christ's humanity will no longer be interposed to keep us back from a closer view of God."[20] When Calvin describes the Son's "humanity" as "no longer to be interposed to keep us back from a closer view of God," he does not at all mean to disparage Christ's human nature. Rather, he recognizes that Christ's human nature serves a particular redemptive purpose that, in that eternal day of heaven, will have been

---

[19] Calvin, *Institutes*, 2.14.3.
[20] Calvin, *Commentary on the Epistles of Paul the Apostle to the Corinthians,* vol. 2, trans. John Pringle (Edinburgh, UK: Calvin Translation Society, 1848), 17.

accomplished. Again, I believe we have biblical and theological reasons to disagree with Calvin here, which will become clear in the following pages, but we should not miss this fascinating turn of events in our historical survey thus far. What is so striking about this feature of Calvin's doctrine is that he here comes close to articulating a position often attributed to Aquinas: a conception of the beatific vision that is christologically deficient. Whether such a charge really sticks for Aquinas is debatable,[21] but perhaps it sticks for Calvin.[22]

Johann Gerhard

The Lutheran tradition is not silent on the beatific vision. Johann Gerhard (1582–1637), the Lutheran-scholastic theologian, treats the topic in a number of places, particularly in volume 34 of his *Theological Commonplaces*, titled *On Eternal Life*.[23] Gerhard's fifth chapter, "On the Material and Form of Eternal Life," addresses the beatific vision from many angles, pulling particularly from Augustine. "You see," writes Gerhard, "anything joyful and good that happens in this life, anything desirable and lovable, all of it is set forth as a foreshadow of the blessedness and happiness of eternal life so that there may be a hint that eternal life is going to be the fullness of all good things, the treasury of every happiness, the end and fulfillment of every desire."[24] After listing one lengthy citation after another of various church fathers and medieval theologians, Gerhard succinctly states: "To include many things in a few words, there will be in eternal life 'the beatific vision' of the most holy

---

[21]Ortlund, "Will We See God's Essence?"
[22]Indeed, Simon Gaine even suggests that, theologically speaking, Thomas is more of a mediating position between Calvin on the one side, with Owen and Edwards on the other, with respect to the role of Christ in the beatific vision. See Simon Gaine, "The Beatific Vision and the Heavenly Meditation of Christ," *TheoLogica* 2, no. 2 (2018), 127-28.
[23]Johann Gerhard, *Theological Commonplaces XXXIV: On Eternal Life*, ed. Joshua J. Hayes and Heath R. Curtis, trans. Richard J. Dinda (St. Louis: Concordia, 2022). Translated from volume 9 of Johann Gerhard, *Loci Theologica*, edited by Friedrich Reinhold Eduard Preuss (Berlin: Hinrichs, 1875).
[24]Gerhard, *On Eternal Life*, 51.93.

Trinity, the putting on of incorruptibility, and the fulfillment of every desire."[25]

Gerhard goes on to explicate this succinct statement with a list of comparisons between this life and the next: "In this life there is pure calamity, in the other pure felicity; here pure captivity, there pure freedom; here pure transience, there pure eternity. There we shall have insatiable satiety and unfailing joy, the blessed sight of God, the restoration of perfect righteousness, the fulfillment of all good things, and the recovery of the divine image."[26] Gerhard's treatment, in fact, is as thorough as any other we have thus far examined. On the question of whether the vision of God is intellectual or ocular, Gerhard is able to consistently affirm both by bringing in a Christological emphasis. On the one hand, Gerhard seems to side with a kind of position articulated by Aquinas when he writes: "The elect will not see God in the same way as one man looks upon another in this life. From such purely external vision he receives perhaps some pleasure but no or very little practical use. However, the vision of God will be especially internal and intimate, providing the elect not only joy and pleasure but also a treasury of all goods things."[27]

On the other hand, Gerhard recognizes the important centrality of Christ in the beatific vision when he goes on to say, "Nevertheless it is certain that the blessed will see Christ, true God and man, with their own corporeal eyes and, consequently, that the bodies of the blessed cannot be totally excluded from the vision of God."[28] Gerhard then seems to approvingly acknowledge "the pious ancients" who attributed "a threefold seeing to the blessed: corporeal, by which they will see the humanity of Christ, the saints in their glorified bodies, and a new heaven and new earth; spiritual,

---

[25]Gerhard, *On Eternal Life*, 53.104.
[26]Gerhard, *On Eternal Life*, 53.104.
[27]Gerhard, *On Eternal Life*, 60.115.
[28]Gerhard, *On Eternal Life*, 60.115.

by which they will see the angels and the souls of the blessed; intellectual, by which they will see God Himself."[29]

As he promises, Gerhard returns to the question in much more detail later on. Before giving his own proposal for how to answer the question, Will the blessed see the divine essence with bodily eyes?, Gerhard helpfully lays out the landscape of how the question has been answered in the past.[30] Gerhard points to "some of the fathers," "the Scholastics and all the Papists," and some of "the Calvinists," including Vermigli and Zanchi, who all answer in the negative.[31] After listing out the arguments the negative position uses from Scripture and from rationality, Gerhard goes on to do the same for "some of our theologians" who "accept the affirmative side of this question," which includes Chytraeus, Schilterus and Cramerus, as well as the Calvinist Alsted.[32] Only after giving full voice to both positions does Gerhard give his own proposal, which is something, at least in his own self-conception, as a mediatorial position between the two. "Here we think that we should stand, so to speak, in the middle of the road," says Gerhard.[33] On the one hand, Gerhard recognizes that "God in His own nature is incorporeal spirit, so also He remains such to all eternity."[34] Creatures do not cease to be creatures in glory, and God does not cease to be what he always is: incorporeal spirit. On the other hand, the Scriptures seem to paint the picture of the blessed doing what they cannot do: seeing in their flesh that which is not flesh. "That the blessed in eternal life will look upon God with the greatest joy is revealed in Holy Scripture," says Gerhard, "but whether the mode of that beatific vision will be only mental and interior or at the same time ocular and exterior, this cannot be discovered definitely."[35]

---

[29] Gerhard, *On Eternal Life*, 60.115.
[30] Gerhard, *On Eternal Life*, 143.239-41.
[31] Gerhard, *On Eternal Life*, 143.239-40.
[32] Gerhard, *On Eternal Life*, 143.240.
[33] Gerhard, *On Eternal Life*, 144.241.
[34] Gerhard, *On Eternal Life*, 144.241.
[35] Gerhard, *On Eternal Life*, 144.242.

To say this much, however, is not a commitment on Gerhard's point to refrain from saying anything further. For he does venture to insist that it cannot and should not "be stubbornly denied that the eyes of the blessed are so much glorified and that through a supernatural light they are so uplifted that they could achieve the very vision of the divine essence."[36] Gerhard, like Augustine before, speculates that perhaps God blesses the saints with an incomprehensible power to do that which is completely lacking in the power of nature. "If God can grant a glorified body other properties of spirit," reasons Gerhard, "why not also this: the ability to see spirit with its own eyes? Surely God is not less infinitely distant from the created intellect than from corporeal vision. But it is clear that supernatural light elevates the created intellect to know God face to face. So why could it not also elevate corporeal vision to see God?"[37]

The profundity of this line of argumentation can scarcely be exaggerated. Most discussions surrounding this issue seem to assume that internal and intellectual knowledge of God is somehow more credible of a prospect than external and ocular vision of God. But Gerhard puts his finger on a fact that is often unacknowledged in these discussions: the creature's perfect knowledge of the incomprehensible God is no less extraordinary or paradoxical than the creature's perfect vision of the invisible God. The infinite chasm between the Creator and the creature means that to embrace one affirmation is just as paradoxical as to embrace the other. "Therefore if the finite intellect can be elevated to the intuitive knowledge of God without harming the infinity of the divine essence," concludes Gerhard, "it seems possible that the glorified eye could also be elevated to a clear vision of God without injury to the spiritualness of the divine essence. Therefore it is more correct to reserve a decision on this question for future experience rather than

---

[36]Gerhard, *On Eternal Life*, 144.242.
[37]Gerhard, *On Eternal Life*, 144.242.

unpleasantly and scrupulously fighting about it."[38] Thus far and no further is Gerhard willing to speculate. With a chastened sense of self-discipline, he concludes, "The rest of the questions the Scholastics have raised about the beatific vision of God are more curious than fruitful and are answered by them more rashly than truly."[39]

FRANCIS TURRETIN

When it comes to discussions on the beatific vision, the great Italian theologian Francis Turretin (1623–1687), while being highly revered in other areas, is not always heralded as a hero. For example, in her essay, "Beholding the Glory of God in the Face of Jesus Christ: John Owen and the 'Reforming' of the Beatific Vision," Suzanne McDonald faults Turretin for what she deems his insufficient attention to Christ in his treatment on the beatific vision: "Christ is quite literally almost invisible throughout his entire discussion on the vision of God in glory. He is mentioned only a handful of times in passing, because reference to the book of Revelation requires it."[40] McDonald goes on to add, further, that "Turretin's account of the beatific vision here is barely Trinitarian at all. On the whole, it seems as though the God whom we are being invited to behold in glory could equally be the Neo-Platonic 'One.'"[41] Kyle Strobel shares McDonald's criticisms toward Turretin, adding that Turretin "posits a glory where Christ's 'imaging' has become irrelevant."[42] Granted, Strobel acknowledges the elenctic nature of Turretin's work: "what we have from him . . . is not a constructive theology of the beatific vision, but a polemical argument concerning how, in his mind, Protestants should conceive

---

[38] Gerhard, *On Eternal Life*, 144.242.
[39] Gerhard, *On Eternal Life*, 145.244.
[40] Suzanne McDonald, "Beholding the Glory of God in the Face of Jesus Christ: John Owen and the 'Reforming' of the Beatific Vision," in *The Ashgate Research Companion to John Owen's Theology*, ed. Kelly M. Kapic and Mark Jones (Burlington, VT: Ashgate, 2012), 154.
[41] McDonald, "Beholding the Glory of God," 154.
[42] Kyle Strobel, "Jonathan Edwards' Reformed Doctrine of the Beatific Vision," in *Jonathan Edwards and Scotland*, ed. Kenneth P. Minkema, Adrian C. Neele, and Kelly Van Andel (Edinburgh: Dunedin Academic Press, 2011), 167.

of the vision of God."[43] Nevertheless, Strobel seems to find even this qualification as reason for further criticism: "his polemical tactics may be just as telling as a robust analysis would be. Owen, it would seem, would have engaged his opposition on the beatific vision with a robust Christology, wielding specifically dogmatic decisions against his opponents. Turretin does not do so."[44] As valuable as Strobel's analysis is, one wonders if this is an example of criticizing a figure for not writing the book one would have preferred for him to write instead of the one he wrote.

For my own part, I prefer to engage Turretin in the catholic and elenctic spirit in which he wrote and will refrain from criticizing him for failing to break new constructive ground on the doctrine of the beatific vision, since that is not what he set out to accomplish. It seems clear that Turretin is concerned primarily with adjudicating where Reformation theology was continuous and discontinuous with other contending conceptions. He is not so much concerned with raising new questions to the fore as he is with answering existing questions from a distinctly Protestant vantage point. This is why, as we will see below, Turretin engages with the Eastern Orthodox, the Roman Catholics, and the Socinians, and why, for example, his primary divergences with Aquinas concern the role of personal merit in the varying degrees of glory among the saints in the next life.[45]

Turretin begins his discussion on the beatific vision in his third volume on the question of whether eternal life "consists in the vision of God or in the love and enjoyment of him?" At the start, Turretin is concerned with noting the continuity between faith in this life and vision in the next: "the life of grace does not differ except in degree from the life of glory, for grace is nothing else than

---

[43]Strobel, "Edwards' Reformed Doctrine of the Beatific Vision," 167-68.
[44]Strobel, "Edwards' Reformed Doctrine of the Beatific Vision," 168.
[45]See Francis Turretin, *Institutes of Elenctic Theology*, 3 vols., ed. James T Dennison, trans. George Musgrave Giger (Phillipsburg, NJ: P&R, 1997), 20.10.1-4.

glory begun, as glory is grace consummated."[46] However, Turretin recognizes the danger of pressing this issue of continuity too far, conflating faith and sight, which is why he quickly emphasizes that the chasm which separates faith now and vision later is bridged by death and resurrection.[47] For Turretin, the blessedness of the beatific vision is nothing other than the saint's enjoyment of divine beatitude: participation in God's own self-happiness. This participation is precisely what lies behind his distinction between "objective blessedness" (i.e., God himself—the source and sum of all blessedness) and "formal blessedness" (i.e., the saint's enjoyment of objective blessedness; the "noblest operation of the soul about God as its supreme good by which it is most intimately united with it and unceasingly and for ever cleaves to him").[48] Formal blessedness is what it is by consequence of objective blessedness—the latter defines the former, but not the other way around.

From here, Turretin addresses the question of whether the beatific vision consists in seeing God or in loving God—in apprehending him with the intellect or with the will. According to Turretin, Aquinas answers with the former, and Scotus answers with the latter. "But both are at fault in this," contends Turretin. "They divide things that ought to be joined together and hold that happiness is placed separately, either in vision or in love, since it consists conjointly in the vision and love of God. Thus neither sight without love, nor love without sight constitutes its [the beatific vision's] form."[49]

One may question how fairly Turretin represents either Aquinas or Scotus, but regardless of how accurate he is in his presentation of the two, casting the question along these lines is what enables his to reflect on how the beatific vision is the perfection of sight, love,

---

[46]Turretin, *Institutes*, 20.8.2.
[47]Turretin, *Institutes*, 20.8.2.
[48]Turretin, *Institutes*, 20.8.3.
[49]Turretin, *Institutes*, 20.8.5.

and joy. "Sight contemplates God as the supreme good; love is carried out towards him, and is most closely united with him; and joy enjoys and acquiesces in him. Sight perfects the intellect, love the will, joy the conscience."[50] From here, Turretin enters into a discussion specifically on the first of this threefold apprehension of God in glory: sight. If sight "contemplates God as the supreme good," and "perfects the intellect," what will be the nature of this contemplation and perfect intellectual apprehension? Turretin answers by contrasting how our contemplation in glory will differ from our contemplation now. In this life, according to Turretin, our knowledge is "specular"—which is to say, we do not comprehend essences but rather the signs and images of those essences mediately portrayed. Further, our sight in this life is "enigmatical"—which is to say, partial and veiled by obscurity. But when "we shall see face to face, this enigmatical and specular knowledge will cease to make room for intuitive vision, which apprehends the thing itself, every veil being removed; not from afar and inverted, but before; not obscurely and enveloped, but most clearly and distinctly; not in part but most fully. . . . However, the distinction between the Creator and the creature is preserved, so that only a similarity, not an equality is denoted."[51]

Like so many others in the tradition before him, Turretin maintains that the vision aspect of the beatific vision differs from faith's apprehension of the same object (God) specifically in its intuitive mode: in the beatific vision, we will no longer have to reason our way to God, but our apprehension of him will be intuitive and immediate and full. Turretin further elaborates that the vision in glory differs from vision on earth in that the former is "mental, intellectual and internal," not "ocular, sensible and external." Vision in glory is "supernatural and spiritual," not the "natural of faith"; it is "intuitive and beatific" and not "symbolic and enigmatic"; it is

---

[50]Turretin, *Institutes*, 20.8.6.
[51]Turretin, *Institutes*, 20.8.8.

"comprehensive and adequate," not "apprehensive and inadequate."[52] "In this life," says Turretin, we see God "by the light of grace and by the specular knowledge of faith; in the other life, however, by an intuitive and far more perfect beatific vision by the light of glory."[53]

However, it is important that we not forget the distinction Turretin made earlier between objective and formal blessedness. That the saints apprehend God intuitively and immediately and fully; this formal blessedness of the beatific vision does not entail that the infinite is somehow circumscribed by the finite: objective blessedness—God himself—does not cease to be "infinitely knowable" in glory (as Aquinas puts it). Thus, I cannot agree with Strobel that Turretin, in his description on the beatific vision, turns "to aspects of anthropology and soteriology as his primary doctrinal import."[54] Such a conclusion fails to deal sufficiently with the load-bearing distinction Turretin makes between objective and formal blessedness. The beatific vision, for Turretin, is not about the saint or the saint's salvation primarily, but about God: God's enjoyment of himself, and the saints enjoyment of him by consequence.[55]

Most considerations of Turretin's notion of the beatific vision are restricted solely here to the first several paragraphs of Turretin's eighth question of his twentieth topic. But Turretin goes on to say much more about the beatific vision and its consequences throughout the rest of his treatment on eternal life. In fact, Turretin would agree with Strobel that "a proper doctrine of the beatific vision should ... hold the language of 'vision' loosely, and reconnect this with other biblical imagery like light, harmony, and communion/fellowship," and even "the New Jerusalem."[56] Turretin

---

[52] Turretin, *Institutes*, 20.8.9-10.
[53] Turretin, *Institutes*, 20.8.14.
[54] Strobel, "Edwards' Reformed Doctrine of the Beatific Vision," 175 (emphasis added).
[55] "He is immortal essentially and of himself by an absolute and perfect impossibility of dying; but the saints are immortal by grace from the beatific vision of God." Turretin, *Institutes*, 20.9.5.
[56] Kyle Strobel, "The Sight of Love: Biblical and Theological Reflections on the Beatific Vision," in *Credo Magazine* 13, no. 3 (2022).

himself emphasizes that "because that unspeakable blessedness can be neither conceived by the mind nor expressed in words, in order to give us some idea of it, the Scriptures are wont to describe it in different ways."[57] He then goes on to innumerate the biblical images and themes that elucidate the beatific vision, including "the absence of all evil,"[58] and the "presence of all good,"[59] as well as emphasizing the biblical imagery of light,[60] and the beatific vision as (1) "the land of Canaan flowing with milk and honey," (2) "the city of Jerusalem," (3) "the tabernacle of Moses and the temple of Solomon," and (4) "the Sabbath."[61] Thus, while Turretin may not deal explicitly with the role of Christ's human nature or the Spirit as the triune bond of love in his treatment of the beatific vision, it is not because "the God whom we are being invited to behold in glory could equally be the Neo-Platonic 'One'" as McDonald says[62]—since he demonstrates a relentless commitment to allow the Scriptures to shape his imagination on the topic—but rather simply because he is concerned with a different set of questions.

Before moving on, we should note that Turretin does enrich the traditional view of the beatific vision with a distinctly Protestant flavor in a way analogous to how McDonald suggests Owen does so with his Christology. Where Owen's "reform" comes in the role of a distinctly christological emphasis in the beatific vision, Turretin's comes with a distinctly Protestant soteriology and conception of merit.

Like much of the tradition before him, Turretin maintains that there will be different degrees of glory among the saints in the beatific vision—different levels of formal blessedness (in fact, Turretin defends this position biblically more thoroughly than perhaps any

---

[57]Turretin, *Institutes*, 20.8.18.
[58]Turretin, *Institutes*, 20.8.18.
[59]Turretin, *Institutes*, 20.8.19.
[60]Turretin, *Institutes*, 20.8.20.
[61]Turretin, *Institutes*, 20.8.11.
[62]McDonald, "Beholding the Glory of God," 154.

figure before him).[63] "Objective blessedness," explains Turretin, "which is placed in God does not admit of degrees because he is the supreme and infinite good. But formal blessedness which is placed in the possession of God and participation of his blessings is not in like manner infinite and nothing prevents it from having degrees."[64]

Turretin emphasizes, with Anselm and Aquinas before him, that such degrees will not be the occasion for envy or pride, since all will be of grace, and the different and differing gifts among the saints will enrich the body of Christ in glory just as God's discriminant gifts enriches the body today.[65] This lack of resentment over discriminant degrees of blessedness in glory is owing to the fact that "the object of blessedness common to all will be God," and each individual saint will enjoy God with all his or her "powers of the soul and all the members of the body" eternally, continuously, and fully, without danger of losing any happiness since every vestige of evil will be equally scrubbed from everyone.[66] All this Turretin affirms in agreement with many before him and with his "papist" contemporaries. But Turretin diverges from them precisely on the reason for discriminant degrees of blessedness. He stridently rejects—in contrast to Aquinas—that personal merit has anything to do with such differing degrees. His rejection is because, according to Turretin on account of his Reformed convictions, "election, justification and adoption are equal in all believers (as also the price of the blood of Christ poured out equally for all the elect)."[67] No one who enjoys the blessedness of heaven, according to Turretin, enjoys any part of it by his own merit, but only on account of the merit of Jesus Christ on his behalf. Turretin maintains, however,

---

[63]Turretin, *Institutes*, 20.10.25.
[64]Turretin, *Institutes*, 20.10.19.
[65]"Now eternal life is not the portion of murmurers, or of the envious, or of those who are rejected and who of the first are made the last; nor does it lead men away from God, but unites them with him; nor is it given to anyone to whom it does not bring a full satiety of joys." Turretin, *Institutes*, 20.10.18.
[66]Turretin, *Institutes*, 20.10.5.
[67]Turretin, *Institutes*, 20.10.20.

that it does not follow from this all-important point regarding merit that the degrees of blessedness that flow from this merit of Christ to his saints must be identical. "Indeed," says Turretin, "the price of the blood of Christ equally expiated the sins of all, but to whom Christ here has given a greater measure of holiness, upon them he will bestow a greater degree of glory also."[68] The distinction may appear subtle and unimportant, but it is the very crux of the Reformational "protest" against Rome's soteriology. If one is after a distinctly Protestant contribution to the beatific vision, this is surely a start.

John Owen

John Owen might be the prototypical catholic reformer. Owen was not alone in his endeavor to thread the theological needle to simultaneously appropriate and reform the Western theological tradition he inherited from the medieval church, but he was certainly one of the very best. In his trinitarianism and Christology, Owen was richly catholic, inheriting the best of the Western tradition up to his day.[69] In his soteriology, he was staunchly Protestant, over and against Rome.[70] Although even here, Owen is able to refrain from repudiating Rome's soteriology wholesale, appropriating Aquinas's notion of "infused habits" and relocating them from the dogmatic realm of justification to their proper home in justification's fruit: sanctification.[71] It should not be surprising, then, to know that Owen very self-consciously appropriates Aquinas in his meditations on the beatific vision (and thereby

---

[68] Turretin, *Institutes*, 20.10.20.

[69] See Alan Spence, "The Significance of John Owen for Modern Christology," and Robert Letham, "John Owen's Doctrine of the Trinity in its Catholic Context," in Kapic and Jones, ed., *Ashgate Companion to Owen*. See also Carl R. Trueman, *The Claims of Truth: John Owen's Trinitarian Theology* (Grand Rapids, MI: Reformed Heritage, 1998).

[70] See John Owen, *The Works of John Owen*, vol. 5, *The Doctrine of Justification by Faith*, ed. William H. Goold (Edinburgh: The Banner of Truth Trust, 1965).

[71] See J. V. Fesko, "Aquinas's Doctrine of Justification and Infused Habits in Reformed Soteriology," in *Aquinas Among the Protestants*, ed. Manfred Svenson and David VanDrunen (Oxford: Wiley Blackwell, 2018), 253-63.

inherits the entire tradition Aquinas assumed by consequence), even while he modifies Aquinas's view with his own Protestant and Reformed theological reflections.[72]

Owen's most concentrated reflections on the beatific vision are found in chapters twelve to fourteen of his book *Meditations and Discourses on the Glory of Christ*.[73] However, much of these reflections are grounded theologically in what he explores in the final chapters of his book, *A Declaration of the Glorious Mystery of Christ*.[74] In the latter, Owen is concerned with describing the ministry of the ascended Christ at present. The importance of this section is that, as Owen emphasizes, "his present state is a state of the highest glory—of exaltation above the whole creation of God, above every name that is or can be named."[75] Which is to say, while this section concerns Christ's ministry in glory on behalf of the church militant, and therefore does not necessarily deal with the beatific vision properly speaking, Christ is nevertheless in the precise state he will occupy in the eschaton. He is awaiting no future glory: what he is right now, he will be forever. Such a point is crucial for Owen because it will help him adjudicate between the continuity and discontinuity of our contemplation of Christ's glory now by the sight of faith, and our vision of his glory in the eschaton by the sight of beatific vision.

---

[72] Although, as Simon Francis Gaine and Hans Boersma have both granted, Owen's modifications likely were not too drastically incompatible with Aquinas's view. Had Aquinas finished his *Summa*, or had he been confronted with Owen's considerations, who knows whether their meditations could have been far closer? Principally, at least, they need not be contrasted too sharply (even if, as I concur with Suzanne McDonald and Hans Boersma, Owen centers Christology in the beatific vision *far more* prominently than Aquinas—such a contrast is genuinely there, but it need not imply an incompatibility between the two). See, Simon Francis Gaine, OP, "The Beatific Vision and the Heavenly Mediation of Christ" in *TheoLogica* 2, no. 2 (2018): 116-28; Hans Boersma, "Thomas Aquinas on the Beatific Vision: A Christological Deficit," *TheoLogica* 2, no. 2 (2018): 129-47; and Gaine, "Thomas Aquinas, the Beatific Vision, and the Role of Christ: A Reply to Hans Boersma," *TheoLogica* 2, no. 2 (2018): 148-67. For more on the debate discussion between Boersma, Gaine, and McDonald, see chap. 5.

[73] John Owen, *Meditations and Discourses on the Glory of Christ*, in *Works of John Owen*, 1:374-415.

[74] John Owen, *CRISTOLOTIA: Or, a Declaration of the Glorious Mystery of the Person of Christ*, in *Works of John Owen*, 1:235-72.

[75] Owen, *A Declaration*, 252.

Owen, like virtually everyone else in the Western tradition, sees a strong continuity between these two "sights" of faith in their object and subject (i.e., the believer—as subject—sees God in Christ—as object), even while there is a strong discontinuity in their mode (i.e., the contrast between faith and sight). And like Aquinas—though to a degree of specificity that is not to be found in Aquinas—there is a causal link between Christ in his glorified state and the beatific vision. It is through the human nature of Christ that human beings enjoy the beatific vision. In glory, "the Lamb, the person of Christ, is the eternal object with that of the Father and the Spirit; the human nature in the Son, admitted into the communion of the same eternal glory."[76] Thus, whatever discontinuity exists between faith now and vision later, no change occurs in the glorious state in which Christ lives at present. What he is now, he will continue to be in our enjoyment of him in the beatific vision.

Having established that Christ persists in his present state into the eschaton, how should we conceptualize the difference between faith and sight for his saints? Suzanne McDonald rightly observes that "Two texts in particular—2 Cor 3:18 and 4:6—plan an important role in this regard," where "the Christological and pneumatological dynamic of the Christian life here and now, and of our eternal salvation, is contained in a nutshell."[77] The image we behold, by which we are transformed "from one degree of glory to another" (2 Cor 3:18), is none other than the "glory of God in the face of Jesus Christ" (2 Cor 4:6). "There is therefore a soteriological trajectory and a transformational continuum," says McDonald, "between beholding the glory of God by faith now and beholding it by sight in eternity."[78] This point Owen is at pains to make time and again.[79]

---

[76] Owen, *A Declaration*, 272.
[77] McDonald, "Beholding the Glory of God," 142-43.
[78] McDonald, "Beholding the Glory of God," 143.
[79] "Both these—namely, faith and sight, the one in this life, the other in that which is to come—have the same immediate object. For they are the abilities of the soul to go fourth unto, and to embrace their object." Owen, *Meditations*, 375.

In tracing out the difference between faith and sight, Owen unsurprisingly uses the language and framework of Aquinas: faith now is "dark—it is but in part. It is but weak, transient, imperfect, partial. It is but little that we can at any time discover of it; it is but a little while that we can abide in the contemplation of what we do discover."[80] By contrast, the beatific vision is "immediate, direct, intuitive."[81] That Owen should self-consciously appropriate Aquinas is to be expected, since, as McDonald points out, "it is Aquinas who sets the agenda for the following nine centuries of reflection on the beatific vision," and "Owen has extensive knowledge of his work," having "a thorough grounding in Aquinas during his Oxford days under Thomas Barlow."[82] Like Aquinas and those who went before him, Owen conceptualized the beatific vision as the culmination of all good and godly desire in this life: "in this perfect state [our soul's faculties] are able to behold and delight in this glory constantly with eternal satisfaction."[83]

Thus, with Aquinas, Owen emphasizes that our vision will be "intuitive" and "immediate" and "direct." Owen even emphasizes, with Aquinas, that this vision will be the vision of God's essence. This last point will be surprising to some, but it is hard to deny in light of Owen's own words: "This beholding of the glory of Christ given him by his Father, is, indeed, subordinate unto the ultimate vision of the essence of God. What that is we cannot well conceive; only we know that the 'pure of heart shall see God.'"[84] Thus, Owen himself does not seem to think that the sum total of the beatific vision can be exhausted by the sight of Christ's human nature. The "ultimate" vision is a vision of the divine essence, which, at present, "we cannot well conceive."

---

[80] Owen, *Meditations*, 378.
[81] Owen, *Meditations*, 378. See also Owen, *Meditations*, 406-7.
[82] McDonald, "Beholding the Glory of God," 144.
[83] Owen, *Meditations*, 406.
[84] Owen, *Meditations*, 385.

However, we would be missing the obvious if we concluded from this that Owen simply inherited, without modifying (or, we might say, enriching) what he received from Aquinas. McDonald is right to point out that Owen adjusts "some of the wider theological presuppositions that inform Aquinas's account to bring them into conformity with the theological perspective encapsulated in the Canons of Dordt."[85] Such adjustments would include Owen's binding his account of the beatific vision explicitly to "the unfolding of God's electing decree," and his "considerably more pessimistic understanding of the effects of sin upon the human capacity for the knowledge of God."[86] Even more drastically, Owen is far more explicit about placing Christ, in his glorified human nature, center stage in his account. Thus, in the passage of Owen quoted above, directly after affirming the "ultimate vision of the essence of God," which "we cannot well conceive," Owen goes on to say: "But it [the vision of Christ's glorified humanity] hath such an immediate connection with it, and subordination unto it, as that without it we can never behold the face of God as the objective blessedness of our souls. For he is, and shall be to eternity, the only means of communication between God and the church."[87]

Thus, Owen does not contrast intellectual vision of the divine essence with ocular vision of Christ's glorified human nature, and even goes so far as to call the latter subordinate to the former. Nevertheless, unlike perhaps any who had come before him, Owen stresses explicitly that all vision of God's essence and glory is communicated through the person and work of Christ. Christ, in the beatific vision, is the preeminent theophanic experience. This has been rightly recognized as Owen's primary contribution to the Western tradition's doctrine of the beatific vision.[88] "Owen," says

---

[85]McDonald, "Beholding the Glory of God," 145.
[86]McDonald, "Beholding the Glory of God," 145.
[87]Owen, *Meditations*, 385-86.
[88]See Boersma, *Seeing God*, 321-26; McDonald, "Beholding the Glory of God."

McDonald on this point, "is therefore drawing out the significance for the doctrine of the beatific vision of that which is axiomatic for his theology as a whole: that God is in himself as he has shown himself to be in his self-revelation, or in his own words."[89] Which is to say, "All knowledge of and union and communion with God now, and everything about our salvation, comes to us through the Son incarnate. So it will be eternally."[90] Such a conclusion is difficult to argue with in light of summary passages like this one from Owen:

> All communications from the Divine Being and infinite fullness in heaven unto glorified saints, are in and through Christ Jesus, who shall forever be the medium of communication between God and the church, even in glory. All things being gathered into one head in him, even things in heaven, and things in earth—that head being in immediate dependence on God—this order shall never be dissolved, Eph. i 10, 11; 1 Cor. iii. 23. And on these communications from God through Christ depends entirely our continuance in a state of blessedness and glory. We shall no more be self-subsistent in glory than we are in nature or grace.[91]

For Owen, everything—including the very cosmological framework of the new heavens and the new earth; the where of our beatific sight of God—depend on and exist through the Son, whose incarnation is everlasting (cf. Col 1:18-20). A vision of the divine essence apart from the incarnate Son is as incomprehensible as a new heavens and earth existing outside of the sustaining and reconciling work of the incarnate Son. Again, McDonald observes how "the significance of Christ's glorified humanity will continue for all eternity, because Christ sums up in himself and holds together in himself the whole glorified creation."[92] Such a central vision of Christ in the beatific vision is, for Owen, the outworking of a strong Chalcedonian Christology, wherein the glory of Christ is not merely

---

[89] McDonald, "Beholding the Glory of God," 149.
[90] McDonald, "Beholding the Glory of God," 149.
[91] Owen, *Meditations*, 414.
[92] McDonald, "Beholding the Glory of God," 153.

the glory of man, but of the God-man, with the glory of the divine essence truly communicated thereby.[93]

Insofar as it goes, this christological and christocentric emphasis can be rightly contrasted with Aquinas from a purely descriptive point of view. One can scarcely argue against the instance that, of the material Aquinas left for us on the beatific vision, he has far less to say (even quantitatively) about Christ's role in the beatific vision. But, as I will argue in the next chapter, I do not believe this necessarily entails that Owen was correcting Aquinas of a christological deficiency. It seems just as plausible (if not more so) that Owen rather considered himself to be filling out and explicitly stating what was implicit and not-yet-unfurled in Aquinas's account. Aquinas never completed his Summa, and there is compelling reason to assume that some of the apparent "Christological deficiencies" of Aquinas's account would have been included in his Christological section on eschatology.[94] But regardless of how fitting it is to portray Owen as correcting Aquinas in his thoroughgoing christocentric account of the beatific vision, we have to conclude that this christocentricism is Owen's most significant and welcome contribution to the church's reception of the doctrine.

Before moving on from Owen, there is one more topic relevant for the beatific vision to which Owen lends clarifying light: the relationship between transformation (or deification or *theōsis*) and the beatific vision. Is it the sight that transforms, or the transformation that enables the sight? On one level, Owen straightforwardly answers with the former: "In the first operation of this light of glory, believers shall so behold the glory of Christ, and the glory of God in him, as that therewith and thereby they shall be immediately

---

[93]See my chapter "Mediated Beauty" in *Irresistible Beauty: Beholding Triune Glory in the Face of Jesus Christ* (Ross-shire, UK: Mentor, 2022) for more on this idea of Christ as the "exegete" of the divine nature.

[94]See Gaine, "Thomas Aquinas and John Owen on the Beatific Vision: A Reply to Suzanne McDonald," *New Blackfriars* 97, issue 1070 (2016): 432-46; "The Beatific Vision and the Heavenly Mediation of Christ," *TheoLogica* 2, no. 2 (2018): 116-28; and "Thomas Aquinas, the Beatific Vision, and the Role of Christ: A Reply to Hans Boersma," *TheoLogica* 2, no. 2 (2018): 148-67.

and universally changed into his likeness."[95] However, because of Owen's emphasis on the continuity between the object of our vision by faith now and by glorified sight later (i.e., the glory of God in the face of Jesus Christ), his answer becomes a bit more complex. The subject of those who will be transformed by beatific vision are only those who have already been transformed (i.e., believers united to Christ). And their transformation came about on account of their beholding the very same object that will transform them in the beatific vision: the glory of God in Christ. This means that the question of whether vision precedes transformation or vice versa, requires another question: Which vision? Which transformation?

For Owen, there is a continuum of three states for the creature, with the transformation from one to another being marked by the vision of the glory of God in the face of Christ. These three states are the state of nature, the state of grace, and the state of glory.

Table 4.1

State of nature	Salvation	State of grace	Glorification	State of glory
Light of *nature*	Vision of *faith*	Light of *grace*	Vision of *sight*	Light of *glory*
	Spiritual resurrection	Light of nature (sanctified)	Physical resurrection	Light of *grace* (glorified)
				Light of *nature* (sanctified)

In each of these states, knowledge is a consequence of a "light" that God grants. The first is "natural light."[96] This light, according to Owen, is powerless in enabling its subject to comprehend the things of God. To know spiritual things, men need more than the light of nature, they need the light of faith and grace.[97] How does a person come by this supernatural light, whereby they are able to comprehend the things of God? *Vision* of the glory of God in the face of

---

[95] Owen, *Meditations*, 412.
[96] Owen, *Meditations*, 382.
[97] Owen, *Meditations*, 382.

Jesus Christ (2 Cor 4:6): "He shines into their hearts, to give them the knowledge of his glory in the face of his dear Son."[98] And yet crucially, this supernatural light does not remove or eradicate the light of nature but rather *sanctifies* this previous light: "Howbeit this new light doth not abolish, blot out, or render useless, the other light of nature, as the sun, when it riseth, extinguisheth the light of the stars; but it directs it and rectifies it as unto its principle, object, and end."[99] This qualification has significant implications for Owen's insistence that Christ's mediatorial revelation of the divine nature will not cease in glory. Like how the light of grace does not abolish nature, the light of glory (i.e., the beatific vision) will not abolish the light of grace (i.e., the light of the glory of God in the *face of Jesus Christ*). "In heaven," says Owen, "there shall be a superadded light of glory, which shall make the mind itself 'shine as the firmament,' Dan. xii. 3," and just as "the *light of grace* doth not destroy or abolish the *light of nature,* but rectify and improve it, so *the light of glory* shall not abolish or destroy the *light of faith and grace,* but, by incorporating with it, render it absolutely perfect."[100] Thus, some kind of God-given light is necessary for knowledge in each state, and the transformation from one state to another (from nature to grace, from grace to glory), is made possible by God graciously granting a new light and vision, and this vision transforms:

> This is the progress of our nature unto its rest and blessedness. The principles remaining in it concerning good and evil, with its practical convictions, are not destroyed but improved by grace; as its blindness, darkness, and enmity to God are in part taken away. Being renewed by grace, what it receives here of a spiritual life and light shall never be destroyed, but be perfected in glory. Grace renews nature; glory perfects grace; and so the whole soul is brought unto rest in God.[101]

---

[98]Owen, *Meditations*, 382. This notion is, in a nutshell, the sum and substance of the thesis of my book, *Irresistible Beauty*.
[99]Owen, *Meditations*, 382.
[100]Owen, *Meditations*, 382.
[101]Owen, *Meditations*, 383.

Thus, the question of whether the vision precedes transformation or transformation precedes vision is not as simple as we might imagine. The beatific vision seems to clearly precede deification (1 Jn 3:2), but this deification is the culmination of what began at conversion, when the believer was made a new creation (2 Cor 5:17). This transformation into a "new creation" began with the sight of the glory of God in the face of Jesus Christ (2 Cor 4:6). And like how the culmination of deification in the eschaton is the completion of the selfsame process begun at conversion, the vision of sight in the beatific vision has the selfsame object as the vision of faith experienced at conversion.[102] Or, as Owen succinctly puts it: "Grace renews nature; glory perfects grace; and so the whole soul is brought unto rest in God."[103]

JONATHAN EDWARDS

Few theologians have made a greater impact on evangelical theology in the Americas like the Northampton pastor Jonathan Edwards. Edwards's influence is surely owing to the fact that he was comfortable—perhaps more comfortable than any figure thus far discussed—carving out innovative articulations of classical doctrines. Edwards was nothing if not a truly creative theologian. His doctrine of the beatific vision is no exception to this rule. This characterization of Edwards, however, should not be taken to mean that Edwards did not *inherit* any theological ideas. Like Gregory of Nyssa, Edwards conceptualized the beatific vision as a pilgrimage of ever-increasing delight and enjoyment. Like Augustine, Edwards saw the beatific vision as the telos of all earthly delight, the natural

---

[102]In the next chapter, I will briefly consider not only how soteriology ties into eschatology as the preceding paragraphs have explored with Owen, but also how creation and protology tie into both. It is not for nothing that Paul's discussion of salvation in 2 Corinthians 3:18-4:6 alludes both to Genesis and creation, as well as Isaiah and the promise of a new creation. Is it not right for us to see *creatio ex nihilo* as the seed that flowers into the *visio Dei*? For a fuller discussion on this passage in 2 Corinthians, see Parkison, *Irresistible Beauty*, 161-74.
[103]Owen, *Meditations*, 383.

destination of every good desire ever awakened.[104] Like Anselm, he believed that joy in the beatific vision would be multiplied by the presence of the saints and angels.[105] And like Aquinas, Edwards believed that the beatific vision would be intuitive and immediate, not a joyous knowledge that one would have to *deduce*.[106]

That being said, Edwards did nevertheless chart new territory. If Owen advanced the beatific vision with a christocentric focus, Edwards followed him and took another step forward with his pneumatological emphasis.[107] Here, I will briefly sketch out Edwards's view, primarily from a sermon he preached in 1735 on Romans 2:10. But before we can meaningfully wrestle with what Edwards says here, it is important to place his reflections within the context of his overall theology proper, which conceptualizes the Trinity as beatitude par excellence.

For Edwards, "God is infinitely happy in the enjoyment of himself."[108] Beatitude is not merely what God experiences or reveals to his creatures—beatitude is essential to Edwards's conception of the divine nature. In God, there is a "perfectly beholding and infinitely loving, and rejoicing in, his own essence and perfections."[109] "Edwards's God," note Oliver Crisp and Kyle Strobel, "is infinite perfection that wills to overflow so that others can partake in the fullness of this perfection. This perfection, following the contours of God's own life, is an overflow of knowledge to be both perceived and loved according to its greatness, goodness, and beauty."[110] The infinite self-happiness of God is, for Edwards, the foundation for all our thinking about theology, even (and

---

[104]See Jonathan Edwards, *The Works of Jonathan Edwards Online*, 72 vols. (Jonathan Edwards Center at Yale University, 2009), 8:393-94.
[105]See, *WJEO* 8:375-77.
[106]See, *WJEO* 50:373, sermon on Romans 2:10, L 43r.
[107]This is a central contention of Kyle C. Strobel in his book, *Jonathan Edwards's Theology: A Reinterpretation* (New York: T&T Clark, 2013). See esp. chap. 3.
[108]*WJEO* 21:113.
[109]*WJEO* 21:113.
[110]Oliver D. Crisp and Kyle C. Strobel, *Jonathan Edwards: An Introduction to His Thought* (Grand Rapids, MI: Eerdmans, 2018), 56-57.

especially) in the way we think about the doctrine of the Trinity. The divine processions of paternity, filiation, and spiration are the outworking of this axiom for Edwards. Put in Anselmian dictum, we might say that for Edwards, God is *that than which none happier can be conceived*, and this divine self-happiness subsists eternally as God perfectly *knowing* and perfectly *loving* himself. God's own delight in God's self is God's eternal generation and spiration. Crisp and Strobel helpfully point out that "the foundation of this view is the psychological analogy, but its architecture is the beatific vision—a vision of God generating perfect happiness. Whereas most theologians focus the beatific vision on the experience that *believers* have in glory, Edwards locates this experience in God's own life of blessedness."[111] God's being pure acts, in other words, as a kind of description of God's experience of his own beatific vision.[112] "God's life is the infinite actuality of divine blessedness—beatitude known and experienced in the eternal fullness of the divine being."[113]

Such a theological vision has immediate and stark implications for the doctrine of the beatific vision—and indeed, our conception of theology as a whole. By consequence of the foregoing, any kind of true knowledge of God is a kind of participation in divine beatitude. This is precisely what Strobel maintains: "Knowing God, for Edwards, is partaking in his self-knowledge of beatific-delight. God's beatific self-knowledge serves as the archetype of all other knowledge. To know God is to behold and delight in him *beatifically*."[114] With this theological vision in place, let us consider Edwards's doctrine of the beatific vision in light of his sermon on Romans 2:10.

---

[111] Crisp and Strobel, *Jonathan Edwards*, 42.

[112] It is worth mentioning that while this feature of Edwards's theology proper is often characterized as incredibly unique and innovative, it is not far from what we have seen above in Turretin; namely, the idea that while "formal beatitude" is the believer's experience of the beatific vision, "objective beatitude" is none other than God himself.

[113] Crisp and Strobel, *Jonathan Edwards*, 42.

[114] Strobel, *Jonathan Edwards's Theology*, 135.

In his 1735 sermon, Edwards considers the "glory and honor and peace for everyone who does good" that Paul mentions in Romans 2:10 and explores this phrase in light of the beatific vision. In his own words, Edwards endeavors to "give a description of the consummate and eternal glory and blessedness of the saints."[115] He gives this description by way of a sustained mediation on the "nature" and "circumstances" of this vision. Beginning with "the nature of it," Edwards considers "the lowest part of it," namely, "the glory of the place."[116] From here, Edwards ramps up in intensity and delightfulness, considering the glorious bodies of the redeemed, the glory of their souls, and the glory of their fellowship. At this point, he pauses and reflects on the apex of glorious fellowship in the heavenly society, wherein the "saints in heaven shall converse" with and "shall see Christ in a twofold sense": namely, they shall "see him as appearing in his glorified human nature with their bodily eyes,"[117] and "they shall see him with the eye of the soul."[118] Like Owen, Edwards stresses the central importance of viewing the glorified body of Christ as the saint's direct object—his glorified body is the direct object of the vision of *their* glorified bodies. In this sense, Christ's glorified human body will be a body among bodies in heaven. Our God shall dwell with us forever. But even here, Christ will stand out as unparalleled. According to Edwards, the

> loveliness of Christ . . . will be a most ravishing thing to them. For though the bodies of the saints shall appear with an exceeding beauty and glory, yet the body of Christ will be the masterpiece of all God's workmanship. . . . The eye will never be cloyed or glutted in beholding this glorious sight. . . . This will be the most glorious sight that the saints will ever see with their bodily eyes. The most glorious sight that ever has been seen as will be seen by my bodily eyes. There will be far

---

[115] Edwards, sermon on Rom. 2:10, L 31r. See an edited excerpt of this sermon in Kyle C. Strobel, Adriaan C. Neele, and Kenneth P. Minkema, eds., *Jonathan Edwards: Spiritual Writings* (New York: Paulist Press, 2019), 185-205.
[116] Edwards, sermon on Rom. 2:10, L 31r.
[117] Edwards, sermon on Rom. 2:10, L 37v-38r.
[118] Edwards, sermon on Rom. 2:10, L 38v.

more happiness and pleasure redounding to the beholders from this sight than any other. Yea the eyes of the resurrection body will be given chiefly to behold this sight.[119]

This last line from Edwards should not be quickly dismissed. According to Edwards, the eyes of the resurrection body of believers exist to behold the glory of God in the new heavens and the new earth, and no ocular vision will be so glorious and so pleasing as will be the vision of *Christ* in his glorified human nature. Thus, Boersma is not wrong to emphasize that "Edwards's teaching on the beatific vision stands out for its remarkable Christ-centeredness: Christ is the central object of the beatific vision."[120] However, this is not all Edwards has to say about the vision of Christ. Not only will the saints see him with the eyes of their glorified bodies, Edwards maintains that the saints will also "see him with the eye of the soul." This sight, according to Edwards, will consist in beholding "that bright image of God that the Father beheld and was infinitely happy in beholding from all eternity."[121] They will participate by grace in God's own beatitude, whereby the Father perfectly *sees* his Son. This should not be taken to mean that Edwards believes the saint will behold the essence of God comprehensively, however. Edwards concurs with Aquinas that such a "comprehensive sight" is "impossible" for "a finite mind."[122] Rather, this vision "shall be perfect in its kind," namely, creatures will see God as far as possible, given their nature. They will see him perfectly according to a creaturely mode of seeing.

Edwards goes on to say that in this vision, the saints "shall see everything in God that tends to excite and inflame love and everything in him that gratifies love."[123] By narrowing his focus on the topic of love in the beatific vision, we anticipate the role of the Spirit. "The means by which God shall grant this vision of himself," says

---

[119] Edwards, sermon on Rom. 2:10, L 38v.
[120] Boersma, *Seeing God*, 363.
[121] Edwards, sermon on Rom. 2:10, L 39v.
[122] Edwards, sermon on Rom. 2:10, L 43v.
[123] Edwards, sermon on Rom. 2:10, L 44r.

Edwards, "is the Holy Ghost."[124] Just as it is by the Holy Spirit that spiritual sight is given in this life, "so tis the same Holy Spirit by which a beatifical vision is given of God in heaven. The saints in heaven are as dependent on God for all their holiness, all their light, as the saints on earth . . . they shall have this beatifical vision of God because they will be full of God, fill with the Holy Spirit of God."[125] According to Edwards, this is why it is fitting for us to recognize the Spirit as the "pure river of water of life" that "thus proceeds from the throne of God and the Lamb (Rev 22:1-5)."[126]

Here in his sermon on Romans 2:10, then, Edwards makes explicit what his doctrine of God requires implicitly: the beatific vision is a way of being brought up into the Trinity's own beatitude, which is God's self-knowing (the Son) and self-loving (the Spirit). Thus, Strobel concludes, "By placing the vision in the context of the triune life, Edwards incorporates his understanding of the beatific nature of the Trinity *ad intra*, and his vision of the believer's participation within that life. It is with the person of Christ, the true mediator between God and humanity, that believers can now see and be seen, as they know and are known."[127]

For Edwards, the beatific vision was a vision of God in Christ by the Spirit, a participation in the divine beatitude of God's self-knowing and self-loving. In the final chapter of this book, we will return to Edwards's reflection on the beatific vision, and heaven more generally, specifically as regards the notion of beatifical friendship. But at this juncture, we should simply point out that Edwards develops an account of the beatific vision that is distinctly *trinitarian*. True, it is a distinctly *Edwardsian* trinitarianism, which means it is sure to be controversial in some quarters.[128] Regardless

---

[124] Edwards, sermon on Rom. 2:10, L 45r.
[125] Edwards, sermon on Rom. 2:10, L 45r.
[126] Edwards, sermon on Rom. 2:10, L 45r.
[127] Strobel, *Jonathan Edwards's Theology*, 143-44.
[128] For a recent defense of the classical bona fides of Edwards's theology proper, see Joseph James Rigney, "Diverse Excellencies: Jonathan Edwards on the Attributes of God," PhD diss., University of Chester, 2019.

of what one makes of Edwards's idiosyncratic terminology, it seems to me that some notion of a distinctly trinitarian model of the beatific vision, wherein the saints behold the glory of God in everything—preeminently in and on the account of—the glorified human nature of Christ, by the Holy Spirit, as a kind of expression of divine love, is compatible with nearly everything that has been said by the historical figures we have thus far surveyed (with perhaps Calvin excepted).

Conclusion

In this chapter, we have examined the testimony of a sampling of figures from the Reformation and post-Reformation era on the beatific vision. We could have appealed to any number of additional figures, but the sampling we have here is sufficient evidence to insist upon the doctrine's precedented ecumenical stature. Of the many theological ideas the Reformers dispensed with, the beatific vision was not one of them. The reclamation of the Scripture's central authority did not come with a corresponding de-emphasis on the blessed hope of the beatific vision because the Reformers recognized what we saw in chapter two: the biblical case for this doctrine is incredibly strong. However, some variations on how to conceptualize the doctrine does begin to develop with the Reformation and beyond. Whatever else this survey demonstrates, we can be certain that the doctrine of the beatific vision has no necessary conflict with evangelical or Reformed theology at the theoretical level, nor at the historical level.

5

RETRIEVAL FOR REFORMED EVANGELICALS

IF THE UBIQUITY OF THE BEATIFIC vision's importance and centrality is as apparent in the Scriptures and the historic witness of the church, as our study thus far indicates, then Hans Boersma is right to conclude that the "reductionism inherent in modernity's abandonment of the beatific vision is . . . much more serious than may at first appear."[1] From popular-level accounts of eschatology and glorification to more thorough systematic treatments, a broadly evangelical and Reformed lack of interest in the beatific vision is apparent.[2] Why might this be, and how might this neglect amount to self-impoverishment? Conversely, what do evangelicals stand to gain by reclaiming the doctrine, and how might their theological distinctives stand to not only inform their reception of the doctrine but also enrich the great tradition more broadly?

This chapter is ambitious in its aspirations to answer these questions in brief. First, I will consider some of the various proposals set forth for why this doctrine has been largely abandoned and ignored in evangelical circles. Along these lines, this chapter will briefly document recent debates regarding the conceptual relationship between Owen and Aquinas and the role of Christology in

---

[1] Hans Boersma, *Seeing God: The Beatific Vision in the Christian Tradition* (Grand Rapids, MI: Eerdmans, 2018), 95.
[2] Consider the relative or outright neglect of the beatific vision in Graham A. Cole, *Glorification: An Introduction* (Wheaton, IL: Crossway, 2022); David A. Höhne, *The Last Things* (Downers Grove, IL: IVP Academic, 2019).

the beatific vision. From there, I will show how the Protestant and Reformed tradition stands to enrich the broader catholic notion of the beatific vision with its distinctive soteriological emphases. And this will position us to consider afresh the relationship between deification (or *theōsis*) and the beatific vision, before concluding with a positive dogmatic definition of the beatific vision.

What Went Wrong?

The neglect of a doctrine like the beatific vision at the popular level is downstream of larger tectonic shifts in the wider modern imagination. There is a reason the classical thinkers of yesteryear never felt compelled to justify their commendation of contemplation as an intrinsic good, while such a notion is met with scoffing and derision today. For example, in his book *The Discarded Image*, Lewis casts a vision for the medieval imagination—one he argues is broad enough to describe the scholar and the serf alike—with what he calls a "mental Model of the Universe."[3] This model, Lewis insists, is marked by two related characteristics: the bookish culture of the medieval world, and the medieval "intense love of system." "This is the medieval synthesis itself, the whole organization of their theology, science, and history into a single, complex, harmonious mental Model of the Universe. . . . Its contents, however rich and various, are in harmony. We see how everything links up with everything else; at one, not in flat equality, but in a hierarchical ladder."[4] In the medieval imagination, searching for harmony in the various corners of the universe and thought found its justification in the central conviction that *such a harmony existed*. Contemplation was not a flight of fancy, it was an exercise of tracing out and embracing reality at its most fundamental and immanent level. In contrast to this vision of reality, the modern imagination suffocates under what Charles Taylor calls

---

[3] C. S. Lewis, *The Discarded Image: An Introduction to Medieval and Renaissance Literature* (Cambridge: Cambridge University Press, 1964), 11.
[4] Lewis, *The Discarded Image*, 11-12. See also Jason M. Baxter, *The Medieval Mind of C. S. Lewis: How Great Books Shaped a Great Mind* (Downers Grove, IL: IVP Academic, 2022).

"the malaise of modernity."[5] Ours is an age tyrannized by a morbid immanentization wherein no harmony exists whatsoever. The banishment of transcendence and realism has eventuated in an imagination impoverished of truth, goodness, and beauty, and by consequence, any motivation or incentive for deep contemplation. This present situation is precisely what Lewis warned about in his prophetic work *The Abolition of Man*,[6] and what others in recent years have ably documented as a realization of Lewis's prediction.[7]

The philosophical shifts in modernity have impacted the church's reception of the beatific vision in other indirect ways as well. Not only is the beatific vision rendered incomprehensible by the stifling atmosphere of secularism and materialism, but the spirit of Enlightenment itself incentivizes innovation and a conscious rejection of tradition. The unseemly union of theology and the spirit of the Enlightenment led to twin sisters. Though they would never acknowledge their common ancestry, biblicist fundamentalism and theological liberalism share common blood.[8] Both uncritically adopt the metaphysical assumptions of modernity. For the theological liberal, this metaphysic leads to an embrace of biblical higher criticism and a hermeneutic of suspicion.[9] For the fundamentalist, while a commitment to the Scripture's divine authority remains, the assumption of this same metaphysic leads to functionally the same hermeneutic, wherein any consideration of the Scriptures that fall

---

[5] See Charles Taylor, *A Secular Age* (Cambridge, MA: Harvard University Press, 2007).
[6] C. S. Lewis, *The Abolition of Man* (New York: HarperCollins, 2001).
[7] See Carl R. Trueman, *The Rise and Triumph of the Modern Self: Cultural Amnesia, Expressive Individualism, and the Road to Sexual Revolution* (Wheaton, IL: Crossway, 2020); Paul Tyson, *Returning to Reality: Christian Platonism for Our Times* (Eugene, OR: Cascade, 2014); Edward Feser, *The Last Superstition: A Refutation of the New Atheism* (South Bend, IN: St. Augustine's Press, 2008); Jordan Cooper, *In Defense of the True, the Good, and the Beautiful: On the Loss of Transcendence and the Decline of the West* (Ithaca: Just and Sinner, 2021).
[8] For a recent case making this point, see Craig A. Carter, *Interpreting Scripture with the Great Tradition: Recovering the Genius of Premodern Exegesis* (Grand Rapids, MI: Baker Academic, 2018).
[9] For the *kind* of hermeneutic of suspicion I have in mind, see Michael C. Legaspi, *The Death of Scripture and the Rise of Biblical Studies* (New York: Oxford University Press, 2010). Also see Samuel G. Parkison, *Irresistible Beauty: Beholding Triune Glory in the Face of Jesus Christ* (Ross-shire, UK: Mentor, 2022), 63-70.

outside of a grammatical-historical lens is strictly banished.[10] In either case, both theological liberalism and her twin sister, biblicist fundamentalism, unceremoniously sever ties with the great tradition and the classical realist metaphysic by which it is characterized. Neither sister has the patience or interest, therefore, to consider a doctrine like the beatific vision.

There is a story to tell behind the beatific vision's abandonment in the Dutch Reformed tradition as well. In addition to, and perhaps alongside, the broader philosophical and theological shifts that took place in the modern world, Michael Allen documents a turn toward what he calls "eschatological naturalism" in his recent book *Grounded in Heaven*.[11] This trend comes from a very different set of concerns than the ones we have been considering here, however. "A variety of authors in recent years have sought to draw Christians away from the dangers of segmenting their lives," notes Allen,

> The maladies can be described under varying terminology: sometimes "Gnosticism" is the label for such dualistic divisions of our lives; sometimes "Platonism" or "Platonizing" serves as the moniker for this mishap whereby we seek flight from our context; sometimes "spiritualism" depicts a malformed view of God's involvement with his creatures, as if the triune God only interacted with us in certain liturgical or religious moments and nowhere else.[12]

In response to these excesses, some theologians call for a strong sense of integration. As Allen points out, even figures far from the Dutch Reformed tradition, as disparate as N. T. Wright and Rob Bell, have put their finger on the problem of disintegration.[13] The emphasis on embodiment and eschatological glorified matter strikes a particular note of resonance with the neo-Calvinist and

---

[10] I have written elsewhere on this hermeneutic in Parkison, *Irresistible Beauty*, 65-72.
[11] Michael Allen, *Grounded in Heaven: Recentering Christian Hope and Life on God* (Grand Rapids, MI: Eerdmans, 2018).
[12] Allen, *Grounded in Heaven*, 3.
[13] Allen, *Grounded in Heaven*, 3-5.

Kuyperian tradition (with which Allen happily identifies).[14] Allen is careful to explain how the "naturalism" in "eschatological naturalism" is used "only in a very specific manner."[15] No one within this tradition can be called a "naturalist," properly speaking, since "they have as wide and deep a notion of divine presence throughout our world and generations as exists in the Christian world."[16] "But," Allen goes on to explain, "when it comes to the climax of redemptive history, neo-Calvinists have often turned from focus upon communion with Christ, the presence of God, or the beatific vision . . . to focus instead upon the resurrection of the body, the shalom of the city, and the renewal of the earth."[17]

In reaction to pietism and spiritualism, Allen points out how even thinkers like Herman Bavinck respond in an uncharacteristically overreactive manner. While "Bavinck manages to glean more from sources traditionally engaged only by Roman Catholics in the late nineteenth- and early twentieth-century context," Bavinck's eschatology, "which forms the culmination of his fourth volume [of his *Reformed Dogmatics*]" nevertheless "focuses not only narrowly but also polemically upon the notion of the new creation over against more spiritual emphases found elsewhere in the Christian tradition."[18] Boersma concurs with this assessment when he observes how "neo-Calvinists sometimes inveigh sharply against traditional views of the hereafter, supposedly characterized by an otherworldly, heavenly outlook, a body-soul dualism, and a benighted captivity to a Christian Platonist mind-set."[19]

---

[14] Although, we must be sure to emphasize that Abraham Kuyper himself was not prone to the same eschatological naturalism as those who have propagated the Kuyperian tradition. See, e.g., Boersma, *Seeing God*, 338-50.

[15] Allen, *Grounded in Heaven*, 7.

[16] Allen, *Grounded in Heaven*, 8.

[17] Allen, *Grounded in Heaven*, 8.

[18] Allen, *Grounded in Heaven*, 6.

[19] Boersma, *Seeing God*, 33. Both Boersma and Allen point to figures like J. Richard Middleton and Anthony A. Hoekema as contemporary representatives of this tendency. See J. Richard Middleton, *A New Heaven and a New Earth: Reclaiming Biblical Eschatology* (Grand Rapids, MI: Baker Academic, 2014); and Anthony A. Hoekema, *The Bible and the Future* (Grand

The judgment that Bavinck's eschatology suffered from a neglect of sufficient attention on the beatific vision has recently been challenged by James Eglinton, Cory Brock, and Nathaniel Gray Sutanto.[20] Each of these figures suggest that such a narrative bespeaks a lack of familiarity with Bavinck's works as a whole, insisting that Bavinck's theological system was the furthest thing from overly this-worldly—in other words, readers will search to no avail for a theocentric *deficit* in Bavinck's work. Sutanto, in particular, has done us all a great service to pull from a wide array of Bavinck's corpus to show that Bavinck *did* in fact develop a positive conception of the beatific vision, and that he was critically aware of Eastern Orthodox theology. This is important, since Boersma suggests that had Bavicnk availed himself to Eastern Orthodox resources or the post-Reformation witness of figures like John Owen, he may have found such resources helpful. Sutanto shows that Bavinck *did* interact with the East and found its theological categories problematic, and that he *did* appropriate Owen to much avail.[21] Thus, while "Bavinck's view may be modest,"[22] he did posit a conception of the *visio* that "should be characterized as Christological, covenantal, ethical and mystical in character."[23]

However, Allen has, in my estimation, responded to the particular challenges of Eglinton and Brock convincingly in a recent article.[24] The question of where Bavinck should be situated as an

---

Rapids, MI: Eerdmans, 1979). For a similar reading of Bavinck, see J. Todd Billings, *Union with Christ: Reframing Theology and Ministry for the Church* (Grand Rapids, MI: Baker Academic, 2011), 75-86.

[20]See James Eglinton, *Bavinck: A Critical Biography* (Grand Rapids, MI: Baker Academic, 2020), 195-96; and Cory Brock, "Revisiting Bavinck and the Beatific Vision," *Journal of Biblical and Theological Studies* 6, no. 2 (2021), 367-82; Sutanto, "Herman Bavinck on the Beatific Vision," in *International Journal of Systematic Theology*, August (2022), https://doi.org/10.1111/ijst.12610.

[21]Sutanto, "Bavinck on the Beatific Vision," 8-15.

[22]Sutanto, "Bavinck on the Beatific Vision," 18.

[23]Sutanto, "Bavinck on the Beatific Vision," 2.

[24]Michael Allen, "On Bavinck, the Beatific Vision, and Theological Practice," in *Reformed Faith & Practice* 7, no. 1 (2022). The question of appropriate proportion when it comes to Bavinck and the beatific vision is still live. While some of Boersma's initial claims may have been overreaching, as seems the case in light of Sutanto's recent article, there still remains a

individual into this discussion is a live one, and Sutanto's and Allen's articles deserve critical attention, but attention should also be given to the question of how Bavinck's system was *received* in subsequent generations.[25]

Regardless of whether one agrees with Allen and Boersma that Bavinck *tilted* toward a kind of eschatological naturalism, the trend among later neo-Calvinists in the Dutch Reformed tradition seems difficult to deny. Out of an effort to rescue thoughts of heaven from the dull picture of ethereal non-materiality, some theologians have consequently overreacted and reduced heaven to the redemption of material and sinless creaturely enjoyment. Of course, these are glorious realities, and any notion of heaven that does not embrace them is an impoverished one. But if the centralizing hope of the blessed vision, without which heaven would not at all be *heaven*, is jettisoned in the process, we are no better off. To reappropriate the words of our Lord, "These you ought to have done, without neglecting the others" (Mt 23:23).

Thus, variegated causes stand behind the present situation of dogmatic neglect of the beatific vision. This means that the work of recentering this blessed hope will have to be likewise variegated. We must cast and embrace a vision for the practical import of the beatific vision. We must learn how to eschew the pragmatism that despises any practice that does not yield immediate use and rather insist upon, and advocate for, theological contemplation as an end in itself. We must learn to interrogate the faulty metaphysical assumptions we inherit, and critically and intentionally appropriate ones that are more hospitable to biblical teaching (including *this* biblical teaching)—for example, what I am calling classical realism.

---

question of how reasonable Bavinck's theological heirs in the Dutch Reformed tradition have been to conclude from his theological emphases that a kind of eschatological naturalism fits.

[25] Although, as Sutanto has pointed out in an email correspondence, the question of the beatific vision in the Dutch Reformed tradition deserves even wider attention. K. Shilder's (1890–1952) work might be fruitfully read on the matter. See Shilder, *Wat is de hemel?* (Barneveld: Nederlands Dagblad, 2009).

We must humbly learn from the past in an earnest attempt to retrieve the theological work of our forefathers of yesteryear for our benefit today. We must avoid muting what the Scriptures and the great tradition proclaim out of a reactionary spirit to avoid overly ascetic and disintegrated tendencies.

Contemporary Debate

Of course, I am not the first person to raise this alarm. In many ways, this book is entering into a contemporary conversation already underway. Thus, before moving on to my own synthesis and proposal, it will be useful for us to get some of the relevant scholarship before us. What follows is a thoroughly in-house debate. As far as I am concerned, the scholars who have elevated the importance of this doctrine in recent years are my allies, and I am grateful for all the work they have done to foreground the blessed hope to this point. This appraisal should therefore be read in a spirit of appreciative critique within a context of broad agreement.

As we have mentioned elsewhere already, Suzanne McDonald's 2012 essay, "Beholding the Glory of God in the Face of Jesus Christ," was something of a Protestant clarion call to rehabilitate the beatific vision in the spirit of what she deems Owen's "reformation" of the doctrine. In this article, McDonald contrasts Owen with previous treatments, particularly that of Thomas and the Thomistic tradition, noting how the beatific vision "was not a major topic of reflection for Reformed theologians either in [Owen's] own generation or earlier."[26] McDonald is quick to acknowledge Owen's indebtedness to Aquinas and highlight Owen's apparent attempt to rehabilitate Aquinas as a useful resource in the Protestant imagination.[27] Nevertheless, it is McDonald's contention that Owen "offers us an utterly and rigorously Christocentric" account that is "beyond

---

[26] McDonald, "Beholding the Glory of God," 141.
[27] McDonald, "Beholding the Glory of God," 144-45.

anything that the earlier Thomist tradition provides."[28] The heart of the contrast between Owen and Aquinas lies in the centrality (or lack thereof) of Christ in either's account of the blessed vision. "In essence," says McDonald, "the difference between Owen and Thomas is that for Aquinas and the Thomist tradition, the emphasis seems to be upon the functional role of Christ—he is instrumental to the possibility of us experiencing the beatific vision—whereas Owen insists that Christ is *also* intrinsic to the essence of the beatific vision itself."[29]

McDonald concludes that Owen's "reformation" or "re-formation" of Aquinas's account of the *visio Dei* is an improvement in that it fills a christological void left by Aquinas, but suggests that even Owen's account leaves room for more of an explicit pneumatology. Since "the Holy Spirit almost entirely fades from view when [Owen] speaks about the consummation of ... sight in heaven," McDonald maintains that "what is needed is a more fully Trinitarian account of the beatific vision."[30] Kyle C. Strobel concurs both with McDonald's assessment of Owen in relation to Aquinas and the need for a more fully trinitarian account, commending Jonathan Edwards's view of the beatific vision as an ideal synthesis, since he "follows the 'Reforming' nature of Owen's [view], but refuses to stop with a Christological re-working of the vision of God."[31] For Edwards, seeing God in the beatific vision is always seeing *through* the Son and his redeeming work, *by* the ministry of the Holy Spirit. Edwards, therefore, "addresses the vision through *participation* in the inner-trinitarian vision of love."[32]

---

[28] McDonald, "Beholding the Glory of God," 145.
[29] McDonald, "Beholding the Glory of God," 150.
[30] McDonald, "Beholding the Glory of God," 158.
[31] Kyle C. Strobel, "Jonathan Edwards' Reformed Doctrine of the Beatific Vision," in *Jonathan Edwards and Scotland*, ed. Kenneth P. Minkema, Adriaan C. Neele, and Kelly Van Andel (Edinburgh: Dunedin Academic Press, 2011), 173.
[32] Strobel, "Jonathan Edwards' Reformed Doctrine," 174. Hans Boersma affirms this depiction of Edwards in relation to Aquinas as well in his essay, "The 'Grand Medium': An Edwardsean Modification of Thomas Aquinas on the Beatific Vision," *Modern Theology* 33, no. 2 (2017): 187-212.

This narrative was problematized, however, by an article published in 2016 by a Dominican scholar named Simon Francis Gaine, titled "Thomas Aquinas and John Owen on the Beatific Vision: A Reply to Suzanne McDonald."[33] Gaine wonders if McDonald's "contrast between Owen and Aquinas" is drawn too "starkly." He notes how, on the one hand, Owen himself says that "beholding the glory of Christ given by the father is indeed subordinate unto the ultimate vision of the essence of God"—a fact acknowledged by McDonald herself in a footnote[34]—and, on the other hand, "for Aquinas, the intellectual act of beatific vision takes as object not only the essence of God but the humanity of Christ also."[35] Gain appeals to Aquinas's *Compendium of Theology* wherein he explicitly states a twofold object of blessed knowledge (in both faith in this life, and vision in the hereafter), "namely, the divinity of the Trinity and the humanity of Christ."[36] In Gaine's reading, Aquinas affirms the vision of Christ's humanity. Granted, this vision is "purely intellectual rather than physical vision," and therefore, unlike Owen, "Aquinas holds that as such it can be enjoyed by souls separated from their bodies before the resurrection," Aquinas nevertheless believes that after the resurrection "there is a further knowledge of Christ's humanity mediated through the glorified senses of the resurrection body of each of the blessed."[37]

Additionally, Gaine highlights an important aspect of Christ's mediatorial role in the beatific vision: the causal relationship between Christ's vision and the saints'. "The grace of the Holy Spirit bestowed on each member of the Body," says Gaine, "is a participation in the grace of Christ the Head. In no way is this participated grace something that, once caused, no longer requires the

---

[33]Simon Francis Gaine, OP, "Thomas Aquinas and John Owen on the Beatific Vision: A Reply to Suzanne McDonald," *New Blackfriars* 97, no. 1070 (2016): 432-46.
[34]McDonald, "Beholding the Glory of God," 150n27.
[35]Gaine, "A Reply to McDonald."
[36]Thomas Aquinas, *Compendium of Theology*, trans. Richard J. Regan (New York: Oxford University Press), 1.2.
[37]Gaine, "A Reply to McDonald."

continuing existence of the grace of Christ."[38] In this way, according to Gaine, Aquinas conceptualizes Christ as the "place" wherein the divine vision is always and ever experienced. Rather than conceptualizing the difference between Owen and Aquinas as the difference between the presence or absence of Christ as a mediator in the beatific vision (since *both* affirm Christ as mediator for the beatific vision in some fashion), Gaine proposes we conceptualize their difference as to the *manner* of mediation:

> Christ is thus the "place" from which God is seen, without him intervening as the lens through which the vision is mediated. There are to be distinguished then two kinds of proposed heavenly mediatorship for Christ, one of which he continually exercises according to Aquinas's teaching [i.e., Christ as the *place*], and the other of which he never does [i.e., Christ as the *medium*—"intervening as a lens through which that vision is mediated"]. The former is not alien to Owen's teaching, as a careful reading of the *Meditations* shows. Where Owen differs from Aquinas is in introducing the latter, where Christ acts as an instrumental means by which divinity is seen.[39]

At this point, Hans Boersma becomes the primary dialogical partner with Gaine taking up and defending McDonald's and Strobel's previously articulated positions in his 2018 work, *Seeing God*. Boersma here finds Gaine's treatment unsatisfying, going so far as to say that "Aquinas does *not* suggest" that the believer's enjoyment of the beatific vision is "by participating in *Christ's* beatific vision."[40] "To be sure," says Boersma, "such a view may be consonant with Aquinas's overall position, but he does not spell this out anywhere. And it seems likely that had this been his actual position, he would explicitly have mentioned it at some point in his relatively prolific writing both on the beatific vision in general and on Christ's own beatific vision."[41] Regardless of what Aquinas may or may not have

---

[38] Gaine, "A Reply to McDonald."
[39] Gaine, "A Reply to McDonald."
[40] Boersma, *Seeing God*, 160.
[41] Boersma, *Seeing God*, 160.

believed on the question, however, Boersma insists that Aquinas's view would *still* constitute a christological deficit, since the question of deficiency depends not strictly on the *how* of the beatific vision, but also on the *what*. Thus, "the Thomist position can only be regarded as insufficiently christological: for Aquinas, the beatific vision is not the vision of Christ but the vision of the essence of God."[42]

In September 2018, the theological journal *TheoLogica* published a series of articles by Gaine and Boersma as an effort to advance the conversation more clearly. The first entry was Gaine's article, "The Beatific Vision and the Heavenly Mediation of Christ," in which he primarily defends his reading of Aquinas on the question of Christ's beatific vision and its causal relationship to the saints. "While I agree that it is true that Aquinas never explicitly spells out what I have proposed," says Gaine, "my aim in this article is to suggest that there is reason to think not only that such a view is *consonant* with Aquinas's overall thought, but that it follows so securely from Aquinas's overall thought, philosophical as well as theological, that Aquinas may be fairly said to endorse it."[43] Gaine defends his position by way of analysis of several places in the *Summa theologiae* where Aquinas tersely appeals to the concept—his terseness owing to the fact that he most certainly planned to elaborate at length in the completion of the *Summa*'s *Tertia Pars*, which he famously never completed. Here, Gaine anticipates Boersma's objection that such further elaboration surely must amount to mere speculation. If Aquinas were planning to say more on the topic, why did he not do so at the various places in the *Summa* where he could have? Gaine suggests that "this has to do with Aquinas's theological method."[44]

That he remains committed to the general doctrine of heavenly enlightenment is confirmed in the *Prima* and *Secunda Pars* where

---

[42]Boersma, *Seeing God*, 161.
[43]Simon Francis Gaine, OP, "The Beatific Vision and the Heavenly Mediation of Christ," *TheoLogica* 2, no. 2 (2018): 116-28.
[44]Gaine, "The Beatific Vision."

he allows for continuation of such illumination in general, besides the beatific vision, up to the day of judgment (*ST* I, q. 106, a. 4, ad 3; II-II, q. 52, a. 3). That he does not mention Christ's particular role here is intelligible in view of the fact that Christ is not properly treated until the *Tertia Pars,* and we can reasonably expect that Aquinas would have treated Christ's place in this illumination toward the end of this unfinished part.[45]

Boersma's response in the same *TheoLogica* issue, "Thomas Aquinas on the Beatific Vision: A Christological Deficit," brings the matter into sharper focus. While Boersma takes issue with Gaine's reading of several key passages in the *Summa,* he nevertheless feels compelled, in light of Gaine's response, to slightly revise his previous assessment that Aquinas likely did not hold to the opinion that Christ's beatific vision *causes* the saints in glory. Specifically, on the second passage Gaine explores—*ST* III, q. 22, a. 5—Boersma comes to agree with Gaine "that Aquinas was very likely thinking here of Christ eternally mediating the beatific vision to the saints."[46] However, "Aquinas's articulation is vague and indirect."[47] While Boersma acknowledges Gaine's point that Aquinas may very well have elaborated on the question at greater length, had he finished the *Summa theologiae,* the question is still speculative in nature. Rather than assessing Aquinas on what one believes he would have said, given the opportunities to expand, we should assess him on what he *did* say, given the opportunities to which he *did* avail himself. Additionally, Boersma repeats his original point that regardless of what Aquinas believed about the relationship between Christ's beatific vision and the saints', the most *crucial* shortfall of Aquinas's view is the absence of Christ as the *content* of the beatific vision: the chief theophanic encounter with God in glory. Thus,

---

[45] Gaine, "The Beatific Vision."
[46] Boersma, "Thomas Aquinas on the Beatific Vision: A Christological Deficit," *TheoLogica* 2, no. 2 (2018): 134.
[47] Boersma, "Aquinas on the Beatific Vision," 134.

according to Boersma, even with the slight revision of his assessment, Aquinas's account of the beatific vision is still christologically deficient because (1) his articulation of Christ's vision and its causal link to the saints' is underdeveloped and (essentially) culpably minimal, and (2) his account of the object of the divine vision is the divine essence instead of Christ.

Gaine is given the final word in the *TheoLogica* issue with his essay, "Thomas Aquinas, the Beatific Vision and the Role of Christ: A Reply to Hans Boersma."[48] In response to the charge that Aquinas's articulation of the beatific vision is christologically deficient on account of its insufficiently developed link between Christ's vision and the saints', Gaine criticizes Boersma's standards for assessment. "Boersma locates the first factor in the *paucity* of Aquinas's actual references to the link between Christ's vision and that of the saints," says Gaine, "and holds Aquinas culpable for it. His current criticism of Aquinas is not that he does not hold the thesis in question, but that he does not mention it very often, and not at all in places where he should have done."[49] Gaine agrees with Boersma that the frequent mention of a theological theme in the work of a theologian (like Owen's repetitious emphasis on the saints' vision of Christ in the beatific vision) indicates that such a theologian places a high value on such a theme. He cannot agree with Boersma, however, with the suggestion that a theologian's *infrequent* mention of a theological theme indicates a lack of importance for such a one.

Thus, in response to Boersma's first charge of christological deficiency in Aquinas, Gaine objects to Boersma's apparent insistence that Aquinas must repeat a theme sufficiently before it is allowed a place of prominence in our assessment of his view. Few references, for Gaine, do not amount to unimportance. Further, Gaine pushes

---

[48] Simon Francis Gaine, OP, "Thomas Aquinas, the Beatific Vision and the Role of Christ: A Reply to Hans Boersma," *TheoLogica* 2, no. 2 (2018): 148-67.
[49] Gaine, "A Reply to Boersma."

back against Boersma's claim that expecting a further treatment on Christ's beatific vision in the unfinished *Tertia Pars* is mere speculation. According to Gaine, such an expectation is not merely permissible, but is rather downright *required* once Aquinas's methodological commitments are accepted. In Gaine's view, one may wish (like Boersma) for Aquinas to elaborate on certain matters in other places in the *Summa*, but Aquinas can hardly be faulted for failing to organize his material according to what *we* think would be more intuitive. Along these lines, Gaine highlights how Boersma minimizes the apparent shared ground between Owen and Aquinas on the sight of the divine essence in the beatific vision. Again, Gaine does not wish for us to forget that it was *Owen* who said, "Beholding the glory of Christ given by the father is indeed subordinate unto the ultimate vision of the essence of God." But since "Boersma makes much of the fact that this is mentioned in only two passages," he "refuses to conclude from these passages that Owen agreed with Aquinas that the beatific vision is directed to the divine essence."[50]

In response to Boersma's second reason for concluding that Aquinas's account of the beatific vision is deficient on account of its focus on the divine essence instead of Christ as its object, Gaine elaborates on what he takes the sight of the divine essence to *include*. According to Gaine, the whole question hinges on Aquinas's account "of God's own knowledge, in which the beatific vision participates."[51] "Since the beatific vision is a created intellect's participation in this divine knowledge through the divine essence," Gaines notes, "it makes no more sense to suppose that the beatific vision's participated focus on the divine essence necessarily excludes knowledge of Christ than does the focus of God's knowledge on himself."[52] Gaine concludes that "since all the saints have Christ as the instrumental cause of their grace and glory, they would in

---

[50]Gaine, "A Reply to Boersma."
[51]Gaine, "A Reply to Boersma."
[52]Gaine, "A Reply to Boersma."

every case have knowledge of Christ in the divine essence, a beatific knowledge of him of a kind that could not be bettered. To focus on the divine essence is thus to *include* Christ as an object of beatific knowledge, not to exclude him."[53] According to Gaine, "Aquinas does not deny heavenly theophanies," but "he does this explicitly in the wider context of theophany throughout the whole of the new creation.... Aquinas envisages heaven as 'theophanic,' where God is eternally manifested in the renewed creation, but above all in the Word made flesh."[54]

Where, then, does the foregoing leave us? It may be tempting to conclude that a stark and sharp choice lies before us: we can have the strictly intellectual and christologically deficient account of the beatific vision espoused by Aquinas, or the enhanced christological and pneumatological accounts of Owen and Edwards, but we may not have both. For my own part, however, I sympathize with Gaine's assessment of the situation. His reading of Aquinas's view seems to me to attend to the nature and structure of the *Summa* more sensitively and fairly than the alternatives. Further, I cannot help but wonder if the minimization of Owen's apparent affirmation of the believer's beatific experience of the divine essence bespeaks a temptation to ascribe motive to Owen that may, in fact, not be there. To regard this expressed belief of Owen's as inconsistent with his christocentric view—as McDonald and Boersma take it to be—is only necessary if one takes Owen's christocentric view as being *consciously contrary* to Aquinas's divine essence view. If, as McDonald and Boersma suggest, Owen is self-consciously *reforming* Aquinas's view of the beatific vision, then a statement like "beholding the glory of Christ given by the Father is indeed subordinate unto the ultimate vision of the essence of God" becomes problematic and must be read as an inconsistency. But I wonder if we are really justified in assuming that Owen is attempting to improve upon

---

[53]Gaine, "A Reply to Boersma."
[54]Gaine, "A Reply to Boersma."

Aquinas here. It would at least be reasonable for one to expect that if Owen intends to correct Aquinas, he would say as much.[55]

Personally, I am not at all convinced that Owen saw himself as correcting Aquinas or filling in a christological void that Aquinas left. Their respective treatments were so different from one another—in scope, in tone, in purpose, in audience—that we should suppose a direct polemic relationship between the two only with extreme reserve and hesitation. Rather than taking this sentence about "the ultimate vision of the essence of God" as an inconsistency on Owen's part, I believe it is far more natural to read it as reflecting the truth that Owen's view is not—either in his own understanding or in reality—radically different from Aquinas's. However, I would like to emphasize that while I am not convinced Owen's christological emphasis (and Edwards's pneumatological emphasis, for that matter) is a *correction* of Aquinas, I do affirm both Owen's and Edwards's emphases as rich contributions to the doctrine.[56] Without erasing the real differences that do exist between Aquinas and Owen, and at the risk of trying to have my cake and eat it too, I want to say "no" to the starkest version of the false choice between Aquinas and Owen, and say "yes" to both. I propose instead a dogmatic synthesis that is big enough for both to live in.

The Way Forward: Inseparable Operations

We can begin to imagine what this might look like with an appeal to the doctrine of *inseparable operations*. This is the doctrine that maintains that since the Trinity is undivided, the operations of the

---

[55]For an example of where Owen does this on another issue, namely, infused grace, see J. V. Fesko, "Aquinas's Doctrine of Justification and Infused Habits in Reformed Soteriology," in *Aquinas Among the Protestants*, ed. Manfred Svensson and David VanDrunen (Oxford: Wiley Blackwell, 2018), 253-63.

[56]By disagreeing with Boersma, McDonald, and Strobel on how to read Aquinas, I do not at all mean to minimize or disagree with the way they insist Owen and Edwards have enriched the great tradition with their reflections on the beatific vision. I do not disagree with the merits they attribute to Owen and Edwards, only on the demerits they attribute to Aquinas.

Trinity are also undivided. For example, while we can recognize the unique appropriation of a single person in a manifestation of the trinitarian missions (e.g., the Son in the incarnation, or the Spirit at Pentecost), we must never consider such appropriation outside the context of the single inseparable operation of the Trinity. The Son is incarnate, not the Father nor the Spirit, but the Son's incarnation is *his* appropriation of the *Trinity's inseparable operation* of redemption. God the Son can be distinguished from God the Father and God the Spirit, but never separated—the Son's assumption of a human nature is his appropriation of a single triune action *as Son*. Considered as a kind of hermeneutical "rule," R. B. Jaimeson and Tyler Wittman appeal to inseparable operations, urging their readers to "learn to count persons rather than actions," since "whenever Scripture mentions only one or two divine persons," we must "understand that all three are equally present and active."[57]

Keeping the doctrine of inseparable operations in view prevents us from creating too sharp a bifurcation between conceptualizing the beatific vision as a spiritual sight of the divine essence on the one hand, and an ocular sight of Christ's human nature on the other. Michael Allen balances these concerns well. On the one hand, Allen emphasizes that any revelation in the divine economy involves some conception of the invisible God making himself visible, highlighting two considerations: "First," says Allen, "it is necessary to note that both incarnation and the event of Pentecost involve divine visibility in some fashion," and "second, the New Testament witness points to the Christological nature of the beatific vision."[58] On the other hand, Allen reads these two considerations in light of inseparable operations as a whole. "The Son's incarnational manifestation before the world stage is not a solo performance. . . . The external works of the Trinity are undivided, though they are differentiated."[59]

---

[57] Jaimeson and Wittman, *Biblical Reasoning*, 106.
[58] Allen, *Grounded in Heaven*, 76-77.
[59] Allen, *Grounded in Heaven*, 78.

Thus, according to Allen, "the Son's own manifestation is a Trinitarian—and not only a Christological—act."[60] In Christ, therefore, "we see *God* and not simply an instrument of or attachment to God in the vision."[61] Again, this means that the choice between the beatific vision as an apprehension of the divine essence—in a mode of knowing, of course, that is fitting to the creature—and the vision of Christ in his human nature is a false choice. The "attendant condition of the humanity of Christ," Allen reminds us, "does not mean that the blessed vision of God in the Face of Christ can be reduced to a vision of his humanity. Rather, we see him: the person of the Son of God, 'God of God, Light of Light, Very God of Very God.' ... The Son as Son is visible. But the Son as Son is visible by means of his humanity."[62]

Therefore, it seems best to conceptualize the beatific vision as a vision of the divine essence in the person and work of Christ, the incarnate Son, by the illuminating and gracious operating principle of the Spirit as the eternal divine subsistence of the Father and Son's love. The beatific vision, in other words, is made possible by the inseparable operations of the Trinity, and is therefore a truly trinitarian vision. We shall behold the *glory of God* in his essence, and we shall behold this glory *in the face of Jesus Christ* by the unveiling and illumining ministry of the *Holy Spirit*.

Protestant-Reformed Contribution: Some Positive Proposals

To maintain that the Protestant-Reformed articulation of John Owen on the beatific vision may not constitute a correction or deviation from the Thomistic tradition he inherited is not to say that he and others did not enrich the tradition in uniquely Protestant-Reformed ways. There is, after all, something to say about the fact

---

[60] Allen, *Grounded in Heaven*, 78.
[61] Allen, *Grounded in Heaven*, 80.
[62] Allen, *Grounded in Heaven*, 79.

that while Owen's christological emphasis broadly fits within a Thomistic portrayal of the beatific vision, it was Owen, the Reformed Protestant, who elucidated this point. Insisting that figures like Owen have enriched the great tradition with key insights on how to articulate the beatific vision is, on one level, a mere matter of historical fact. The Protestant tradition not only stands to benefit the great tradition as a whole, it already has. And yet we can say even more, for it is not only that the Protestant-Reformed tradition has happened to contribute to the church catholic's doctrine of the blessed hope—as if its being Reformed and Protestant were accidental or irrelevant to its contribution—but also that it has done so precisely because of its Protestantism. While the christological emphasis of Owen and Edwards's notion of the beatific vision as participation in intra-trinitarian love may be consonant with a Thomistic conception, a Reformed understanding of justification and union with Christ is not. But their being at odds with one another on justification and union with Christ does not, as is often maintained, amount to the difference between realism versus nominalism.[63] On this point, it is not uncommon to pit a participatory notion of soteriology against a Protestant emphasis on forensic righteousness. But such a contrast is fiction, both theologically and historically. The mistaken argument may be summarized in this way.

The highly forensic nature of a Protestant conception of justification by faith alone—with its notion of imputed righteousness—is foreign to the great tradition of Christianity and owes much of its intellectual support to nominalism.[64] Sola fide is all about the punitive reality of breaking a law, and not about the restorative quality of healing humanity. The doctrine is deeply individualistic—it

---

[63] See Barrett, *Reformation as Renewal*, chap. 5.
[64] The following section contains reworked and expanded material from a column I wrote for *Credo Magazine* titled, "Further Up and Further In: Appreciating the Platonic Tradition and the Reformed Conception of Union with Christ," vol. 12, no. 1 (March 2022), as well as my article, "'One Baptism for the Remission of Sins': Exploring the Harmony Between Christian Platonism, Reformed Soteriology, and Credobaptism," in *Perichoresis*, vol. 21, no. 2 (2023).

involves the arbitrary legal fiction of swapping the currency of the guilty for that of the innocent. Because of its reliance on nominalism and volunteerism, it has no category for participation.

What are Reformed Protestants, who so deeply admire and appreciate the thick realism of the Christian Realist tradition, to do? Are we to forfeit our doctrine of justification or the prominent classical realist metaphysic of the great tradition? The good news is that if we think carefully and consistently, we need not choose either option. Not only is it untrue that the great tradition lacked emphasis on the penal and substitutionary aspects of atonement,[65] it is also the case that there is no necessary conflict between Christian Realism and penal substitution or imputed righteousness. This much we can be confident of without even working out all the details by simply standing firmly on this rock-solid truth: God does not contradict himself, and both metaphysical realism and imputed righteousness are truly taught in the Scriptures (Ps 19:1-6; 148:1-14; Col 1:17; Heb 1:3; cf. Is 53:4-6; Rom 3:21-26; 2 Cor 5:21; Gal 5:15-21). If we have a problem reconciling these two doctrinal convictions, we can take comfort knowing that we are the problem, so long as both are undeniably and clearly taught in Scripture (and they are). Therefore, we should contemplate these truths, searching for their harmony with the disposition of faith seeking understanding.

And when we do, lo and behold, they do cohere. The forensic nature of justification by faith alone is only a nominalist doctrine if we affirm two things that we ought to most stridently deny: first, that the moral law, which man transgresses and so thereby incurs

---

[65]See Michael A. G. Haykin, "We Trust in the Saving Blood: Definite Atonement in the Ancient Church," in *From Heaven He Came and Sought Her: Definite Atonement in Historical, Biblical, Theological, and Pastoral Perspective*, ed. David Gibson and Jonathan Gibson (Wheaton, IL: Crossway, 2013); Raymond A. Blacketer, "Definite Atonement in Historical Perspective," in *The Glory of the Atonement: Biblical, Historical, and Practical Perspectives. Essays in Honor of Roger Nicole*, ed. Charles E. Hill and Frank A. James III (Downers Grove, IL: InterVarsity Press, 2004); and Steve Jeffery, Michael Ovey, and Andrew Sach, *Pierced for Our Transgressions: Rediscovering the Glory of Penal Substitution* (Wheaton, IL: Crossway, 2007), 161-84.

guilt, is arbitrary, and second, that imputation is impersonal. Let us consider each of these bad ideas in turn.

First, the notion that justification is a mere matter of legality. If fallen man were guilty of transgressing a law that just so happened to be there, but which could have been different if God arbitrarily declared that the legal boundaries were rearrangeable, then yes, the amount of emphasis Protestants place on the sinner's legal guilt—and Christ's legal imputation of righteousness—would appear to be a nominalism-square-peg we are trying to fit into a realism-round-hole. But this is not the Protestant claim. We recognize that the heart of the sinner's guilt before God is not a mere matter of legality—it is rebellion against God himself. God's moral law typifies his changeless holy character; it is not an arbitrary standard. To ask if sin is a matter of legal infraction in need of a punitive response or a matter of metaphysical suicide in need of a renovative response is to pose a false choice. The answer is yes, because the legal line guilty sinners cross is not an external or creaturely accident; it runs straight down the heart of God. The legality of sin could no more be considered a concept of nominalism than could the character of God himself.

Second, and related, the notion that the imputation of Christ's righteousness is impersonal. Again, if this imputation was a kind of legal fiction, it would bespeak an arbitrariness that has no place in the great tradition's heritage of realism. And to be fair, imputation is often described in impersonal, cold and legal terms. But this is not an essential component of the doctrine. It is only described this way exclusively when Christ's work is abstracted from his person. But the best of the Reformed tradition has always insisted that this must not be the case. The "forgiveness of sins"—a legal concept—is one of the many blessings the believer has (i.e., one of the "heavenly blessings") in Christ (Eph 1:3-14). In other words, the imputation of Christ's righteousness in justification by faith is only a nominalist "legal fiction" if it is set at odds with—or detached from—union with Christ. Since the Reformed tradition has not done this historically, there is nothing at odds between its adherence to *sola fide* and a participatory soteriology that culminates in deification and the beatific vision.[66]

GETTING JUSTIFICATION RIGHT

But we can say even more than this. Not only is the Reformed tradition not at odds with participation and the beatific vision, it enriches the tradition by untangling the knot of justification, infusion, sanctification, and merit it perceives Roman Catholicism as tying over the centuries. The fault of Rome, from a Reformed perspective, is not on its insistence that the beatific vision, justification, infused grace, and merit all interrelate at the most essential level. Rome's vital error is in the conflation and confusion of these categories.

Reformed Protestant theology agrees with Rome that in Christ and by the Spirit, the believer is infused with gracious habits whereby he grows in godliness, culminating in the beatific vision and ultimate participation: deification. They also agree with Rome that all of this intimately relates to justification and merit. They disagree with Rome, however, about what justification is, its grounds, and by what merit it is rendered. According to the Reformed tradition, justification is a legal verdict declared by God, which he renders to a believer only on behalf of the merits of Christ—on account of his active and passive obedience as the righteousness he imputes—which the believer receives by faith alone. In Christ and by the Spirit, the believer does receive an infusion of grace upon conversion, but this grace is distinct from the gracious verdict he receives on behalf of Christ's righteousness imputed to

---

[66]Recent scholarship has helpfully documented that deification, properly understood, need not be considered at odds with Protestant and Reformed convictions, since a proper conception of *theōsis* or deification need not give way to a blending of Creator and creature. E.g., see Donsun Cho, "Deification in the Baptist Tradition: Christification of the Human Nature Through Adopted and Participatory Sonship Without Becoming Another Christ," *Perichoresis* 17, no. 2 (2019); and Joanna Leidenhag, "Demarcating Deification and the Indwelling of the Holy Spirit in Reformed Theology," *Perichoresis* 18, no. 1 (2020).

him. Together, the grace of justification and the grace of sanctification are the *duplex gratia* (double grace) the believer receives in Christ alone. The former grounds the latter, so that the righteous deeds of the believer—the evidence of gracious infusion—are the fruit of justification. In this way, the beatitude of the beatific vision is enjoyed on account of merit, but only the merit of Christ. Not only does such a formulation account well for how the various elements of soteriology relate to one another, it also safeguards the exclusive praise of Christ in heaven. Every bit of enjoyment the saints experience in the beatific vision is in and on account of Christ alone. In his glorification, the saints are glorified.

"Superadded" Gift or "Concreated" Gift?

Another way the Protestant-Reformed tradition offers a unique approach to the beatific vision has to do with the relationship between teleology and protology; the glorification of man and the creation of man. Thomas Aquinas, following Augustine, emphasized that man was created with God as his final cause. "Eschatology," Matthew Barrett notes, "framed Thomas's participation teleology from beginning to end. For those made in the likeness of God, final causality reaches its apex in the beatific vision, where eternal blessedness and happiness is found in God."[67] For Thomas, this end of human nature is something that lies outside of human nature itself—man's telos is something infinitely beyond the grasp of its nature. Thus, man was created with a *donum superadditum*—a superadded gift—of grace. Grace perfects nature—God's grace completes human nature and brings it to its final consummation. According to Thomas and his medieval contemporaries, the *donum superadditum* was lost at the fall. But how and when God initially granted this *donum superadditum* was not entirely agreed upon, even among medieval theologians. For example, "Thomas

---

[67] Barrett, *Reformation as Renewal*, 147.

maintained the Augustinian emphasis on the primacy of grace by claiming the superadded gift was inseparable from man's constitution, even given to man at creation . . . never was there a time when Adam was without it."[68] Thus, "the donum superadditum could be distinguished in the mind of the theologian but in Adam's experience such a gift was inseperable from the start."[69] This view can be sharply contrasted with that of Bonaventure and Scotus, who "severed" the creation of man from his reception of the *donum superadditum*, conditioning the superadded gift upon man's merit.[70]

Even though most within the Reformed Protestant tradition have decidedly shared sympathies with Thomas over and against Bonaventure and Scotus on the *donum superadditum*, they still maintained that Thomas's conception continued to too sharply separates nature and grace. Rather than espousing the *donum superadditum*, they posited instead a *donum concreatum*, a concreated gift (or *donum naturale*, natural gift; or *donum intrinsecum*, inward gift). Muller summarizes the situation clearly:

> The Protestant argument was that the donum gratuitum, the utterly free gift, or [original righteousness] was part of the original constitution of humanity and therefore a donum concreatum . . . rather than something superadded to the original human constitution. By extension, the loss of the [original righteousness] in the fall was the loss of something fundamental to the human constitution that could be resupplied only by a divine act.[71]

How might this inform our conception of the beatific vision? We might say that the beatific vision, in agreement with Aquinas, is the telos of human nature. But it is a telos that is graciously, yet

---

[68] Barrett, *Reformation as Renewal*, 148.
[69] Barrett, *Reformation as Renewal*, 148.
[70] Barrett, *Reformation as Renewal*, 148.
[71] Richard A. Muller, *Dictionary of Latin and Greek Theological Terms, Drawn Principally from Protestant Scholastic Theology*, 2nd ed. (Grand Rapids, MI: Baker Academic, 2017), 97-98. See also Petrus van Mastricht, *Theoretical-Practical Theology*, vol. 3, *The Works of God and the Fall of Man*, ed. Joel R. Beeke, ed. Todd M. Rester (Grand Rapids, MI: Reformation Heritage, 2021), 1.3.9, 291-95.

intrinsically, realizable apart from the fall. In other words, it is inconceivable—not just historically, as Aquinas would maintain, but also metaphysically—that an unfallen creature would long for a telos outside the possibility of his nature. Human nature before the fall did not need a superadded grace; human nature before the fall was constituted by grace, such that "unfallen nature" and "graciously constituted nature" are virtually synonymous. The fall does not render man's telos an impossibility simply by removing something extra and then burdening humanity with concupiscence; rather, the fall renders man's telos an impossibility because it handicaps him at the essential level of human nature.

Thus, the grace of redemption not only perfects nature, it restores nature, such that the final state of beatific enjoyment is more truly human than the state we experience at present. Incidentally, this Protestant portrayal of human nature also explains why saints in the intermediate state, who are perfected with respect to the fall's curse and corrupted human nature, are nevertheless incomplete in their beatifical enjoyment. It may be true that they experience the beatific vision in a sense, being "absent from the body" and "present with the Lord" (cf. 2 Cor 5:8), but the final consummation of the beatific vision requires the glorified soul's reunion with its glorified body. Saints who have come to life with Christ, having experienced the first resurrection and enjoying beatific delight in the presence of their Lord, still await the second resurrection, when "what is mortal will be swallowed up by life" (2 Cor 5:8). Their end is not Revelation 20:4-6, when with Christ, safe from the threat of the second death, they "come to life" and "reign with Christ," but rather Revelation 22:4-5, when resurrected to inhabit the new heavens and the new earth, "they will see his face." The final telos of human nature is not realizable once it lacks original righteousness, nor is it realizable when it lacks the union between body and soul.[72]

---

[72]Unfortunately, a defense of this take on Revelation 20 and the nature of the millennium is beyond the scope of this present work. For a thorough and convincing defense of what I take

Ocular or Intellectual Vision?

On the matter of whether this vision is ocular or intellectual, it seems to me that a strict dichotomy of these two is less than helpful. For humans, one is never possible without the other. Every part of our existence is anchored to the physical and visible world. Even our most abstract thinking forms in our minds with images. We cannot think or speak devoid of spatial categories. Even the previous sentence demonstrates this principle with use of the word *devoid*. What other word might I have chosen? *Without? Apart from? In the absence of?* All these make use of spatial categories. So, our thinking always involves the use of images, and our ocular vision is never isolated from the intellect. We bring images into our intellect, and we view images intellectually. This way of thinking and knowing is a created reality that God deems "good," and is therefore not a consequence of the fall. Rather than imagining this feature of our thinking and knowing is a deficiency that we will be rid of in the resurrection, it seems better to think of it as an analog to an even greater experience of thinking and knowing in glory. Thus, it is possible to maintain some notion of distinguishing between "mediate" knowledge of God's essence now, and "immediate" knowledge of God's essence in the beatific vision, since the former is the fruit of reasoning from creation to God, and the latter is intuitively seeing God from creation.

Likewise, I share with Owen the sense that Christ must be insisted upon as the central ocular object of the beatific vision. But this must never be contrasted too sharply with an intellectual account of the beatific vision. Denying any aspect of the intellectualist account of the beatific vision would seem to imply that at no point in the eternal Sabbath of life in the new heavens and the new earth will the saint look at anything but Christ. But I cannot imagine why

---

for granted here, see G. K. Beale, *The Book of Revelation* (Grand Rapids, MI: Eerdmans, 1999), 991-1021. For a shorter description, see Brian J. Tabb, *All Things New: Revelation as Canonical Capstone* (Downers Grove, IL: IVP Academic, 2019), 90-95.

we cannot, so to speak, take our perfect vision of Christ with us everywhere else we look. We can do this in part even now. I have seen the time-lapse videos of flower buds unfolding to unfurl their consummate loveliness in full bloom, for example. And while I walk through a flower garden, I see flowers at various stages in that bloom process, but the image I have seen from the time-lapse videos stays with me. I look at the flower bud and can see what it will be, and I look at the flower in full bloom and can see what it was, in partial and incomplete ways. It does not seem plausible to me that in our glorified bodies we will be able to do less, rather than more, of what we can do now. Is it not reasonable to assume that in the resurrection, "intellectual" and "ocular" vision will be more perfectly wedded than now? If so, choosing between "an intellectual" and an "ocular" vision of the divine essence (in the face of Jesus Christ by the illumination of the Spirit) is unnecessary. I find it plausible that in our glorified flesh, we shall see, by the Spirit, the divine essence in the glorified humanity of Christ, and we shall never cease to see him even when we see his operations of creating and sustaining everything else that we see. Already, we have seen other figures, like Johan Gerhard in the previous chapter, appeal to a "both/and" account of the beatific vision along these very lines.

If God can grant a glorified body other properties of spirit, why not also this: the ability to see spirit with its own eyes? Surely God is not less infinitely distant from the created intellect than from corporeal vision. But it is clear that supernatural light elevates the created intellect to know God face to face. So why could it not also elevate corporeal vision to see God?[73]

Indeed, it appears that Owen himself would agree with the above rejection of either "intellectual" or "ocular." After emphasizing that the beatific vision will surely involve a corporeal sense in beholding Christ "immediately" and "in his own person," he goes on to qualify:

---

[73]Gerhard, *On Eternal Life*, 144.242.

"But principally, as we shall see immediately, this vision is intellectual. It is not, therefore, the mere human nature of Christ is the object of it, but his divine person, as the nature subsisteth therein."[74]

Admittedly, this is all rather opaque and speculative, and "what we will be is not yet known," but this vision seems to me the best way to conceptualize the glorification (including the amplification) of that which is good about creation (i.e., that which is not the status quo on account of the fall, but rather what is the case by virtue of being creaturely), while also holding fast to the incomprehensible blessed hope of the beatific vision. These considerations can also be helpful as a corrective for those who worry that too much focus on the beatific vision can abstract the hope of heaven from the recreation of the heavens and the earth. As we have granted earlier, this is a crucial component of our heavenly hope, and we hear with appreciation the groans of creation for the consummation (cf. Rom 8:19-25). Far be it from the Christian to adopt a vision of the eschaton that amounts to a Buddhist concept of nirvana. However, the overly carnal Muslim depiction of paradise is no better. In a truly Christian vision of the eschaton, with the beatific vision central, the choice between bodily existence and the spiritual vision of God is a false one. As I mentioned at the conclusion of chapter two, the beatific vision does not find its consummate fulfillment in the intermediate state, which means the beatific vision cannot be rightly understood—in a final sense—without bodily existence. While the relationship between ocular vision and intellectual vision is deeply mysterious, and we are consigned, in one sense, to speculation, since we are like seeds contemplating what it will be like once we sprout and are fully grown (cf. 1 Cor 15:35-44), we can nevertheless insist in the strongest possible terms that such a relationship emphatically does exist. "In my flesh," we say with Job, "I shall see God" (Job 19:26).

---

[74]Owen, *Meditations*, 379.

Does the Beatific Vision Cause Deification (or Vice Versa)?

While there are no doubt unbiblical notions of deification (or *theōsis*),[75] it most certainly has its Reformed articulations as well.[76] The opposition some tend to have toward this language comes from a fear of confusing the Creator-creature distinction, or the idea that the doctrine posits the dissolution of the saint, as if to be deified is to be absorbed up into the divine essence.[77] While such notions would be problematic, we need not imply any of them when we use the language of the believer being "deified" or experiencing *theōsis*. In its most general sense, the doctrine describes the believer's transformation—on account of his union with Christ—in glorification. This transformation is a result of participation in Christ, and it is as such the believer's coming to share in the glory of God by grace. God, in Christ, makes the believer to be a "partaker of the divine nature" (2 Pet 1:4), transforming him with his glory. As Robert Letham notes, "This is not a union of essence—we do not cease to be human and become God or get merged into God like ingredients in an ontological soup. This is not *apothēosis*."[78] Nor do we "lose our personal individual identities in some universal generic humanity,"[79] nor are we "hypostatically united to the Son,"[80] we are rather "united with Christ's person," and "since the assumed humanity of Christ participates in the eternal Son, is sanctified and glorified in him, and since we feed on the flesh and blood of Christ

---

[75] See Joel R. Beeke and Paul M. Smalley, *Reformed Systematic Theology*, vol. 2, *Spirit and Salvation* (Wheaton, IL: Crossway, 2019), 257-59.

[76] See Carl Mosser, "Recovering the Reformation's Ecumenical Vision of Redemption as Deification and the Beatific Vision," *Perichoresis* 18, no. 1 (2020); Robert Letham, *Union with Christ: In Scripture, History, and Theology* (Phillipsburg, NJ: P&R, 2011), 122-28.

[77] And to be fair to those who are nervous along these lines, this kind of metaphysical monism seems to be exactly what figures like David Bentley Hart mean by the term *theōsis*. See, e.g., David Bently Hart, *You Are Gods: On Nature and Supernature* (Notre Dame, IN: University of Notre Dame Press, 2022).

[78] Letham, *Union with Christ*, 123.

[79] Letham, *Union with Christ*, 123.

[80] Letham, *Union with Christ*, 126.

[by faith], we, too, in Christ are being transformed into his glorious likeness."[81] Or, as Calvin puts it, Christ "makes us, ingrafted into his body, participants not only in all his benefits but also in himself," so that "he grows more and more into one body with us, until he becomes completely one with us."[82] Thus, deification is simply the way of describing the transformation which marks the final, eschatological expression of the believer's union with Christ.

Regarding the question of whether the transformation of the saint in glory causes the beatific vision, or vice versa, it is probably best to think of this as a kind of chicken-or-egg dilemma. Only those who are justified will behold the beatific vision, and in that sense, the work of salvation and the double grace of justification and sanctification fit us for the beatific vision. The work of transformation—of renewing creation (cf. 2 Cor 5:16), which is consummated in the final state of the eschaton—begins now. In other words, there is a sense in which the believer, by virtue of his union with Christ, is deified at conversion. So, in that sense, deification comes first. However, this "deification" of the double grace of justification and sanctification began when the very same object of our beatific vision (i.e., the glory of God in the face of Jesus Christ) was apprehended by faith in this life. In that sense, it was a kind of beatific vision in this life—the vision of faith, wherein faith is conceptualized as beholding the glory of God in the face of Jesus Christ—that was the instrument for receiving the double grace of justification and sanctification. The vision of faith is the instrument whereby we secure the forensic right and transformed ability to enjoy another kind of vision—the beatific vision of God's essence in glory—in the next life. The vision of God always transforms.

So, in one sense, the question, "Does deification cause the beatific vision or does the beatific vision cause deification?" is simple: 1 John 3:2 is clear enough that vision causes transformation. However, the

---

[81] Letham, *Union with Christ*, 126-27.
[82] Calvin, *Institutes*, 3.2.24. Quoted in Letham, *Union with Christ*, 128.

only people who will experience eschatological vision leading to defying eschatological transformation are those who have experienced another kind of transformation—the *duplex gratia* of justification and sanctification—in this life. Those who will be transformed in glory by beholding the beatific vision are those who have been transformed in this life by beholding the glory of God in the face of Jesus Christ by faith. By the vision of faith, the sinner is transformed into the saint, and because he is a saint, he will experience the vision of glorified sight, which will subsequently transform him into "we know not what" (cf. 1 Jn 3:2). In both visions, the object and subject of the vision are the same: the saints (subjects) behold the glory of God (object). In both visions, the subject of the vision is transformed by its object: beholding the glory of God transforms the saint. Yet, the mode of the vision differs: in this life, we behold the glory of God by faith, mediately, partially, and indirectly; in the next we shall behold the glory of God in the beatific vision, immediately, fully (that is, entirely according to our creaturely mode of knowing), and directly. Additionally, the precise *nature* of the transformation differs: in this life, beholding the glory of God in the face of Christ by faith transforms in the *duplex gratia* of justification and sanctification; in the next, the beatific vision will transform the believer into "we know not what."

Christ's Experience of the Beatific Vision

Another potential debate related to our study involves the nature and scope of Christ's experience of the beatific vision. We have already noted, in agreement with Aquinas, that the believer's experience of the beatific vision occurs in union with Christ—the saint comes to participate in Christ's own beatific vision. The Word can save humanity and begrace the race of mankind with the experience of beatitude, in part, on account of the hypostatic union. When believers are united to Christ, they are united to the Word-made-flesh, who preeminently experiences and realizes humanity's telos.

But the question remains: when does Christ come to experience this beatific vision? Upon his conception, resurrection, or ascension?

According to Thomas Joseph White, traditional Catholic theology, in line with Thomas Aquinas, has historically insisted that "Christ as man possessed the immediate, intuitive knowledge of his own deity, the divine life that he shared with the Father and the Holy Spirit," and therefore "Christ in his earthly existence possessed the beatific vision or immediate knowledge of God."[83] While some contemporary Roman Catholic theologians have challenged this notion on the supposed ground that it "compromises the reality of the humanity of Jesus" and "the unity of his filial personhood,"[84] White insists that "the affirmation of the beatific vision of the historical Christ was and is essential for maintaining the unity of his person in and through the duality of his natures, and most particularly in safeguarding the unity of his personal agency in and through the duality of his two wills."[85] White rightly identifies the crux of the matter in the area of ontology and the nature of Christ's hypostatic union. Because the Word is hypostatically united to a created human nature, which—body and soul—functions as the instrument of the divine will, there must be a perfect and perpetual agreement between Christ's two wills (his human will and his divine will). Thus, White argues, "The human intentions and choices that Christ makes as a man are indicative of his divine personal will, intentions, and choices. It is this cooperation of the two wills that permits the human willing of Christ to take on its filial mode of expression."[86]

In this way, White makes an important and valuable point. If the Son incarnate "reveals in and through his human actions the will of the Father and the activity of the Spirit" throughout his entire

---

[83] Thomas Joseph White, *The Incarnate Lord: A Thomistic Study in Christology* (Washington, DC: The Catholic University of America Press, 2017), 237.
[84] For White's interactions with Jean Galot and Thomas Weinandy, both of whom argue against the idea that Christ experienced the beatific vision from conception, see *The Incarnate Lord*, 240-46.
[85] White, *The Incarnate Lord*, 238.
[86] White, *The Incarnate Lord*, 254.

life, then "he must be humanly aware of what the Father who sent him wills and of what he wills with the Holy Spirit, so that he can express this in his human actions and choices."[87] This does not preclude the Son from truly growing in his human nature, but the human nature—at whatever level of creaturely development we might consider at any given moment in the life of Christ—always perfectly reveals the divine will in such a mode of creaturely existence. The infant in Bethlehem perfectly revealed the divine will as an infant. Adonis Vidu can say, in agreement with White, "on the one hand Christ has the vision of God from conception," and yet go on to insist that "on the other hand throughout his earthly life he discovers (as man) the manifold ways in which God may be participated in and experienced, particularly through the experience of loss and want characteristic of the human condition."[88] Such a conception precludes the notion that Christ's expressed ignorance in the Gospels amounts to a defect or the inability to express the divine will perfectly with his human will. And insofar as it goes, we can agree. Christ, as human, truly grows, and that growth is consonant with his perfect knowledge and expression of the divine will.

But is this all there is to say on the matter? The choice that White presents us with is that Christ experienced either the immediate knowledge of the beatific vision, or knowledge accessible through the grace of the theological virtue of faith. "Necessarily," says White, "outside of the vision, all knowledge of God is through effects, and only faith permits a quasi-immediate contact with God, through love."[89] But is the choice truly this stark? Either we conceptualize Christ's knowledge of the divine will as the beatific vision or as his exercise of faith?

---

[87]White, *The Incarnate Lord*, 255.
[88]Adonis Vidu, *The Same God Who Works All Things: Inseparable Operations in Trinitarian Theology* (Grand Rapids, MI: Eerdmans, 2021), 273.
[89]White, *The Incarnate Lord*, 258, emphasis original.

On this matter, post-Reformation orthodoxy might be of some help. In the first of his four-volume magnum opus, *Post-Reformation Reformed Dogmatics*, Richard A. Muller lays out various categories of theology as described by the Protestant orthodox.[90] On the one hand, there is archetypal theology—which is God's knowledge of himself— and on the other, there is ectypal theology—creaturely knowledge of God. Ectypal theology can be subdivided into additional categories, which would include "theology of union," the "theology of the blessed," and "theology in via" (on the way). We might describe this last kind of theology—the kind we experience in this life—as "pilgrim theology." A "theology of union" is most relevant for our present discussion. Threading the needle between White's stark choice (i.e., Christ's knowledge of the divine is either beatific or learned according to faith), the Reformed orthodox proposed a theological knowledge that Christ experienced on earth by virtue of the hypostatic union. "Christ's knowledge of God, in view of the uniqueness of his person," says Muller, "represents a separate category of theology to be contrasted with the theology of angels and of men either in via or in partia."[91] Many of the concerns surrounding the Reformed orthodox discussion of this theology of union are virtually identical with the concerns White lays out for emphasizing Christ's earthly experience of the beatific vision. Divine wisdom, insisted the Reformed orthodox, is communicated to Christ not by "revelation strictly so-called" (i.e., the wisdom that comes through the exercise of faith, or the kind of wisdom that is characteristic of our pilgrim theology), but is rather communicated by union. Muller explains,

> This communication does not mean—as the ubiquitarians would have it—that infinite divine wisdom is transformed into a human intellect.

---

[90]Richard A. Muller, *Post-Reformation Reformed Dogmatics*, 4 vols., 2nd ed. (Grand Rapids, MI: Baker Academic, 2003), 1:248-69. Although, the category of "archetypal theology" is probably less preferable, terminologically, than the more straightforward identification of "archetypal *knowledge*," since "theology," as a kind of *science*, is a fundamentally *human* enterprise. I am grateful to James Dolezal who pointed this out to me in a conversation.
[91]Muller, *PRRD*, 1:249.

Rather Christ's mind was enlightened extraordinarily by the Holy Spirit because of the power of union with the divine nature ... that union takes place without commixture or comingling, without a confusion of the natures, and thus without either a communication of divinity to humanity or a transference of the divine attributes to the human nature. Thus Jesus has two natures, two wills, two intellects—a divine and a human—and each has the knowledge that is proper to it.[92]

Thus, the theology of union, experienced only by Jesus, is not archetypal knowledge (God's knowledge of God), but is rather a unique kind of ectypal theology (man's knowledge of God)—a kind of ectypal theology only experienced by the Word-made-flesh. While it is clear that this conception of Christ's knowledge differs from the Lutheran picture of the communication of properties (*communicatio idiomantum*), it may not at first glance appear to contradict with the Roman Catholic insistence that Christ experienced the beatific vision in this life. How do beatific theology and a theology of union differ? Is this merely a distinction without a difference? The Reformed orthodox answer has everything to do with soteriology and Christ's role as our second Adam.

As Muller emphasizes, "Christ's knowledge ... was a knowledge suited to his life—and not an existence beyond passion and death. Scientia beata, blessed or beatific knowledge, is therefore excluded, leaving two principles (species) of knowledge, scientia infusa [infused knowledge] and scientia acquisita [acquired knowledge]."[93] In other words, beatific knowledge is knowledge that befits the resurrected and glorified human nature, which Christ did not possess until his resurrection and glorification. White, of course, would stridently deny the possibility that Christ's knowledge was in any way an infused or acquired (gracious) knowledge, but this seems to be because the only category he has for this kind of knowledge is the kind that we believers possess in this life—which is to say,

---

[92] Muller, *PRRD*, 1:250.
[93] Muller, *PRRD*, 1:253.

partial, incomplete, progressive, wanting, and progressively perfected by love.[94] But the Reformed orthodox, such as Turretin, conceive of Christ's theology of union differently. "The infused knowledge," explains Muller, "is a supernatural disposition that knows heavenly things by the light of grace—in the case of Christ, it is given or infused by a special grace of the Spirit that utterly sanctifies his human nature and fills it with the gifts of grace."[95] Thus, White's concern that any knowledge short of beatific knowledge in the humanity of Christ would somehow compromise the integrity of the hypostatic union and the perfect agreement of Christ's two wills is averted by the Reformed notion of *theologia unionis*. His knowledge is utterly sanctified and perfect. It has not deficiency, and it is complete in its proper mode, which we might summarize as a "pre-resurrection," "pre-glorification" mode. Additionally, such a notion avoids stripping Christ's earthly ministry of its soteriological impact. Again, Muller presents the matter well, and so we quote him at length here:

> Christ's knowledge of God as infused by the Holy Spirit and acquired during his life and ministry by the exercise of his intellect must be a true and perfect knowledge of God, higher than that of any sinful man and perfected in and for the sake of the hypostatic union, but—if it is to be true to scriptural passages like Luke 2:52 and Mark 13:32—it must lack, at least during Christ's earthly life, some of the wisdom of the blessed. In addition, it must conform to the condition or state of Christ so that it reflects first his humiliation and then his exaltation and thereby provides a basis first of the theologia viatorum [the theology of the saints in this life] and then for the theologia beatorum [the theology of the blessed]. . . . If Christ's knowledge of God were the visio beatifica [beatific vision], his theology a theologia beatorum sive visionis, it would be identical with the theology of the redeemed in heaven and, in effect, the terminus ad quem of human theology, nothing more. . . . This view, however, the Reformed almost universally rejected: they

---

[94]See, e.g., White, *The Incarnate Lord*, 258-60.
[95]Muller, *PRRD*, 1:253-54.

maintained the continuance of Christ's mediation into the eschaton, arguing that our union with Christ as mediator provides the basis for our union with God eternally, insofar as our union with God must always be in Christ. Even so, our vision of God, the theologia visionis, must ultimately rest on Christ's relation to God and his knowledge of God for us, the theologia unionis. The purpose or goal of this theology of union, then, corresponds with the purpose or goal of Christ, the anointed one.[96]

We might make this point more succinctly by casting it in its covenantal context. If the beatific vision is the promise held out as the fulfillment of the covenant of works, it is the reward for obedience. This reward is the very thing that Adam forfeited for himself and all his posterity, and which Christ secured with his active and passive obedience for his posterity. He was born "under the law, to redeem those who were under the law" (Gal 4:4-5). To be under the law is to not yet enjoy the beatific vision. To insist that Christ experienced this non-beatific state of being under the law is not to insist on some kind of kenotic self-emptying of his divine nature, nor is it to say that Christ's knowledge was in any way deficient or hampered by the mark of sin, but is simply to stress that Christ leads his posterity through obedience to the covenant of works to the reward of the beatific vision. We reap the benefits of obedience to the covenant of works not because we have obeyed, but because Christ has for us. United to him, his obedient righteousness (which brings the benefit of obedience—the beatific vision) is imputed to us. Christ comes to where we are to bring us to our final end in him. When Christ did come to experience the beatific vision, the transition from humiliation to exaltation was not marked by a mere quantitative leap (as if he lacked sufficient knowledge of God before and now had it), but rather the qualitative difference between theological knowledge pre- versus post-resurrection.[97]

---

[96] Muller, *PRRD*, 1:255.
[97] Even if one agrees with insisting that Christ's knowledge leading up to the cross was a theology of union and not that of beatific knowledge, there remains a question, of course, of

Synthesis and Definition

Before concluding this chapter, it will be helpful to summarize and synthesize all that we have said thus far into a single descriptive definition. Here, I shall affirm the key central components of the beatific vision articulated throughout the great tradition, as well as include the distinctly Protestant and Reformed contributions explored above. In this way, this definition should be read not only as an attempt to be historically rooted, but also as a constructive and dogmatic proposal for the doctrine.

The beatific vision is the telos of humanity: the vision of God the saints will enjoy in the eschaton. The beatific vision is a vision of love, a participatory vision of God's essence, in resurrected bodies, wherewith we will see this vision immediately and everywhere, particularly in the person of Christ, on account of our union with him. The object of our contemplation by faith now (i.e., God in Christ) will be the object of this beatific vision forever—him whom we delight to behold by faith now we will continually delight to behold in glorified vision hereafter. United to Christ, his perfect vision of God will be our perfect vision of God, for he is the author and perfector of our faith, our forerunner and perfect federal head and restorative source. This vision is the full satiation of every creaturely desire and the absolute telos of the image-bearer. Every happiness that has partial fulfillment here will be realized in full in this vision, since this vision is the destination to which all natural desires lead. The realization of this hope is one of perpetual growth and expansion—where the saint's capacity for delight in the blessedness of God grows with his reception of that delight, and his thirst increases simultaneously with his satiation. Thus, the saint is full to the brim with satisfaction even as his capacity for satisfaction grows forevermore. The "formal blessedness" of the finite creature forever

---

whether Christ's experience of the beatific vision began in his descent to hades, in his resurrection, or in his ascension. I am inclined to answer with the latter option, but good arguments might be marshaled for the other two as well.

increases to ever-apprehend the infinite "objective blessedness," which is God himself. This vision never moves beyond the person of Christ, because the person of Christ never ceases to be Emmanuel; all the fullness of God is pleased to dwell in him, so our increasing delight in God's essence is an increasing delight in the Son who is forever hypostatically united to human nature. It is his blood that purchases the beatific vision for the saints, and they will therefore never tire of crying out, "Worthy are you! For you were slain, and by your blood you ransomed a people for yourself." The beatific vision is the consummation of the believer's bond to God—who is Christ—which means it is the consummate fellowship and communion with the believer's bond to Christ—who is the Spirit. Thus, the beatific vision is a spiritual vision of divine love—where the believer is brought by the Spirit into the Trinity's own beatitude, further up and further in, forever. This vision is described and signaled to in the Scriptures in a number of ways: it is the culmination of every biblical hope for the Promised Land, for the new Jerusalem, for communion with God in his glory on the holy mountain, for entrance into the Edenic presence of God in the Temple and the Holy of Holies, and for the eternal rest of Sabbath. Furthermore, this vision is the perfect realization of fellowship; both the saints' fellowship with God, and subsequently, the saints' fellowship with each other. The individual saint's delight of this vision is enhanced by the presence of other saints and angels, for there love will be perfectly expressed, and true love for neighbor will overwhelm the individual saint with delight—the joy of neighbor will increase the joy of oneself. In this way, the beatific vision is the final and absolute enjoyment of the Trinity's beatitude, and the celebration of God's being all in all.

6

THE BEATIFIC VISION AND THE CHRISTIAN LIFE

ONE MAY BE TEMPTED TO identify this final chapter on the beatific vision and the Christian life as the practical chapter, or the useful chapter, or—God forbid—the relevant chapter. "Here," one might assume, "the long-winded author finally brings the 'so what' of all this speculative theologizing." The often unstated assumption behind this formulation is that contemplation of God is a good only insofar as it impacts the everyday life of a Christian. "Give me something that is relevant for my life" is often the orienting posture toward the topic of theology. But if what we have maintained thus far is true, contemplation of God is no means to an end, but is rather the ultimate end itself. Theology is not practical in the sense that it becomes a service to some daily pursuit. Rather, for creatures who are made *for* God, theology is practical by definition. This is *the singular* telos of the human being: his delighted contemplation of God. Theology's practicality, therefore, begins more fundamentally than its tendency to delight the soul that contemplates the blessed Trinity.

Therefore, this chapter should not be read as a final effort to justify the preceding chapters, as if commending the eschatological hope of the beatific vision requires a defense anchored in carnal concerns. If the blessed hope of seeing God is situated properly, it needs no support. It is its own intrinsic defense. Cultivating a soulish hope for the beatific vision is *the most practical* thing an image-bearer can do, given his nature and telos. All other pursuits and concerns, therefore, rightly orbit around the beatific vision. This chapter offers a handful of examples for how setting our hopeful gaze toward God in the beatific vision illuminates and enlivens the Christian life. Rather than propping up the beatific vision with practical implications, I seek to show how the beatific vision, rightly understood, transfigures the way we engage with concerns in our present pilgrimage. To that end, I will consider how the beatific vision shapes and informs the way we understand prayer, corporate worship, sin and sanctification, missions, suffering, and friendship.

Prayer

Prayer is spiritual oxygen for the Christian. A Christian life without prayer is a life dying of suffocation. This is why Christopher Holmes can go so far as to say, "There is no greater call in this life than that of the call to prayer."[1] Prayer is thus perhaps the most basic Christian practice to orient organically around the beatific vision. A common misconception regarding prayer is that the practice is a form of therapeutic escape from the real world. However, according to a classical realist metaphysic and a thoroughly biblical anthropology—with its corresponding teleological emphasis on the beatific vision—the practice of prayer is an exercise in reality. Indeed, a Christian in the act of praying engages in something more real than anything else he can possibly do on earth. For all the discontinuities that exist between life in this world and life in the next, prayer is one unmistakable continuity. In prayer, the saint taps into an ultimate and transcendent mode of existence: he is communing with the triune God for whom he was made. This is because "in prayer we receive existence afresh, true likeness to God. We become truly human, reflecting the existence of God, who is pure goodness

---

[1] Christopher R. J. Holmes, *A Theology of the Christian Life: Imitating and Participating in God* (Grand Rapids, MI: Baker Academic, 2021), 139.

itself."[2] Such "reception" and "reflection" will mark the saint in glory forever. Therefore, when he prays, he practices his future. "We will never finish with God."[3]

Prayer is therefore a form of communion that orients the Christian toward his ultimate and truest end. Holmes, again, puts the matter well: "Prayer reorients our desires in such a way that we begin to desire God, our Father, who is supremely good. Prayer perfects our appetites. We begin to desire, more and more what is good for us, which is God!"[4] This desire finds its final and constant satiation in the beatific vision. God has made us for himself—he has made us to enjoy and communion with and participate in himself, such that our deepest delight and the realization of our created purpose is to receive the fullness of life from the fullness of life—deep cries out to deep. God, as the infinite, boundless plenitude of life and light and love, is the good for which our soul was created. In prayer, this future reality breaks into our souls in this life. All this is true for every Christian, regardless of whether he or she is conscious of the beatific vision in the act of prayer. But when the doctrine is held explicitly in view, how could it not aggravate the Godward longing of the soul in prayer even more? Indeed, the psalmists seem to stir their own souls up into a frenzy, desperately longing for this end for which they are created, throughout the Psalter. Psalm 27:4 is, in this way, the entire biblical psalter in one verse: "One thing have I asked of the Lord, that will I seek after: that I may dwell in the house of the Lord all the days of my life, to gaze upon the beauty of the Lord and to inquire in his temple." Small wonder, then, why Anselm's great journey toward the beatific vision in the *Proslogion* is a prayer:

> I pray, O God, that I may know You and love You, so that I may rejoice in You. And if I cannot do so fully in this life may I progress gradually

---

[2] Holmes, *A Theology of the Christian Life*, 31.
[3] Holmes, *A Theology of the Christian Life*, 31.
[4] Holmes, *A Theology of the Christian Life*, 31.

until it comes to fullness. Let the knowledge of You grow in me here, and there [in heaven] be made complete; let Your love grow in me here and there be made complete, so that here my joy may be great in hope, and there be complete in reality.[5]

In light of what we have seen in this book regarding the beatific vision, this prayer from Anselm is thoroughly understandable. Indeed, it is the prayer that seems to rise unbidden from the soul that embraces the beatific vision as its true end. The beatific vision therefore has a purifying effect on the prayers of the conscious saint. The light and heat of God's essence in heaven shines forth into the heart of the praying saint, continually purging his prayer of desires and requests unbecoming of his future. "Hallowed be Thy name" becomes his deep, guttural ache. With his gaze set toward heaven, he, with increasing measure, prays accordingly.

It seems fitting, before concluding this section on prayer, to offer an example of what a prayer shaped by the beatific vision might look like. The following is the prayer I wrote in preparation for this very volume. Once a week, when I sat down to work on this book, this is the prayer I offered up to God:

> O my Lord, blessed Trinity—Father, Son, and Holy Spirit—blessed be your name now and forevermore. I praise you for your boundless beauty. You are full of splendor and glory. You are light, inexpressible. You are a depthless deep. Your majesty is ineffable and boundless. You are a fire of pure, white-hot holiness, and I long to be consumed by you. You have, by your mysterious and kind providence, granted for me to write on the blessed hope of gazing upon your beauty in this book. Though I do not feel equal to the task, Lord, I am invigorated by it. Overcome the snares that threaten to keep me from faithfully kindling hope in my readers. Lord Jesus, you have said that the pure in heart are blessed, for they shall see God, and I know all too well the sight-obscuring effects of sin and corruption. Purify me, that I might see you truly. Give to me the joy of saying with David truly, "One thing have I

---

[5]Anselm, *Proslogion*, in *Anselm of Canterbury: The Major Works*, ed. Brian Davies and G. R. Evans (New York: Oxford University Press, 1998), 26.103-4.

asked of the Lord, that will I seek after: that I may dwell in the house of the Lord all the days of my life, to gaze upon the beauty of the Lord and to inquire in his temple." Holy Spirit, sanctify my heart and mind—consecrate my office as I read and write there, and may it be a place of sweet contemplation. May I encounter the heat of holy, triune beatitude there. Forbid that I should ever approach the subject with a cold heart. May I ever be drawn by you, the pure Divine Fire who burns unceasingly as unbegotten Father, eternally begotten Son, and spirated Spirit. Holy Spirit, illumine your Scriptures to me. Show me, even as through a glass darkly lit, what we are to set our hopeful gaze upon in this life. May my writing be to me a grace, wherein I consume your nourishing words and commune with you in happy fellowship, my God and my love. May my writing be worship.

Protect me, O God, and prevent me from saying anything that is dishonoring to you or unbecoming of your goodness. Keep the desire to see you—and the desire to lovingly invite many others to see you—as the engine of my work. Forbid that I should write to be praised. Forbid that I should write to be recognized. Forbid that I should dishonor my fellow image-bearer by misrepresentation or by hastily drawing conclusions. For I want to love my neighbor as I love myself by letting each of my consulted sources speak truly for themselves, instead of merely forcing them to say what I wish for them to say for the sake of an argument's expediency. In all these ways and more, O God, I am dependent on you. Stir my affections for you and the blessed hope of the beatific vision, and use my words to do the same in the hearts of others, in the name of Jesus Christ, to the glory of the Father, Son, and Holy Spirit. Amen.

Corporate Worship

Our reflections on the beatific vision are incomplete if they do not materialize into an act of corporate beholding of God. The beatific vision is not a private hope: it is the hope of all the blessed. Therefore, practicing for the beatific vision should be the activity not merely of the individual Christian, but also of the gathered church. Matthew Barrett puts the point powerfully when he says, "Gazing at the beauty of the Lord is the premier ambition of the theologian, but the theologian's task is incomplete if his heavenly gaze is for himself alone."[6] This, in fact, is why the local church gathers. She gathers to worship her bridegroom, where she hears his address and sees his glorious face (cf. 2 Cor 3:12-4:6). It is no coincidence that the two most important verses for John Owen's formulation of the beatific vision (2 Cor 3:18; 4:6) describe the glory of God in Christ shining forth from the Scriptures in the context of *public Scripture reading and proclamation*. The local church gathers to see the glory of God in the face of Jesus Christ *together*. It gathers as one body to sing with one voice the praises of its King—the one it longs to "see in his beauty" (cf. Is 33:17). She gathers to hear her good shepherd address her, as he leads her with his voice into the Promised Land. "The church will drink from the well of contemplation if the soul of the church is defined not only by its present but future *telos*," says Barrett, "which is nothing less than doxology. The church exists and operates within God's economy as saints forming an embassy of praise—from redemption to restoration, from union to communion, from consecration to contemplation."[7]

What might it look like for a local church to allow for the transformative effect of the blessed hope to function in its gathered assemblies? Much can be said about the topic, but here we treat how this principle ought to determine how a church carries out (1) its ministry of the Word (i.e., reading, preaching, and teaching Scripture), and (2) its ministry of the sacraments (baptism and communion).

The ministry of the Word. Consider 2 Corinthians 4:6. Although the emphasis of this verse is soteriological in nature, the context for the passage as a whole has major implications on hermeneutics.[8] Paul says essentially that there is a right way to read the Scripture

---

[6]Matthew Barrett, "Classical Theology: A Spiritual Exercise," *Journal of Classical Theology* 1 (2022): 6.
[7]Barrett, "Classical Theology," 9.
[8]For more of a thorough treatment see Samuel G. Parkison, *Irresistible Beauty: Beholding Triune Glory in the Face of Jesus Christ* (Ross-shire, UK: Mentor, 2022), 191-98.

(in this instance, the Old Testament in particular), and there is a wrong way. Those who see the glory of God in the face of Jesus Christ "whenever Moses is read" are reading with "the veil removed"—they read *rightly*. The glory of God in the face of Jesus Christ is *there* in the Scriptures, and they can see it. Those who are unable to see this glory are encumbered not by anything found in the text, but rather by the satanic veil that keeps them from seeing what is truly there (2 Cor 3:14-15; 4:4)—they read *wrongly*. This means that the dogged insistence of beholding the glory of God in the face of Jesus Christ by staring at any part of the Scripture is not a hermeneutic style—indeed, it is a grace. God's glory on Christ's face objectively shines forth from the text, which means that any hermeneutic that fails to appreciate this glory is incomplete.[9] As I have attempted to show throughout this volume, this glory the saint beholds by faith in this life is precisely the very same glory he will behold by beatifical vision in the next.

While this theological principle alone does not answer all the questions it might raise about hermeneutics, it at least establishes this much: as the local church gathers around the inscripturated Word of God, it should do so with the express conviction that what it will find there is the glory of God in the face of Jesus Christ—the *same* glory that will transfix its attention for all of eternity in the beatific vision. This is not wishful thinking or theological imposition on its part; it is rather its effort to believe what Scripture says about itself. As a "creature of the Word,"[10] when the church hears in the proclamation of the text that the glory of God in the face of Jesus Christ emanates in an objective sense from its pages, and is seen by those unencumbered by a satanic veil with the eyes of faith (2 Cor 3:12-4:6), it *believes what it hears and sees*. And its hopeful

---

[9] A splendid example of what this looks like in the pulpit is Iain Duguid, "Preaching Christ from Proverbs," *Unio Cum Christo* 5, no. 1 (2019): 173-89.

[10] This phrase comes from Kevin J. Vanhoozer, *The Drama of Doctrine: A Canonical-Linguistic Approach to Christian Theology* (Louisville, KY: Westminster John Knox, 2005), 230.

longing for heaven compels it to see with eagerness what it can see of that future *now*.

All this is punctuated in the church's ministry of preaching and teaching. If the local church gathers around the Word to see in it the glory of God in Christ, such glory must be set plainly before them in the sermon. The new covenant ministry is a ministry of *proclamation*, and the subject of this proclamation is none other than the glory of Christ. There are two reasons for this. First, preachers must set the glory of Christ before the congregation in their proclamation of Scripture because the glory of Christ is legitimately to be found there. They have not truthfully proclaimed the Scripture if they have not proclaimed how it radiates Christ's beauty. Second, getting a collective eye-full of Christ's glory is how the church will grow up into maturity. No gimmicks or pragmatic initiatives will do for the local congregation what a sermon reveling in the excellencies of Christ will do. The body of Christ is "nourished and knit together through its joints and ligaments," and "grows with a growth that is from God" only when it holds "fast to the Head" (Col 2:19). This is how it is transformed into the image of Christ from one degree of glory to another, forever.

The ministry of the sacraments.[11] "Baptism and the Lord's Supper belong to the very essence of the church."[12] This is the first of Michael Haykin's six concluding theses in his recent work, *Amidst Us Our Beloved Stands: Recovering Sacrament in the Baptist Tradition*, and if he is correct, the beatific vision's doctrinal impact on these sacramental practices can scarcely be exaggerated. If the church is a heaven-bound bride, the sacramental marks of her identity must be conceived as heaven-bound as well. Of course, describing these two ordinances as sacraments is sure to rub many

---

[11] The following section contains reworked and expanded material from my article, "'One Baptism for the Remission of Sins': Exploring the Harmony Between Christian Platonism, Reformed Soteriology, and Credobaptism," in *Perichoresis*, Volume 21, issue 2 (2023).

[12] Michael A. G. Haykin, *Amidst Us Our Beloved Stands: Recovering Sacrament in the Baptist Tradition* (Bellingham, WA: Lexham, 2022), 120.

evangelicals wrongly, particularly those who—like myself—affirm a credobaptist understanding of baptism. Not only will many of my own Baptist brethren balk on the designation, some within high-church traditions will be mystified by my language as well. I use the term to emphasize the reality that when the church practices these ordinances, *God* does something real in them. He is an *actor* in these practices—using them to orient their practitioners to their final end in the beatific vision. He comes from that future telos, so to speak, and pulls them to their true homeland as they receive these glorious gifts.

Is it right for a Baptist to talk in this way? Not according to many, particularly when baptism is in view. Since the Baptist view essentially conceptualizes baptism as a form of personal self-expression (so the argument goes), it stands in stark opposition to the great tradition, which, although incredibly diverse with how the particulars work together, has *always* insisted on layers of meaning in baptism. Though there has not been complete agreement on how, to what degree, and what kind of divine grace is communicated to the baptized in the physical act of water baptism, the great tradition is uniform in at least this much: whatever constitutes as baptism, God uses it as an effective means of grace. This sacramentalism draws from the kind of classical realist metaphysic described in chapter one, wherein meaning transgresses the boundaries of material form. The cosmos and actions within it mean more than their physical dimensions. In this participatory metaphysic, Christians have nearly always insisted, God has ordained to sovereignly administer a certain kind of gracious blessing on the right administration of baptism (whatever constitutes as "right administration" and "baptism"). If this is the case, baptism as mere symbolic, individualistic *self-expression* assumes a very different kind of metaphysic, and therefore has no place within the classical realist tradition.

So goes the argument against the notion that credobaptists can be, in any sense, sacramental. And to the degree that such a formulation exhausts the credobaptist position, I would agree. Fortunately, such a reductionistic view of baptism is not necessarily *the* Baptist position. To be fair, critics of Baptist ecclesiology and the Baptist tradition have a point when they argue along these lines. It is not difficult to find voices to enthusiastically confirm such a stereotype, and though such a point would be difficult to substantiate, I think it is fair to assume that this view is at least dominant—if not *default*—for most self-identified Baptists on the planet. But the mere, self-expressive view of baptism is historically and theologically accidental to the Baptist tradition. It is not an essential Baptist distinctive. "Baptist sacramentalism" is no oxymoron, historically or theologically.[13]

Even if one is not willing to embrace what we might call the "high sacramentalism" of figures like David F Wright, George Beasley-Murray, and Everett Ferguson, who argue for a kind of "credobaptismal regeneration," one is not thereby necessarily consigned to a merely symbolic notion of baptism.[14] To assume as much is to assume that the only kinds of grace God grants through his sacraments are *regenerative*. But this is an unnecessary leap; "regenerative grace" and "means of grace" are by no means synonyms. Bobby Jamieson, for example, offers a formidable argument for what he calls baptism as "the initiating oath-sign of the new covenant."[15] Baptism is a grace in the sense that through it, God offers all kinds of assurances to the believer, as he legitimizes the believer's inclusion in the new covenant by offering his stamp of approval

---

[13]See Haykin, *Amidst Us Our Beloved Stands*; Anthony R. Cross and Philip E. Thompson, eds., *Baptist Sacramentalism 1* (Eugene, OR: Pickwick, 2003); Stanley K. Fowler, *More Than a Symbol: The British Baptist Recovery of Baptismal Sacramentalism* (Eugene, OR: Wipf and Stock, 2002); D. B. Riker, *A Catholic Reformed Theologian: Federalism and Baptism in the Thought of Benjamin Keach, 1640–1704* (Eugene, OR: Wipf and Stock, 2009).

[14]See David F. Wright, *Infant Baptism in Historical Perspective* (Eugene, OR: Wipf and Stock, 2006); George Beasley-Murray, "Baptism and the Sacramental View," *The Baptist Times*, February 11, 1960; Everett Ferguson, *Baptism in the Early Church: History, Theology, and Liturgy in the First Five Centuries* (Grand Rapids, MI: Eerdmans, 2013).

[15]Bobby Jamieson, *Going Public: Why Baptism Is Required for Church Membership* (Nashville: B&H Academic, 2015), 80.

through his earthly emissary: the local church. The grace of baptism need not be regenerative in order to be real. Jamieson goes on to say,

> It is an enacted vow whereby a person formally submits to the Triune Lord of the new covenant and pledges to fulfill the requirements of the new covenant. . . . The new covenant creates a visible people, and one becomes a visible member of that people through baptism. One may not be counted among the people of the new covenant until one has undergone its initiating oath-sign.[16]

In Jamieson's view, baptism is not simply the act of indicating invisible realities with a visible sign. Rather, the visible sign *effects* the visible manifestation of the invisible reality. Put in classical realist dictum, the universal form or idea of the church is, in part, made manifest in this-worldly fashion through the sacrament of baptism. This is how the church uses the keys to the kingdom of heaven (cf. Mt 16:18-19; 18:18; 28:19) to bind on earth that which is bound in heaven. There is only one institution on the planet that has been so deputized by divine order to manifest those heavenly realities in their earthly form, and that is the local church. God, through the deputized local church sacrament of baptism, formally ushers his elect into the local expression of Christ's body, whereby he feeds, spiritually, on Christ himself. When the new believer comes to Christ by faith, he feeds on Christ in a sense—but God feeds Christ to the believer in quite another, more tangible sense, after he has been baptized into his earthly body. For there, in that local expression of the universal body of Christ, the believer's faithful feasting on Christ is punctuated in a physical dimension; he is *spiritually* nourished with *physical* bread and wine as he continues to feed on Christ *by faith*.[17]

There is something to be said about the fact that some of the most crucial New Testament passages describing union with Christ are

---

[16] Jamieson, *Going Public*, 80.
[17] Richard C. Barcellos, *The Lord's Supper as a Means of Grace: More Than a Memory* (Ross-shire, UK: Mentor, 2013), 55-71.

draped in baptismal language (e.g., Rom 6:1-11; Gal 3:27-29). Some have understandably taken these tight connections to mean that the Spirit's regenerative baptism and the church's water baptism are at least coterminous, if not synonymous. While I do not share this view, I do agree with its central insistence that Spirit baptism and water baptism are inextricably related. To be united to Christ and separated from his body—or baptized *into* Christ by the Spirit, but not baptized by water into Christ's earthly body (the local church)— is a foreign category to the Scriptures. And this is precisely where the beatific vision ought to rightly orient baptism. When the local church baptizes a new believer, it is saying, with the authority of God himself, "*You* are coming with *us* into the promised land of heaven. Now that you have crossed the Jordan River, we march on toward the New Jerusalem." The practice of baptism ought to therefore be oriented toward the future hope of the blessed vision.

The Lord's Supper also ought to have this heavenward orientation. In his outstanding work on communion, *Remembrance, Communion, and Hope*, J. Todd Billings considers the sacrament in a threefold fashion.[18] In this "emblem of the gospel," says Billings, the church *remembers* Christ's work in the gospel, *communes* with Christ and his people in the present, and *hopes* for the culmination of her union and communion in the future. This final perspective is most relevant for our present purposes. "For as often as you eat this bread and drink the cup, you proclaim the Lord's death *until he comes*" (1 Cor 11:26, emphasis added). With these words, the apostle Paul orients the Lord's Supper directionally to a distinct point: the coming of Christ. "This is why the Lord's Supper is so central for reorienting the hope of Christian congregations today," says Billings. "It focuses our attention, our affections, our communities, upon being nourished by God's promises in Jesus Christ. . . . We feed upon Jesus Christ, who is our foretaste of heaven, and will

---

[18] J. Todd Billings, *Remembrance, Communion, and Hope: Rediscovering the Gospel at the Lord's Table* (Grand Rapids, MI: Eerdmans, 2018).

be the heavenly bridegroom in the age to come."[19] What the believer receives as a foretaste in the Lord's Supper is not merely life after death—the "first resurrection" or the intermediate state (cf. Rev 20:4; 2 Cor 5:9; Phil 1:23). Billings is right to note how "the Lord's Supper thus reminds us that even [the intermediate state] is not the consummation of God's covenantal promises. Neither Eden nor the paradise that Jesus promises the thief on the cross is exalted and yet earthly enough."[20] Rather, communion is a foretaste of the "second resurrection," the arrival of New Jerusalem, in the renewed new heavens and new earth (cf. Rev 21). The beatific vision is consummated *there*, at the wedding feast of the Lamb, when the souls of those who have experienced the first resurrection are reunited with their now-glorified bodies in the second resurrection—when God will "wipe every tear from their eyes" (Rev 21:4), and with those eyes, they will "see his face" (Rev 22:4). The consummation of our earthly enjoyment of the Lord's Supper is the very thing Jesus himself waits for (cf. Lk 22:16), and as we partake of this meal today, we are oriented along with Christ toward that final meal. Here, on this side of the resurrection, we continue to eat, but our meals are meager tables, spread for us by our good shepherd in the wilderness, in the presence of our enemies, as we walk through the valley of the shadow of death (cf. Ps 23). Billings, again:

> At the table, we gather as hungry, broken communities to eat and drink together, to taste and see the goodness of the Lord, and to experience a foretaste of a dusty yet heavenly banquet. Even now, we may be able to see a sparkle of the loveliness in Christ that will clothe us all in our new, Spirit-animated bodies. For now, embodied worship of the crucified and risen Lord is our highest act of praise in this life. Likewise, embodied worship of the Lamb who was crucified will be our highest act of praise after the second advent. . . . Our theology will no longer be theology on pilgrimage, but theology of face-to-face encounter.[21]

---

[19]Billings, *Remembrance, Communion, and Hope*, 174.
[20]Billings, *Remembrance, Communion, and Hope*, 191.
[21]Billings, *Remembrance, Communion, and Hope*, 195.

All our celebrations of the Lord's Supper here, then, are shadows of the substance: the great feast of the beatific vision.

Taken together, we can see how these earthly signs of baptism and communion are divinely ordained signs and seals of heavenly realities, and to insist on having heavenly realities apart from their earthly manifestations is to attempt to tear asunder what God has joined together. In other words, it is not as if the ordinary means of grace are mere earthly responses to heavenly realities, they are rather the earthly windows into heavenly realities. Heaven and earth meet, for those who are in Christ, here: at the proclamation of the Word, the administration of water, and the consumption of bread and wine. By faith (and never without it), Word and Sacrament are true meeting places for communion with the Trinity and are thus trustworthy promises of the truest meeting place for our communion with the Trinity in heaven, where we will commune fully in the beatific vision.

Missions

"Missions exist because worship doesn't." This is the central thesis of John Piper's seminal book, *Let the Nations Be Glad!*, which takes its title from the resounding petition of Psalm 67:4.[22] The missionary spirit, according to Piper, is motivated by the desire to see God glorified among all the nations. Driven both by the positive desire to see God worshiped rightly, and the negative desire of being heartbroken by the nations' idolatry, the church takes her goodness—that which will make the nations *glad*—to those that do not know or believe the love of God in Christ. Missions therefore flows directly from what we have said above: namely, that the blessed hope of the beatific vision is *not* the hope of the isolated individual. The teleological contrast between the garden in Genesis 1 and the garden's intended culmination in the new Jerusalem in

---

[22] John Piper, *Let the Nations Be Glad!: The Supremacy of God in Missions*, 4th ed. (Grand Rapids, MI: Baker Academic, 2022), 3.

Revelation 21 helpfully illustrates the point. God's final intention was not to grant Adam the beatific vision, but rather to grant the beatific vision to Adam *and his posterity*—a *multitude*, a *people*.

Exaggerating the centrality of God's intention to save a multitude of peoples, an omni-ethnic bride from all tribes and tongues, is difficult. We see this plan unfurl from God's creation of man and the command to "multiply and fill the earth" (Gen 1:26-28), to his promised seed to come from the woman in order to crush the head of the serpent (Gen 3:15), who would come from the line of Abraham to (Gen 12:1-3; 15:5-6; 17:6-8), Isaac (Gen 26:4-5), Jacob (Gen 28:13), Judah (Gen 49:10), and David (1 Sam 16:1-13) in order to bless the nations, such that "Israel will be third with Egypt and Assyria, a blessing in the midst of the earth, whom the Lord of hosts has blessed, saying 'Blessed be Egypt my people, and Assyria the work of my hands, and Israel my inheritance'" (Is 19:24-25). This seed, we discover in the New Testament, is Christ himself (Mt 1:1-17; Gal 4:16-18), and it is thus *through Christ* that the eschatological church is formed. Revelation 7:9-12 reveals the fruit of Christ's accomplishment: a "great multitude that no one could number, from every nation, from all tribes and peoples and languages, standing before the throne and before the Lamb, clothed in white robes, with palm branches in their hands, and crying out with a loud voice, 'Salvation belongs to our God who sits on the throne, and to the Lamb!'" This is the end to which all the history of redemption develops. Paul makes this point clear when he pens Romans 15:8-13, quoting from the Law (Rom 15:10; cf. Deut 32:43), the Prophets (Rom 15:12; cf. Is 11:10-11), and the Writings (Rom 15:9, 11; cf. 2 Sam 22:50 and Ps 117:1), to show how all the Old Testament testifies to God's intention to receive praise from the nations. Indeed, this very notion of praise among all peoples seems to be the very thing that motivates Paul in his missionary zeal. God's intended means to the end of Revelation 7:9-12 is the faithful proclamation of his ambassadors (2 Cor 5:16-21), who serve as Christ's mouthpiece, lending him their voice so that through them he might draw his scattered sheep into his fold (Jn 10:16). Thus, behind the missional call of the church lies the freight of the entire biblical narrative.

The beatific vision relates to this missionary zeal in a number of ways. On one level, a simple love of neighbor compels the church to live on mission. She looks at those who are perishing in contrast to the blessed hope that awaits her, and she burns with desire to see the lost saved. Because her members' hopes are set in heaven, they can count all the sacrifices required to fulfill the mission of taking the gospel to the nations as less than nothing. What could the saints possibly lose in the pursuit of obeying Christ and inviting many others to experience what they anticipate in glory? The cost of such a pursuit does not diminish one bit the prize of the beatific vision.

But on another, related level, the beatific vision is *enriched* by missions, and therefore transposes missionary zeal to an even higher key. In other words, it is not merely that believers' hope in the beatific vision compels them to look with pity on the nations who lack this hope, it is also the fact that extending this hope to the nations *increases* the prize of heaven, which *increases* the blessedness of the blessed hope. In his recent book *Mission Affirmed*, Elliot Clark highlights this central point regarding the missionary motive. Paul, Clark shows, was single-mindedly focused on *receiving a crown of glory* from God in heaven—and that crown was the faith of those whom he brought to Christ (Phil 4:1; 1 Thess 2:19). Illustrating Lewis's insights from his sermon "The Weight of Glory," Clark writes:

> This is the glory that we seek: not just giving praise to God but receiving praise from God. Such honor is tangible, relatable, and desirable. But so often when we talk of glory, or hear it taught, the concept sounds impersonal, unattainable, and irrelevant. To many of us, the joys of heaven are ethereal and the glory of God esoteric. As a result, the Bible's many promises about glory feel disconnected from our greatest desires. But listen to Lewis's logic: our innermost longings point to a world

where those desires can be fulfilled. Our hunger for praise from others is a hunger satiated by God himself.[23]

This point is why Paul could shamelessly pursue a "crown of boasting" in the conversion of unbelievers. He desired for nothing more than to receive God in heaven—to bask in the "well done" of his beloved. This principle is illustrated strikingly in Romans 15:16, where he describes his ministry among the Gentiles in priestly terms, as he offers a sacrifice before God. Shockingly, the sacrifice in this instance are *the Gentiles themselves*—the Gentiles he ministers to, as sanctified by the Holy Spirit, *are* his offering to God. Paul ministers to the Gentiles as an act of sacred worship to God. Their Spirit-wrought holiness is what he revels in before God, not in a self-justifying way but in a grateful and adoring way. It is as if he is saying, "Lord you have entrusted these people to me, and I offer them back to you having taught them the gospel, adorned by the holiness of your Spirit. Here they are, my pride and joy!" Their progress in the gospel—their joy in God—is his great delight and aspiration as a minister. Thus, we should not imagine that Paul is so motivated by heavenly beatitude that he is willing to do hard things for the spread of the gospel among the nations. Rather, he sees a direct correlation: heavenly beatitude will be *more* enriched by his ministry among the nations.

Sin and Sanctification

Christians are called to a life of holiness. Since this holiness is what John Webster calls a "communicated holiness," it is "not transferred or possessed . . . but derived."[24] All his sanctification originates in and is derived by the God of holiness. This is because God alone is holiness simply. All other forms are holy derivatively in relation to him. "The Christian's sanctity is in Christ," Webster stresses, "in the

---

[23]Elliot Clarke, *Mission Affirmed: Recovering the Missionary Motive of Paul* (Wheaton, IL: Crossway, 2022), 46.

[24]John Webster, *Holiness* (Grand Rapids, MI: Eerdmans, 2013), 78.

Spirit, not *in se*; it is always and only an alien sanctity."[25] Because the Christian's life of holiness is a life unto God—the inexhaustible and ineffable mystery of Father, Son, and Spirit—we should not be surprised by its profundity.

If the beatific vision is the vision of the all-holy One himself, a necessary relationship between the holiness of the viewer and the holiness of his object is unavoidable. To approach God is to approach the eternal firey holiness—his presence, by necessity, burns away the dross of sin and impurity. As we live ever more to God, we ever receive more of his holiness—like iron in a furnace, the heat of the fire is communicated to the heat of the iron, such that their heat is one of distinction, a true *receptivity* (the iron does not make the fire hot, it is the other way around), and yet there is also a true *participation* (the heat of the fire becomes, truly, the heat of the iron). This is why Franciscus Junius (1545–1602) can describe the beatific vision (or, the "theology of vision") as "that which has been communicated with the angels, and with the spirits of the saints made holy or perfect in heaven."[26] The communication is from the all-holy one to his creatures—we share in his vision of himself by grace, which means we must be made like him to see what he sees. We must be made holy to see that which is holy. Junius therefore goes on to expand his definition in this way: "The theology of the blessed or the exalted theology is the wisdom of divine matters communicated in the Spirit of God according to the measure of Christ with those who dwell in heaven; according to this theology they enjoy the eternal, gracious, and glorious vision of God for his glory."[27] "From Him," Junius concludes, "all light, grace, and glory are shed abroad to created things, and He is also the end of those things and of every created thing."[28] The

---

[25] Webster, *Holiness*, 83.
[26] Franciscus Junius, *A Treatise on True Theology: With the Life of Fransiscus Junius*, trans. David C. Noe (Grand Rapids, MI: Reformation Heritage), 130.
[27] Junius, *True Theology*, 133.
[28] Junius, *True Theology*, 134.

implications on the present life of the believer and his pursuit of purity are therefore replete.

The New Testament persistently ties holy living to eschatological ends. Sometimes the relationship is one of motivation, both negative and positive. Negatively, the reality of judgment and wrath soberly strip sinful temptations of their luster and loveliness. Living on the edge of eternity, we are urged to consider our actions and inclinations in the light of hellfire and judgment (cf. Mt 5:29-30; 1 Jn 2:15-17; 1 Cor 6:9-10). Positively, the promise of "seeing God" is explicitly held out to those who are "pure in heart," and the desire to commune with the Lord in happy, holy fellowship forever serves as a motivation for resisting present temptation and steadfastly pursuing holiness (cf. Mt 5:8; Heb 12:1-2, 12-14).

The New Testament authors also routinely cast the present conduct of believers in the most urgent of backdrops: the impending return of Christ. Since the Lord Jesus is returning to retrieve his pure bride, ought we not then live in a sense of urgent expectancy, resenting the thought of him returning to the saints in a poor and pitiful position of lethargy and sinful stagnations (cf. 1 Thess 4:1-7; 5:8-11)? Ought we not live in such a way that all our hopes are set on his return (cf. 1 Tim 6:12-16; 2 Tim 4:7-8; Titus 2:11-14; 2 Pet 3:11-13; 1 Jn 3:1-6)? And, perhaps most important, the New Testament authors—and Paul in particular—roots the *progressive sanctification* of the believer's life of obedient holiness within the *definitive sanctification* of his redemption in Christ. In Christ, the believer is a new creation—holy, sanctified, consecrated unto God. In Christ, the believer *is* in heaven—his truest form is his final one, the one into which the Spirit is conforming him: the image of Christ (cf. Rom 6:5-14; 1 Cor 6:10-11; Gal 5:1, 16-26; Col 3:1-11).

Thus, the essence of the New Testament Christian ethic can be summarized in the seeming paradox: *be who you are*. In Christ, you are holy—a partaker of the divine nature (2 Pet 1:4); live like it.

In Christ, you have died to sin and live in Christ, therefore put to death the deeds of the body and live in holiness. This is the New Testament's message for believing pilgrims, on their way to the Promised Land. Therefore, the believer's own salvation has an irreducibly eschatological flavor. To be a Christian is to be bound by the Spirit, in Christ, *to heaven*. His future reaches backward to the present to pull him forward, and the means by which the Spirit does this pulling is the slow, godly plod of obedience through suffering (more on suffering below).

In this scheme, sin is a temporary and unwelcome intruder to the believer, whose fundamental identity is now determined by holiness, not by virtue of his own efforts, but *ontologically* as a new creation. Therefore, believers' eschatological enjoyment of the beatific vision relates to their life of holiness in every way. As a motivation, the beatific vision keeps them from the scandal of satisfying themselves with sinful water from muddy cisterns—they are motivated to choose the better portion of the fountain of living waters in the beatific vision (cf. Jer 2:12-13). With their hearts set in their true homeland, they resist the temptation of befriending the world, despising its transient promises and treasuring instead the permanence of beatifical fellowship (cf. 1 Jn 2:15-17). But even more than a motivation, the beatific vision effects the believer's life of sanctification as its *final cause*. In his letter to the Colossians, for example, Paul fully expects that 3:5-11 will flow *directly* from 3:1-4. "Put to death *therefore* what is earthly among you," he says. Meaning, because of 3:1-4, put to death what is earthly among you. In other words, because "you have been raised with Christ" and are therefore seeking "the things that are above, where Christ is, seated at the right hand of God," and because "you have died, and your life is hidden with Christ" will "appear with him in glory," *put to death what is earthly among you*. What is earthly among the believer, then, is *not* indicative of his truest state. His truest state is his union with Christ in heaven, which will be finally and fully consummated upon his return in glory, when the believer will enjoy the beatific vision forever.

Since that is the believer's destiny—not just in a *state of mind*, but truly and unalterably in Christ and by the Spirit—not only is he *willing* to shed what is earthly among himself, he is *able* to do so. Putting what is earthly and sinful in himself to death is no longer suicide, because that which is earthly and sinful in himself is no longer definitional—he is *new* in Christ, and his newness is indelibly tied to his future of beatific bliss. When he loses his "deeds of the body"—no matter how ingrained in his flesh by habit—he loses nothing of himself, but rather becomes a truer human. He is destined for heaven, and heaven is where his heart is, so in increasing measure, he lives in such a way that is evermore *befitting* to that happy and holy land. Junius, again:

> As the righteous await this perfection, indeed, they grow up through their advances into the perfect man, unto the measure of the full-grown Christ, and they rise up to the perfect vision of Him (Eph 4:13). And last, the final cause of this whole wisdom is the *glory of God*. Here first the glory of our faith, that is of us who believe, is fully set forth; but afterward, however, in the heavens it will be a glory to be enjoyed as completely as possible in God our Father and the Lord Jesus Christ.[29]

Applying the beatific vision to the arena of resistance to sinful temptation is anything but abstract. A colleague of mine recently shared with me how over a decade ago, the beatific vision was *the* doctrine that eventuated in his victory over multiple years of struggle with pornography. As a young believer, he was unable to gain any substantial ground over the stranglehold of his lust. It was not until he interrogated the depth of his sinful desire that he began to gain ground in this area of spiritual discipline. "I kept asking, 'Why do I even keep doing this? I hate it, and get no real joy out of it,'" he explained, "but I eventually realized that my sinful desire was

---

[29] Junius, *True Theology*, 138-39.

a perversion of a much deeper desire; a faint whisper of something better. I realized that it wasn't even *sex* that I ultimately longed for, but rather communion with God in the beatific vision. As soon as I came to understand that I was far more motivated to fight for a joyful vision of God—I replaced my desire for porn with a desire for God." We could reproduce many stories like this. Of course, the beatific vision is not a doctrine that will function as a "silver bullet" for every believer struggling with every kind of besetting sin, but its orienting character can and should be used to much avail for the believer in the throes of earthy temptations. What such a believer needs is a break in the clouds and a burst of light to cut through the firmament—a hope and a joy that *transcends* the suffocation of temporal fleshly desires. This is precisely how the beatific vision functions in the life of a believer.

Suffering

The Scriptures consistently connects a Christian's suffering to hope of glory. In 2 Corinthians in particular, Paul develops, perhaps more thoroughly than anywhere else in the whole of Scripture, a theology of suffering. Second Corinthians 4:7–5:10 has made it into more pastoral counsel conversations than I can count, and for good reason, because in these verses we are given promises for the suffering saint from God himself. The two greatest mistakes we can make when thinking about suffering are, on the one hand, to minimize or trivialize, and, on the other hand, to catastrophize and despair. Paul will not let us to either with 2 Corinthians. He lets our suffering weigh as heavy as it is, and he refuses to ever let us label it as pointless. There is no such thing as wasted suffering for the believer. Suffering is real, and it is sanctifying. Paul's words in this passage conspire to create the kind of people who are "sorrowful yet always rejoicing" (2 Cor 6:10)—the kind of people who have biblical reflexes when it comes to suffering. These reflexes compel us to not flinch from acknowledging suffering as suffering, but also to look immediately with hopeful expectation for what God intends to do through suffering.

Paul does not say, "For this light and momentary affliction may prepare for us an eternal weight of glory, provided we look on the bright side or respond a particular way toward our circumstances." No, rather, in Christ all our suffering is at work. In Christ, suffering has been irreversibly transformed into an instrument for sanctification and glory. "For this light and momentary affliction is preparing for us an eternal weight of glory beyond all comparison, as we look not to the things that are seen but to the things that are unseen. For the things that are seen are transient, but the things that are unseen are eternal." The effect of Paul's words are staggering if their logic is applied consistently in the face of hardship. Paul does not minimize suffering, but he relativizes it in light of the glory to which suffering, under God's providence, contributes. In other words, it is not as if Paul says that suffering will be worth it because glory will be better. Rather, Paul goes so far as to say that somehow, in God's providence, present suffering will make future glory more glorious. In this way, the tables are turned on suffering. The greater the suffering, the greater the promise of glory. Here, then, is one way that the beatific vision impacts the believer's relationship to suffering. Suffering, for the believer attentive to biblical logic, holds promise for unspeakable joys. The beatific vision therefore infuses suffering with meaning, which makes it endurable.

And yet, suffering also causes the believer to feel an acute homesickness in this world, causing him to pine after his heavenly homeland. Suffering makes him rightly dissatisfied with life in the present world, which makes the prayer, "Come, Lord Jesus!" (Rev 22:20) increasingly native to his own experience. This is why Paul's section on suffering in 2 Corinthians 4:7-18 is immediately followed by his section on heaven in 5:1-10. "For while we are still in this tent," says Paul, "we groan, being burdened—not that we would be unclothed, but that we would be further clothed, so that what is mortal may be swallowed up by life" (2 Cor 5:4). We see the same logic reflected in Romans 8:18-26 and Hebrews 12:1-29. Suffering has a purifying effect in the life of the believer. It relativizes his priorities and rearranges his hopes—in the face of loss and suffering and tragedy, he begins to ache for a kind of permanence that is only found in heaven. He satisfies himself with nothing but "a kingdom that cannot be shaken" (Heb 12:28). In the furnace of affliction, God purifies our desires and fits us increasingly for heaven. The promise of God wiping every tear from every eye, after all, is only intelligible as a consolation with the presence of sorrowful tears (Rev 21:4).

What else can explain the phenomenon of saints in the history of the church facing excruciating pain in their final agonizing moments with a spirit of resolved joy and hope? Consider the final words of Helen Starke, a Protestant martyr who was put to death in 1543 for "not having accustomed herself to pray to the Virgin Mary, more especially during the time she was in childbed."[30] She was sentenced to death along with her husband and several other men, who spent their final moments "comforting [one] another, and assuring themselves that they should sup together in the Kingdom of Heaven that night," and so "they condemned themselves to God, and died constantly in the Lord."[31] Although Helen was not allowed to be hung with her husband, she nevertheless walked with him to the place of his execution, and kissed him, saying, "Husband, rejoice, for we have lived together many joyful days; but this day, we must have joy forever; therefore I will not bid you good night, for we shall suddenly meet with joy in the Kingdom of heaven."[32] Following this, Helen gave her little baby to a nearby nurse, and she was then put into a sack by the authorities and subsequently drowned. The history of Christianity has countless such stories.

---

[30] John Fox, *Fox's Book of Martyrs: A History of the Lives, Sufferings and Triumphant Deaths of the Early Christian and the Protestant Martyrs*, ed. William Byron Forbush (Grand Rapids, MI: Zondervan, 1967), 200.
[31] Fox, *Fox's Book of Martyrs*, 200.
[32] Fox, *Fox's Book of Martyrs*, 201.

The unmistakable theme that arises from their sum is one of heavenly hope: they, like their Savior, endured the pain for the joy that was set before them (cf. Heb 12:2).

FRIENDSHIP

To make the central concern of heaven the enjoyment of God in Christ is more than appropriate. This is the "one thing" for which David pines (Ps 27:4), and every other delight of heaven is subsumed by this all-expanding one: the enjoyment of beholding *God*. And yet the theocentricity of the beatific vision does not render other heavenly joys nonexistent. Instead, they take their rightful place in the hearts of heaven's inhabitants. Whereas joy in God often fades in the background of this life, decentered by lesser loves vying for unbefitting significance, all of our loves in heaven will be rightly ordered. There will be no excessive love for that which is not God, for everything that we love we will love for God's sake, and as an extension and expression of our love for God. Therefore, all that is right and good in this life will not be obliterated by the beatific vision, but rather resurrected and transfigured. While there is much we cannot say about that reality—since we are like seeds speculating about our future properties as flowers in full bloom—we can know that certain continuities will remain. One of which is the companionship of friends and siblings in Christ. It has never been "good" for man to be alone (Gen 2:18), and in the eschaton, we see a glimpse of what the creation mandate in full looks like. The garden has grown to a city, and man has been fruitful in his multiplication (Rev 7:9-17; 21:1-22:5; cf. Gen 1:28).

Of all the figures we have examined in this book, none have spoken on the topic of friendship and the beatific vision as affectively as Anselm of Canterbury and Jonathan Edwards. Toward the height of his *Proslogion*, Anselm turns his attention to the presence of saints and angels in glory, and reflects on the contribution their presence will offer in his enjoyment of the beatific vision:

Ask your heart whether it could comprehend its joy in its so great blessedness? But surely if someone else whom you loved in every respect as yourself possessed that same blessedness, your joy would be doubled for you would rejoice as much for him as for yourself. If, then, two or three or many more possessed it you would rejoice just as much for each one as for yourself, if you loved each one as yourself. Therefore in that perfect and pure love of the countless holy angels and holy men where no one will love another less than himself, each will rejoice for every other as for himself.[33]

In his sermon "Heaven is a World of Love," taken from 1 Corinthians 13:8-10, Jonathan Edwards reflects in much the same way on the presence of others in heaven. Edwards situates the centrality of love in heaven with the enjoyment of God: "Everything which is to be beheld there is amiable."[34] Why? Because "The God, who dwells and gloriously manifests himself there, is infinitely lovely. . . . All the persons who belong to that blessed society are lovely. The Father of the family is so, and so are all his children. The Head of the body is so, and so are all the members."[35] God will be loved as the loveliest object of heaven, and everything else will be loved for God's sake, since their loveliness derives from God. "The saints there love God for his own sake," says Edwards, "and each other for God's sake, for the sake of the relation which they bear to God, and that image of God which is upon them."[36] This, Edwards reflects, the saints will do with perfect execution. With no remainder, we shall love each other purely and wholeheartedly, and never in any manner with lack of propriety. Edwards goes to summarize,

> There shall be no remaining enmity, distaste, coldness and deadness of heart towards God and Christ; not the least remainder of any principle of envy to be exercised towards any angels or saints who are superior

---

[33] Anselm, *Proslogion*, in *Anselm of Canterbury: The Major Works,* ed. Brian Davies and G. R. Evans (New York: Oxford University Press, 1998), 25.102.
[34] Jonathan Edwards, *The Works of Jonathan Edwards Online*, 72 vols. (New Haven: Jonathan Edwards Center at Yale University, 2009), 8:371.
[35] Edwards, *WJEO*, 8:371.
[36] Edwards, *WJEO*, 8:375.

in glory, no contempt or slight towards any who are inferior. . . . Such a sweet and perfect harmony will there be in the heavenly society, and perfect love reigning in every heart towards everyone without control, and without alloy, or any interruption. And no envy, or malice, or revenge, or contempt, or selfishness shall enter there, but shall be kept as far off as earth and hell are from heaven.[37]

With painstaking clarity, Edwards continues in his exploration, describing how the heavenly love among the saints will be perfect in its circumstances. Love, there, will be (1) mutual and reciprocal (unrequited love will not be found there), (2) uninterrupted by jealousy without, (3) uninterrupted by internal deficiencies, (4) expressed "with perfect decency and wisdom" (i.e., proportionately and fittingly), (5) unrestrained by distance or external threats to intimacy (there will be no disappointment), (6) uniting for all in heaven, (7) properly possessive (we will all have a rightful share in one another's affections), (8) entirely prosperous, (9) multifaceted, with an endless supply of reasons conspiring to love one another, and (10) endless.[38]

These reflections have significant implications on how we handle the question of varying degrees of blessedness in the beatific vision. While we may agree with Aquinas and Turretin with their biblical reasoning for affirming such,[39] we may be tempted to affirm such a notion reluctantly, only on account of its biblical and logical cogency. But once this teaching is considered in the light of these reflections on friendship in the beatific vision, the prospect of varying degrees of beatitude becomes a delight. For one thing, we should be reassured that those who have lesser degrees of blessedness *lack nothing*. Their lesser degree of beatitude is simply a reflection of the capacity they have for joy—a capacity that will certainly expand over time in perpetuity forever, which means that

---

[37]Edwards, *WJEO*, 8:377.
[38]Edwards, *WJEO*, 8:378-84.
[39]See their respective sections in chaps. 4 and 5.

they will experience the joy of expanded enjoyment, walking in the footsteps of those beloved saints they admire for God's gracious sake as they move further up and further in, and those "*ahead*" of them will experience the delight of watching their beloved reach those vistas of delight with which those ahead are already acquainted. Indeed, we experience reflections of this phenomenon even in this life. When we see those who are less mature in the faith stumbling forward in godliness, we *delight* to see their progress. Our love for them turns *their* joy into *our* joy. Of course, such delight is often mingled—even in the faintest way—with pride and smugness; but that sensation is a reflection of "the old man," whom we hate and whom we love to put off with increasing consistency. In glory, no vestige of pride of boasting will even shadow our hearts with a hint of temptation—we will perfectly fulfill the law of love, and therefore, as we behold our beloved brothers and sisters reach degrees of blessedness that we have already reached, our delight will expand.

Likewise, at our best moments in this life, the dignity and godliness of our fellow saints is an occasion for *joy*. We delight to see the grace of God in their lives; we look to their example as an occasion to pray to God, and as an inspiration to follow their example. True, the progress of our peers often occasions envy, resentment, and despair. But this, too, is a reflection of our imperfect hearts at their worst. As we grow in godliness, we come to hate the parts of us that envies the joys of progressive holiness in those around us, and we are comforted by knowing that in glory, we who are behind, so to speak, will *also* perfectly fulfill the law of love. Our heavenly neighbors we will love as we love ourselves, and their greater capacity for blessedness will occasion nothing but joy in our hearts as our own capacity expands to "catch up" to theirs.

The reality of friendship in the beatific vision also infuses our present pilgrimage with hope and assurance in light of the aches of distance, the ebbing and flowing of relationships, and even estrangement. At this point in my own life, I have lived nineteen years in Kansas, one year in Southern California, ten years in Missouri, and at the time I am writing this, nearly one year in Abu Dhabi. Each home is indelibly marked with relationships, some of which reach great heights of intimacy. Those relationships forged "in Christ" particularly stand out. God the Holy Spirit is faithful to knit hearts together in love (cf. Col 2:2), and I have experienced many deep-woven friendships—enriched with the hard-won jewels of strain and resolution, confrontation and repentance, suffering and consolation.

And yet, as I reflect on these sweet relationships, they are suffused with a conspicuous note of bitterness, with distance having made their sweetness *temporal* and *seasonal* rather than permanent. In this earthly pilgrimage, we collide into one another, knit our hearts together in love, experience great consolations and comfort, and then the sinews tear as we depart—partially or entirely—from one another's lives. "We will stay in touch," we assure ourselves, knowing that despite our best intentions, distance inevitably demotes relationships in their intimacy. Death, as well, no matter how predictable, never fails to come as a surprise. The absence of loss leaves an *imposing* and unfillable void.

In other words, it is not simply our communion with *God* that is partial and incomplete in this life, it is also our communion with *one another* that is never quite complete. Living in Abu Dhabi, I will get homesick from time to time—longing for the consolation of friendships I had in our previous season of life. And yet, many of those friends have moved on to other places and other seasons as well. Were I to return, the sense of loss would not fully abate. Besides, any significant time spent in our previous "home" would, before long, give way to homesickness for Abu Dhabi. We are all pilgrims on this side of the New Jerusalem. No home is *truly* home.

Additionally, some relationships are severed not only by distance and death, but unresolved conflict begets the altogether different loss of estrangement. I have experienced the unwelcome pain of broken relationships with friends and colleagues over theological and interpersonal differences. In my time as a pastor, for example, I have born the sacred responsibility of leading a local congregation through the heartbreaking reality of church discipline. On more than one occasion, the excommunicated was a one-time cherished friend. Thinking back on such cases is a jarring and wounding experience. I can hardly exaggerate the heart-wrenching gravity of leading a congregation to essentially say to one once loved and trusted, "We can no longer affirm your confession of faith. Given your persistence in unrepentant sin, we must revoke the affirmation we gave upon your baptism and/or admission into membership and, with heavy hearts, express our concern for the danger of your soul." Such a reality is almost too much to bear.

What does the hope of the beatific vision offer in the face of such heartache? More than we can describe! If Edwards is right to identify heaven as a world of love, we can also identify it as a world of loose-ends tied up. In this life, the unspeakable joy of Christian fellowship always ends with a letdown. Not because there is anything deficient about earthly Christian fellowship in itself, but because such friendship is intended to awaken a desire that will only finally be consummated in glory. In that world, never will we feel the absence of friends separated by time and distance. Never will we feel the absence of beloved ones stolen by death. Never will we feel homesick. Even estranged relationships, in Christ, shall be mended.

With the beatific vision in mind, I am inspired to continue praying for these individuals, even those estranged, disciplined, and excommunicated. None of our stories are yet complete, and who knows what the Lord will work in our lives between now and then? Even the act of excommunication, after all, is not an infallible or efficient expulsion from heaven. Rather, it is a Christ-sanctioned judgment call, liable to fallibility and ignorance. "Based on all that we can judge by," the church says, "it seems that this person is not bound in heaven, so we therefore *loose* them here on earth" (cf. Mt 16:19; 18:15-20). Perhaps Christ will graciously use excommunication to bring unbelievers to true repentance and faith. Perhaps he will graciously use the sting of church discipline to bring true believers back from their backsliding waywardness. Perhaps in God's providence, time will heal the wounds of disagreement and estrangement. And perhaps none of these things will be resolved in this life. But I am assured of this much: all true believers are *my* siblings in Christ, and their presence in the eschaton will enhance my enjoyment of the beatific vision. And I am reminded to live with an open heart—in such a way that I do not blush at the thought of celebrating in the glories of Christ with those who have broken my heart in this life. In her song, "We Will Feast in the House of Zion," Sandra McCracken writes:

"He has done great things!" We will say together

We will feast and weep no more[40]

What splendid consolation it is to know that "He has done great things" will be the joyful declaration of all of heaven's inhabitants—even among those whose relationships were irrecoverably strained on earth. Before the face of God, we will trace out the great and marvelous things he wrought through all our suffering and confusion and tensions. We will piece together the chords of sanctification he wove through heartbreak, and church discipline, and death, and separation, and we shall all be enriched. We will regret nothing. We will resent nothing. We will harbor no bitter grudges. Instead, we will glory in the beatific vision, side by side, with all the saints, forever.

Conclusion

The beatific vision, if appropriately considered, enlivens and enlightens the Christian life in the areas of prayer, corporate worship,

---

[40]Sandra McCracken, "We Will Feast in the House of Zion" in her album, *Psalms* (2015).

missions, the reality of sin and sanctification, suffering, and friendship. We could, of course, innumerate countless other examples of how the beatific vision might impact the Christian life, but what we have seen here is sufficient to demonstrate that a Christian life lived with no consideration of the blessed hope of the beatific vision is unnecessarily impoverished. If I have succeeded in this volume, Christians who read this—particularly those of the Reformed and evangelical stripe—will have been convinced of the biblical warrant for affirming this doctrine, the blessed hope of the beatific vision. They will also be compelled by the rich historical pedigree this doctrine enjoys, and they will be convinced of its theological and devotional importance. And all this will contribute to their everlasting doxology. I conclude this work, therefore, with a simple prayer:

O triune God—Father, Son, and Holy Spirit—glorify yourself through this modest contribution to your church. Use it to arouse the desires of your saints for you, and bring any inaccuracies or unbecoming reflections to nothing. Grant us confidence in Christ, our most precious object of the sight of faith in this life, and may we ever be fitted for heaven, where we shall behold the glory of God in the face of Jesus Christ by the sight of glorified vision. Sustain those reading this volume in their blessed hope, until we cross over the "Jordan River" of this age into our heavenly Promised Land, where we will commune with you forever. In the name of Jesus, to the praise of the Trinity. Amen.

Postscript

THE BEATIFIC VISION AND GLOBAL CHRISTIANITY

I LIVE AND MINISTER in the heart of the Arabian Peninsula, surrounded by people from all over the world. Forty nationalities are represented in the local church to which I belong, and an analogous demographic is represented in the student body of the school where I teach theology. English is not the primary language for the vast majority of my students, who hail from (to name a few) Jordan, India, Pakistan, the Philippines, Indonesia, Nigeria, Egypt, Angola, Lebanon, Colombia, Scotland, Ethiopia, and South Africa. As such, ours is a perfect context to ascertain the relevance of the beatific vision on Global Christianity. Is this doctrine applicable in a Global Christian context, or does it belong uniquely to the province of the West?

Even apart from considering my abnormally diverse context, the contents of this book itself provides us with ample data to interrogate. In a major way, we might answer the question of the beatific vision's relevance on Global Christianity by simply pointing out that it *is the product* of Global Christianity, in the truest sense. For those of us in the English-speaking world, we can occasionally fall victim to the inaccurate assumption that since the reservoir of theological resources in English is so rich and varied, it must be itself the *fruit* of the English-speaking world. But nothing could be further from the truth. While there is no shortage of significant theological works produced by English-speakers, most of the voices we consulted in this book were not among them. Gregory of Nyssa was a Greek-speaking Cappadocian in the fourth century. Augustine was a fifth-century Latin-speaking North African. Boethius, Anselm, and Aquinas, who spanned the middle and medieval periods, were all Latin-speaking Italians. Gregory Palamas was a fourteenth-century Greek-speaker, born in Constantinople. Calvin and Turretin were sixteenth- and seventeenth-century Swiss theologians, who wrote in French and Latin. Johan Gerhard was seventeenth-century German. And Bavinck was a nineteenth-century Dutch-speaker from the Netherlands. Their collective witness is anything but culturally monolithic, let alone Western.

Of course, the modern West has so many of these great thinkers as a part of its heritage, but that does not mean that they are a unique heritage of the English-speaking world. Only a naive view of history and civilization should lead us to conclude that distinctives of Western *theology* will only flourish in Western contexts. In many ways, when classical theology makes its way from the West to the Global South by the hands of Western Christians, we are merely witnessing the theology that *grew* out of the Global South "returning home."[1] So, at the most basic level, the beatific vision need not *become* relevant for Global Christianity, it is itself a *Global Christian doctrine*.

Still, regardless of how this doctrine relates to Global Christianity at the level of historical development, it is still worth considering how this doctrine might land in diverse religious settings. One way to get at this point is simply to compare the beauty of the doctrine to the competing eschatologies and teleologies of other religions. How does the beatific vision compare, say, with the essentially carnal and hedonistic portrayal of Paradise in Islam? Or the essential dissolution of consciousness and individuality in a

---

[1]For more on this, see Thomas C. Oden's important book, *How Africa Shaped the Christian Mind: Rediscovering the African Seedbed of Western Christianity* (Downers Grove, IL: IVP Books, 2007).

Buddhist conception of Nirvana? Or the endless cycle of reincarnation in Hinduism and some forms of South American and African animistic religions? The superior universal beauty of a Christian eschatology in general, and the beatific vision in particular is, in my estimation, undeniable.

As Christians, we can recognize the fact that all human beings, as made in the image of God, desire the end for which they are made, even if that desire has been obstructed and perverted by sin, demonic deception, corruption. Regardless of the variegated differences in aesthetic taste and cultural values represented across this planet, a *longing for some kind of telos* is irreducibly human. Christianity gives an account not only for where such longing originates (*imago Dei*), and what such longing ultimately exists for (beatific vision), but also for how such longing is corrupted in other religions (sin, idolatry, and demonic deception). Christianity, in other words, *affirms* some things basic to the desire of all teleological longings, *accounts for* those basic things affirmed, and *subverts* such teleological longings where they go wrong. In other words, the Christian faith shows where good longing *fits*, over and against the system of belief or religious practice where such longing is erroneously expressed.[2]

With the Islamic portrayal of Paradise, Christianity agrees with the goodness of creation and creaturely experience of pleasure, but sharply contrasts with its base carnality. In affirmation of Buddhism's promise of a higher experience of transcendence, Christianity affirms such in the beatific vision, but without the baggage of an impersonal, desire-less absorption into the void in an endless state of Nirvana. Christianity affirms the longing for life after death that drives Hinduism and animism with their doctrine of reincarnation—even affirming the desire for the causal "fairness" that is distorted by the notion of Karma—but these longings find their

---

[2]For a similar account of what I am here describing, see Daniel Strange, *Their Rock Is Not Like Our Rock: A Theology of Religions* (Grand Rapids, MI: Zondervan, 2014).

true and fulfilling expressions in the promise of divine judgment, resurrection, and life eternal in the experience of beatific bliss for the redeemed. In other words, the beatific vision is relevant for Global Christianity because it tells a better story than the ones that compete with it across the globe. It addresses the desires not merely of the Westerner, but of the *human*.

But can we say even more? I think so. I have seen firsthand how life-giving and doxologically stirring the Classical Christian Trinitarianism that marks the Western tradition is in a global context. While there is no shortage of theologically erroneous baggage some students bring into the classroom (ironically, as a result of poor theology outsourced from the Western world, including errors ranging from theistic personalism and mutualism to the poison of the Prosperity Gospel), my students here—just as those whom I taught in the United States—flourish like flowers in full bloom under the sunshine of the God of Classical Christian Trinitarianism when he is set before them in all his brilliance.[3] Global Southern Christians, like all Christians, are predisposed to loving biblical *truth*, regardless of who brings it to them.

---

[3] For an example of the kind of theological vision I mean to cast here, over and against its common counterparts today, see James E. Dolezal, *All That Is in God: Evangelical Theology and the Challenge of Classical Christian Theism* (Grand Rapids, MI: Reformation Heritage, 2017); Carter, *Contemplating God with the Great Tradition: Recovering Trinitarian Classical Theism*; Steven J. Duby, *God in Himself: Scripture, Metaphysics, and the Task of Christian Theology* (Downers Grove, IL: IVP Academic, 2019); Matthew Barrett, "Classical Theology: A Spiritual Exercise," *Journal of Classical Theology* 1 (2022).

BIBLIOGRAPHY

Alighieri, Dante. *The Divine Comedy: The Inferno, The Purgatorio, The Paradiso*. Translated by John Ciardi. New York: New American Library, 2003.

Allen, Michael. *Grounded in Heaven: Recentering Christian Hope and Life on God*. Grand Rapids, MI: Eerdmans, 2018.

———. "On Bavinck, the Beatific Vision, and Theological Practice." *Reformed Faith and Practice* 7, no. 1 (2022).

Allen, Michael, and Swain, Scott R. *Reformed Catholicity: The Promise of Retrieval for Theology and Biblical Interpretation*. Grand Rapids, MI: Baker Academic, 2015.

Ames, William. *The Marrow of Theology*. Edited by John D. Eusden. Grand Rapids, MI: Baker Books, 1968.

Anitolios, Khald. *Retrieving Nicaea: The Development and Meaning of Trinitarian Doctrine*. Grand Rapids, MI: Baker Academic, 2011.

Aquinas, Thomas. *Summa Theologiae*. Translated by The Fathers of the English Dominican Province. Westminster, UK: Christian Classics, 1983.

———. *Compendium of Theology*. Translated by Richard J. Regan. New York: Oxford University Press, 2009.

Barcellos, Richard C. *The Lord's Supper as a Means of Grace: More Than a Memory*. Ross-shire, UK: Mentor, 2013.

Barrett, Matthew. "Classical Theology: A Spiritual Exercise." *Journal of Classical Theology* 1 (2022).

———. *Reformation as Renewal: Retrieving the One, Holy, Catholic, and Apostolic Church—An Intellectual History*. Grand Rapids, MI: Zondervan Academic, 2023.

———. ed. *Reformation Theology: A Systematic Summary*. Wheaton, IL: Crossway, 2017.

Bavinck, Herman. *Reformed Dogmatics*. 4 vols. Edited by John Bolt. Translated by John Vriend. Grand Rapids, MI: Baker Academic, 2003–2008.

Baxter, Jason M. *The Medieval Mind of C. S. Lewis: How Great Books Shaped a Great Mind*. Downers Grove, IL: IVP Academic, 2022.

Beale, G. K. *The Book of Revelation*. Grand Rapids, MI: Eerdmans, 1999.

———. *We Become What We Worship: A Biblical Theology of Idolatry*. Downers Grove, IL: IVP Academic, 2008.

Beasley-Murray, George. "Baptism and the Sacramental View." *The Baptist Times.* February 11, 1960.

Beeke, Joel R., and Paul M. Smalley. *Reformed Systematic Theology.* Vol. 2, Spirit and Salvation. Wheaton, IL: Crossway, 2019.

Bennett, Thomas Andrew. *1-3 John: The Two Horizons New Testament Commentary.* Grand Rapids, MI: Eerdmans, 2021.

Billings, J. Todd. *Remembrance, Communion, and Hope: Rediscovering the Gospel at the Lord's Table.* Grand Rapids, MI: Eerdmans, 2018.

———. *Union with Christ: Reframing Theology and Ministry for the Church.* Grand Rapids, MI: Baker Academic, 2011.

Boersma, Hans. *Five Things Theologians Wish Biblical Scholars Knew.* Downers Grove, IL: IVP Academic, 2021.

———. *Heavenly Participation: The Weaving of a Sacramental Tapestry.* Grand Rapids, MI: Eerdmans, 2011.

———. *Seeing God: The Beatific Vision in the Christian Tradition.* Grand Rapids, MI: Eerdmans, 2018.

———. "Thomas Aquinas on the Beatific Vision: A Christological Deficit." *TheoLogica,* vol. 2, no. 2 (2018).

Boethius. *The Consolation of Philosophy.* Translated by Victor Watts. New York: Penguin, 1969.

Bradshaw, David. *Aristotle East and West: Metaphysics and the Division of Christendom.* New York: Cambridge University Press, 2004.

Briggs, Charles A., and Emilie Briggs. *Psalms.* London: T&T Clark, 2000.

Brock, Cory. "Revisiting Bavinck and the Beatific Vision." *Journal of Biblical and Theological Studies* 6, no. 2 (2021).

Brown, Adam Stewart. "The Isaiah Apocalypse: A New Form Critical Look at the Genre, Structure, Content, and Function of Isaiah 24–27." PhD diss., McMaster Divinity College, 2016.

Calvin, John. *Harmony of the Evangelists, Matthew, Mark, and Luke.* Vol. 2. Translated by William Pringle. Edinburgh: Calvin Translation Society, 1848.

———. *Commentaries on the Catholic Epistles.* Translated by John Owen. Edinburgh: Calvin Translation Society, 1855.

———. *Commentary on the Epistles of Paul the Apostle to the Corinthians.* 2 vols. Translated by John Pringle. Edinburgh: Calvin Translation Society, 1848.

———. *Harmony of the Law.* Vol. 3. Translated by Charles William Bingham. Edinburgh: Calvin Translation Society, 1852.

———. *Institutes of the Christian Religion.* 2 vols. Edited by John T. McNeill. Translated by Ford Lewis Battles. Louisville, KY: Westminster John Knox, 1960.

———. *Institutes of the Christian Religion: Translated from the First French Edition of 1541.* Translated by Robert White. Edinburgh: The Banner of Truth Trust, 2014.

Card-Hyatt, Carsten. "Christ Our Light: The Expectation of Seeing God in Calvin's Theology of the Christian Life." *Perichoresis* 18, no. 1 (2020).

Carter, Craig A. *Contemplating God with the Great Tradition: Recovering Trinitarian Classical Theism*. Grand Rapids, MI: Baker Academic, 2021.

———. *Interpreting the Scriptures with the Great Tradition: Recovering the Genius of Premodern Exegesis*. Grand Rapids, MI: Baker Academic, 2018.

Chesterton, G. K. *St. Thomas Aquinas*. London: Hodder and Stoughton, 1943.

———. *The Everlasting Man*. Moscow, ID: Canon, 2021.

Cho, Donsun. "Deification in the Baptist Tradition: Christification of the Human Nature Through Adopted and Participatory Sonship Without Becoming Another Christ." *Perichoresis* 17, no. 2 (2019).

Clarke, Elliot. *Mission Affirmed: Recovering the Missionary Motive of Paul*. Wheaton, IL: Crossway, 2022.

Cole, Graham A. *Glorification: An Introduction*. Wheaton, IL: Crossway, 2022.

Cooper, Jordan B. *In Defense of the True, the Good, and the Beautiful: On the Loss of Transcendence and the Decline of the West*. Ithaca: Just and Sinner, 2021.

Crisp, Oliver D., and Kyle C. Strobel. *Jonathan Edwards: An Introduction to His Thought*. Grand Rapids, MI: Eerdmans, 2018.

Cross, Anthony R., and Philip E. Thompson, eds. *Baptist Sacramentalism 1*. Eugene, OR: Pickwick, 2003.

Dahood, Mitchel. *Psalms 1–50*. New Haven, CT: Yale University Press, 1995.

Davison, Andrew. *Participation in God: A Study of Christian Doctrine and Metaphysics*. New York: Cambridge University Press, 2019.

Dawkins, Richard. *The Selfish Gene*. New York: Oxford University Press, 1978.

deClaissé-Walford, Nancy, Rolf A. Jacobson, and Beth LaNeel Tanner. *The Book of Psalms*. Grand Rapids, MI: Eerdmans, 2014.

Dolezal, James E. *All That Is in God: Evangelical Theology and the Challenge of Classical Christian Theism*. Grand Rapids, MI: Reformation Heritage, 2017.

———. *God Without Parts: Divine Simplicity and the Metaphysics of God's Absoluteness*. Eugene, OR: Pickwick, 2011.

Doolan, Gregory T. *Aquinas on the Divine Ideas as Exemplar Causes*. Washington, DC: The Catholic University of America Press, 2008.

Duby, Steven J. *Divine Simplicity: A Dogmatic Account*. New York: T&T Clark, 2015.

———. *God in Himself: Scripture, Metaphysics, and the Task of Christian Theology*. Downers Grove, IL: IVP Academic, 2019.

Duguid, Iain. "Preaching Christ from Proverbs." *Unio Cum Christo* 5, no. 1 (2019).

Edwards, Jonathan. *The Works of Jonathan Edwards Online*. 72 vols. New Haven: Jonathan Edwards Center at Yale University, 2009.

Edwards, William R., John C. A. Ferguson, and Chad Van Dixhorn, eds. *Theology for Ministry: How Doctrine Affects Pastoral Life and Ministry*. Phillipsburg, NJ: P&R, 2021.

Eglinton, James. *Bavinck: A Critical Biography*. Grand Rapids, MI: Baker Academic, 2020.

Ferguson, Everett. *Baptism in the Early Church: History, Theology, and Liturgy in the First Five Centuries*. Grand Rapids, MI: Eerdmans, 2013.

Feser, Edward. *Five Proofs of the Existence of God*. San Francisco, CA: Ignatius, 2017.

———. *The Last Superstition: A Refutation of the New Atheism*. South Bend, IN: St. Augustine's Press, 2008.

Fesko, J. V. *Adam and the Covenant of Works*. Ross-shire, UK: Mentor, 2021.

———. *Last Things First: Unlocking Genesis 1–3 with the Christ of Eschatology*. Ross-shire, UK: Mentor, 2007.

Fowler, Stanley K. *More Than a Symbol: The British Baptist Recovery of Baptismal Sacramentalism*. Eugene, OR: Wipf and Stock, 2002.

Fox, John. *Fox's Book of Martyrs: A History of the Lives, Sufferings and Triumphant Deaths of the Early Christian and the Protestant Martyrs*. Edited by William Byron Forbush. Grand Rapids, MI: Zondervan, 1967.

Fuqua, Jonathan, and Robert C. Koons, eds. *Classical Theism: New Essays on the Metaphysics of God*. New York: Routledge, 2023.

Gaine, Simon Francis. "The Beatific Vision and the Heavenly Mediation of Christ." *TheoLogica* 2, no. 2 (2018).

———. "Thomas Aquinas and John Owen on the Beatific Vision: A Reply to Suzanne McDonald." *New Blackfriars* 97, issue 1070 (2016): 432-46.

———. "Thomas Aquinas, the Beatific Vision, and the Role of Christ: A Reply to Hans Boersma." *TheoLogica* 2, no. 2 (2018).

Gerhard, Johann. *Theological Commonplaces XXXIV: On Eternal Life*. Edited by Joshua J. Hayes and Heath R. Curtis. Translated by Richard J. Dinda. St. Louis, MO: Concordia, 2022.

Gerson, Lloyd P. *From Plato to Platonism*. Ithaca: Cornell University Press, 2013.

———. *Platonism and Naturalism: The Possibility of Philosophy*. Ithaca: Cornell University Press, 2020.

Gibson, David, and Jonathan Gibson, ed. *From Heaven He Came and Sought Her: Definite Atonement in Historical, Biblical, Theological, and Pastoral Perspective*. Wheaton, IL: Crossway, 2013.

Gregory of Nyssa. *Homilies on the Song of Songs*. Translated by Richard A. Norris Jr. Atlanta: Society of Biblical Literature, 2012.

———. *The Life of Moses*. Translated by Abraham J. Malherbe and Everett Ferguson. New York: HarperCollins, 2006.

Grenz, Stanley J., and Roger E. Olson. *20th-Century Theology: God and the World in a Transitional Age*. Downers Grove, IL: InterVarsity Press, 1997.

Hapton, Alexander J. B., and John Peter Kenny, eds. *Christian Platonism: A History*. New York: Cambridge University Press, 2021.

Haykin, Michael A. G. *Amidst Us Our Beloved Stands: Recovering Sacrament in the Baptist Tradition*. Bellingham, WA: Lexham, 2022.

Hill, Charles E., and Frank A. James III, eds. *The Glory of the Atonement: Biblical, Historical, and Practical Perspectives. Essays in Honor of Roger Nicole*. Downers Grove, IL: InterVarsity Press, 2004.

Hodge, Charles. *Systematic Theology*. 3 vols. Peabody, MA: Hendrikson, 2016.

Hoekema, Anthony A. *The Bible and the Future*. Grand Rapids, MI: Eerdmans, 1979.

Höhne, David A. *The Last Things*. Downers Grove, IL: IVP Academic, 2019.

Holifield, E. Brooks. *Theology in America: Christian Thought from the Age of the Puritans to the Civil War*. New Haven, CT: Yale University Press, 2003.

Holmes, Christopher R. J. *A Theology of the Christian Life: Imitating and Participating in God*. Grand Rapids, MI: Baker Academic, 2021.

Jamieson, R. B., and Tyler R. Wittman. *Biblical Reasoning: Christological and Trinitarian Rules for Exegesis*. Grand Rapids, MI: Baker Academic, 2022.

Jamieson, Bobby. *Going Public: Why Baptism Is Required for Church Membership*. Nashville: B&H Academic, 2015.

Jeffery, Steve, Michael Ovey, and Andrew Sach. *Pierced for Our Transgressions: Rediscovering the Glory of Penal Substitution*. Wheaton, IL: Crossway, 2007.

Jones, Mark, and Kelly M. Kapic, eds. *The Ashgate Research Companion to John Owen's Theology*. Burlington, VT: Ashgate 2016.

Junius, Franciscus. *A Treatise on True Theology: With the Life of Fransiscus Junius*. Translated by David C. Noe. Grand Rapids, MI: Reformation Heritage Books, 2014.

Kant, Immanuel. *Practical Philosophy*. Edited by Mary J. Gregor. New York: Cambridge University Press, 1996.

Kidner, Derek. *Psalms 1–72: An Introduction and Commentary*. Downers Grove, IL: InterVarsity Press, 1973.

King, Jonathan. *The Beauty of the Lord: Theology as Aesthetics*. Bellingham, WA: Lexham, 2018.

Kirkpatric, A. F. *Psalms*. New York: Cambridge University Press, 1912.

Legaspi, Michael C. *The Death of Scripture and the Rise of Biblical Studies*. New York: Oxford University Press, 2010.

Leidenhag, Joanna. "Demarcating Deification and the Indwelling of the Holy Spirit in Reformed Theology." *Perichoresis* 18, no. 1 (2020).

Leithart, Peter J. *The Promise of His Appearing: An Exposition of Second Peter*. Moscow, ID: Canon, 2004.

Levering, Matthew. *Engaging the Doctrine of Creation: Cosmos, Creatures, and the Wise and Good Creator*. Grand Rapids, MI: Baker Academic, 2017.

Letham, Robert. *Union with Christ: In Scripture, History, and Theology*. Phillipsburg, NJ: P&R, 2011.

Lewis, C. S. *Essay Collection and Other Short Pieces*. Edited by Lesley Walmsley. San Francisco: HaperSanFrancisco, 2000.

——— . *God in the Dock: Essays on Theology and Ethics*. Translated by Walter Hooper. Grand Rapids, MI: Eerdmans, 1970.

——— . *Mere Christianity*. New York: HarperCollins, 2001.

——— . *Surprised by Joy: The Shape of My Early Life*. Orlando, FL: Harvest, 1958.

——— . *The Abolition of Man*. New York: HarperCollins, 2001.

——— . *The Discarded Image: An Introduction to Medieval and Renaissance Literature*. Cambridge: Cambridge University Press, 1964.

——— . *The Last Battle*. New York: HarperCollins, 1994.

——— . *The Voyage of the Dawn Treader*. New York: HarperCollins, 1994.

——— . *The Weight of Glory*. New York: HarperCollins, 2001.

Llizo, Robert. "The Vision of God: St. Thomas Aquinas on the Beatific Vision and Resurrected Bodies." *Perichoresis* 17, no. 2 (2019).

Lossky, Vladimir. *The Mystical Theology of the Eastern Church*. Crestwood, NY: St. Vladimir's Seminary Press, 1957.

Marenbon, John. *Medieval Philosophy: A Very Short Introduction*. New York: Oxford University Press, 2016.

Markos, Louis. *From Plato to Christ: How Platonic Thought Shaped the Christian Faith*. Downers Grove, IL: IVP Academic, 2021.

Middleton, J. Richard. *A New Heaven and a New Earth: Reclaiming Biblical Eschatology*. Grand Rapids, MI: Baker Academic, 2014.

Miller, Ike. *Seeing by the Light: Illumination in Augustine's and Barth's Reading of John*. Downers Grove, IL: IVP Academic, 2020.

Minkema, Kenneth P., Adrian C. Neele, and Kelly Van Andel, eds. *Jonathan Edwards and Scotland*. Edinburgh: Dunedin Academic Press, 2011.

Mosser, Carl. "Recovering the Reformation's Ecumenical Vision of Redemption as Deification and Beatific Vision." *Perichoresis* 18, no. 1 (2020).

Motyer, J. Alec. *The Prophecy of Isaiah: An Introduction and Commentary*. Downers Grove, IL: IVP Academic, 1993.

Muller, Richard A. *Dictionary of Latin and Greek Theological Terms: Drawn Principally from Protestant Scholastic Theology*. 2nd ed. Grand Rapids, MI: Baker Academic, 2017.

——— . *Post-Reformation Reformed Dogmatics*, 4 vols. 2nd ed. Grand Rapids, MI: Baker Academic, 2003.

Oden, Thomas C. *How Africa Shaped the Christian Mind: Rediscovering the African Seedbed of Western Christianity*. Downers Grove, IL: IVP Books, 2007.

Ortlund, Gavin. *Anselm's Pursuit of Joy: A Commentary on the* Proslogion. Washington, DC: The Catholic University of America Press, 2020.

———. *Theological Retrieval for Evangelicals: Why We Need Our Past to Have a Future*. Wheaton, IL: Crossway, 2019.

———. "Will We See God's Essence? A Defence of a Thomistic Account of the Beatific Vision." *Scottish Journal of Theology*, issue 1070 (2021).

Oswalt, John N. *The Book of Isaiah: Chapters 1–39*. Grand Rapids, MI: Eerdmans, 1986.

Owen, John. *The Works of John Owen*. 16 vols. Translated by William H. Goold. Edinburgh: The Banner of Truth Trust, 1968.

Palamas, Gregory. *The Triads*. Edited by John Meyendorff. Translated by Nicholas Gendle. Mahwah, NJ: Paulist Press, 1983.

Parkison, Samuel G. "Further Up and Further In: Appreciating the Platonic Tradition and the Reformed Conception of Union with Christ." *Credo Magazine* 12, no. 1 (March 2022).

———. *Irresistible Beauty: Beholding Triune Glory in the Face of Jesus Christ*. Ross-shire, UK: Mentor, 2022,

———. "It's All in Lewis, All in Lewis, Bless Me!: The Resplendent Christian Platonism of C. S. Lewis." *Credo Magazine* 12, no. 1 (2022).

Pelikan, Jaroslav. *Christianity and Classical Culture: The Metamorphosis of Natural Theology in the Christian Encounter with Hellenism*. New Haven, CT: Yale University Press, 1993.

———. *The Christian Tradition: A History of the Development of Doctrine*. 5 vols. Chicago: The University of Chicago Press, 1971–1989.

Pieper, Franz. *Christian Dogmatics*. Vol. 3. St. Louis, MO: Concordia, 1953.

Piper, John. *Desiring God: Meditations of a Christian Hedonist*. Rev. ed. Colorado Springs: Multnomah, 2011.

———. *Let the Nations Be Glad!: The Supremacy of God in Missions*. 4th ed. Grand Rapids, MI: Baker Academic, 2022.

Plumer, William S. *Psalms: A Critical and Expository Commentary with Doctrinal and Practical Remarks*. Edinburgh: Banner of Truth Trust, 1978.

Rigney, Joseph James. "Diverse Excellencies: Jonathan Edwards on the Attributes of God." PhD diss., University of Chester, 2019.

Riker, D. B. *A Catholic Reformed Theologian: Federalism and Baptism in the Thought of Benjamin Keach, 1640–1704*. Eugene, OR: Wipf and Stock, 2009.

Schaff, Phillip. *History of the Christian Church*. 8 vols. Grand Rapids, MI: Eerdmans, 1907.

Schreiner, Patrick. *The Transfiguration of Christ: An Exegetical and Theological Exploration*. Grand Rapids, MI: Baker Academic, 2024.

Schreiner, Thomas R. *1 & 2 Peter and Jude*. Nashville: B&H Academic, 2003.

———. *1 Corinthians: An Introduction and Commentary*. London: Inter-Varsity Press, 2018.

Smalley, Stephen S. *1, 2, and 3 John: Word Biblical Commentary*. Rev. ed. Grand Rapids, MI: Zondervan Academic, 2006.

Strange, Daniel. *Their Rock Is Not Like Our Rock: A Theology of Religions*. Grand Rapids, MI: Zondervan Academic, 2014.

Strobel, Kyle C. *Jonathan Edwards's Theology: A Reinterpretation*. New York: T&T Clark, 2013.

———. "The Sight of Love: Biblical and Theological Reflections on the Beatific Vision." *Credo Magazine* 13, no. 3 (2022).

Strobel, Kyle C., Adriaan C. Neele, and Kenneth P. Minkema, eds. *Jonathan Edwards: Spiritual Writings*. New York: Paulist Press, 2019.

Sutanto, Nathaniel Gray. "Herman Bavinck on the Beatific Vision." *International Journal of Systematic Theology*, August (2022). https://doi.org/10.1111/ijst.12610.

Svenson, Manfred, and David VanDrunen. *Aquinas Among the Protestants*. Oxford: Wiley Blackwell, 2018.

Swain, Scott R. *The Trinity: An Introduction*. Wheaton, IL: Crossway, 2020.

Tabb, Brian J. *All Things New: Revelation as Canonical Capstone*. Downers Grove, IL: IVP Academic, 2019.

Taylor, Charles. *A Secular Age*. Cambridge, MA: Harvard University Press, 2007.

Trueman, Carl R. *The Claims of Truth: John Owen's Trinitarian Theology*. Grand Rapids, MI: Reformed Heritage, 1998.

———. *The Rise and Triumph of the Modern Self: Cultural Amnesia, Expressive Individualism, and the Road to Sexual Revolution*. Wheaton, IL: Crossway, 2020.

Turretin, Francis, *Institutes of Elenctic Theology*. 3 vols. Edited by James T. Dennison. Translated by George Musgrave Giger. Phillipsburg, NJ: P&R, 1997.

Tyson, Paul. *Return to Reality: Christian Platonism for Our Times*. Eugene, OR: Cascade, 2014.

van Mastricht, Petrus. *Theoretical-Practical Theology, Volume 3: The Works of God and the Fall of Man*. Edited by Joel R. Beeke. Translated by Todd M. Rester. Grand Rapids, MI: Reformation Heritage, 2021.

Vanhoozer, Kevin J. *The Drama of Doctrine: A Canonical-Linguistic Approach to Christian Theology*. Louisville, KY: Westminster John Knox, 2005.

Vidu, Adonis. *The Same God Who Works All Things: Inseparable Operations in Trinitarian Theology*. Grand Rapids, MI: Eerdmans, 2021.

———. "Triune Agency, East and West: Uncreated Energies or Created Effects?" *Perichoresis* 18, no. 1 (2020).

Vos, Geerhardus. *Biblical Theology: Old and New Testaments*. Grand Rapids, MI: Eerdmans, 1948.

———. *Reformed Dogmatics*. Translated by Richard B. Gaffin Jr. Bellingham, WA: Lexham, 2012–2016.

Webster, John. *God Without Measure: Working Papers in Christian Theology*. 2 vols. New York: T&T Clark, 2018.

———. *Holiness*. Grand Rapids, MI: Eerdmans, 2013.

Weiser, Artur. *Psalms*. London: SCM, 1962.

Wenkel, David H. *Shining like the Sun: A Biblical Theology of Meeting God Face to Face*. Bellingham, WA: Lexham, 2016.

White, Thomas Joseph. *The Incarnate Lord: A Thomistic Study in Christology*. Washington, DC: The Catholic University of America Press, 2017.

———. *The Trinity: On the Nature and Mystery of the One God*. Washington, DC: The Catholic University of America Press, 2022.

Witsius, Herman. *The Economy of the Covenants Between God and Man: Comprehending a Complete Body of Divinity*. 2 vols. Translated by William Crookshank. Grand Rapids, MI: Reformed Heritage, 2021.

Wittman, Tyler R. *God and Creation in the Theology of Thomas Aquinas and Karl Barth*. New York: Cambridge University Press, 2019.

Wright, David F. *Infant Baptism in Historical Perspective*. Eugene, OR: Wipf and Stock, 2006.

Zwingli, Huldrych. *The Latin Works of Huldreich Zwingli*. Vol. 2. Edited by William J. Hinke. Philadelphia: Heidelberg, 1922.

GENERAL INDEX

Accommodation
   see Divine accommodation
Alighieri, 62, 88-92
Allen, 4-5, 8, 55, 141-43, 155-56
analogia entis, 16-18
Anselm, 62, 77-84, 92, 99, 109, 121, 132, 180-82, 202-3, 212
Aseity, 8-11
Aquinas, 5, 10, 16, 19-20, 62, 83-88, 99, 102, 109, 111-12, 116-17, 118, 121-26, 128, 132, 135, 138, 145-55, 161-63, 169-70, 204, 212
Barcellos, 188
Barrett, 22, 47, 104, 157, 161-62, 182-83, 214
Bavinck, 9-10, 55, 142-44, 212
Beale, 36, 164
Beasley-Murray, 187
Beatitude, 17, 19, 24, 51, 81, 85, 88, 117, 132-33, 161, 169, 177, 194, 204
Beatific vision
   Anselm on, 77-83
   Augustine on, 71-77
   Aquinas and Owen on, 145-54
   biblical foundations of, 22-60
   definition of, 1-3, 176-77
   Calvin on, 106-11
   Christ's experience of, 169-75
   corporate worship and, 182-91
   Dante on, 88-92
   deification and. See Deification
   Edwards on, 131-37
   friendship and, 202-9
   Gerhard on, 111-15
   global Christianity and, 211-14
   Gregory of Nyssa on, 64-70
   Gregory Palamas on, 92-103
   missions and, 191-94
   ocular or Intellectual, 164-66
   Owen on, 122-31
   prayer and, 179-82
   sin and sanctification and, 194-99
   suffering and, 199-202
   Thomas Aquinas on, 83-88
   Turretin on, 115-22
Beauty, the beautiful, 3, 14, 18-19, 36-41, 49, 51-54, 67-68, 76, 132, 134, 140, 180-83, 185, 212-13
Beeke, 162, 167
Billings, 143, 189-90
Boersma, 8, 12, 16, 55, 64, 70-71, 75, 101, 106, 108, 124, 126, 128, 135, 139, 142-44, 146, 148-54
Bradshaw, 97, 100, 102
Brock, 55, 143
Brown, 24, 32-34
Calvin, 42-43, 62, 104-11, 137, 168, 212
Card-Hyatt, 106-8
Carter, 12, 16, 140
Causation
   formal, efficient, material, and final, 16-19
Christian Platonism, 12-14, 16, 140, 157
Clarke, 194
Cole, 138
Cooper, 140
Contemplation, 1, 18, 59, 64 72, 83, 92, 94, 118, 123, 125, 139-40, 144, 176, 178, 182-83
Creation, 16-18, 36, 49, 51, 73, 123, 127, 164, 213
Crisp, 132-33
Davison, 12, 16-17, 19-20, 51
Dawkins, 14
Deification, 40, 95-96, 99-100, 128, 167-69
Desire, 1-3, 19-21, 24, 29, 43, 54-55, 64-65, 69, 76-81, 85, 89, 108-12, 125, 176, 180-82
Divine accommodation, 31, 45
Divine energies, 64-103
Divine infinity, 11-21, 57, 64-114

Dolezal, 10, 172, 214
Donum superaditum, 85, 161-63
Duby, 8, 10
Duguid, 184
Edwards, 3, 14, 15, 62, 111, 115-16, 119, 132-37, 140, 146, 153-54, 157, 202-4, 206
Eglinton, 143
Faith, 57-58, 74-75, 108, 116-19, 123-31, 160-61
Ferguson, 65, 187
Feser, 15, 140
Fesko, 24, 122, 154
Fowler, 187
Fox, 201
Gaine, 111, 123, 128, 147-53
Gerhard, 61, 111-15, 165, 212
Gerson, 15
Gibson, 158
Good, goodness, and the Good, 65-67, 180
Gregory of Nyssa, 31, 59-70, 212
Gregory Palamas, 92-102, 108, 212
Hapton, 13, 16
Haykin, 158, 185, 187
Hill, 158
Hoekema, 142
Holmes, 179-80
Incarnation, 37, 91, 127, 155, 213
Incomprehensibility, 43, 55-57, 63-64, 80, 84, 89, 94-96
Inseparable Operations, 154-56
Intermediate state, 58-60, 163, 166, 190
Jamieson, 31, 187-88
Jeffery, 158
Jones, 106, 115, 122
Junius, 105, 195, 198
Justification, 121, 122, 157-61
Kant, 4
Kenny, 13, 16
King, 37
Legaspi, 140
Leidenhag, 160
Leithart, 43
Levereing, 12
Letham, 122, 167-68
Lewis, 1, 3, 13-14, 21, 54-55, 110, 139-40, 193
Light, 34-39, 43-44, 47-57, 76, 80-84, 88-100, 100, 114, 119-20, 127-37, 141, 156, 165, 180-81
Llizo, 87
Lossky, 95-98, 101
Love, 3, 11-12, 18, 28, 38, 39, 41, 67, 75, 81-83, 91, 116-20, 135, 137, 156, 176-77, 180-82, 191, 193, 202-7
Loveliness, 134, 165, 190, 196, 203

Markos, 12, 15, 18
Mediation, 3, 75, 79-81, 103, 122-32, 148, 166
Middleton, 142
Miller, 38
Minkema, 115, 134, 146
Modernity, 5, 7, 138-40
Mosser, 167
Motyer, 35
Muller, 10-11, 17, 162, 172-75
Nominalism, 14-15, 157-59
Oden, 212
Ontology, ontological, 12, 65, 79, 167, 170, 197
Ortlund, 5, 78-83, 84, 86, 105, 111
Oswalt, 32
Owen, 57, 62, 106-7, 111, 116, 120, 122-32, 134, 138, 143, 145-48, 151-54, 156-57, 165-66, 183
Parkison, 36, 37-38, 41, 49, 53, 132, 140-41, 183
Participation, 12, 16-20, 51, 67, 94, 117, 121, 133, 136, 146-48, 152, 157-58, 160-62, 167, 195
Pelikan, 64-66, 71, 83
Piper, 3, 191
Realism, 12, 14-16, 71, 140, 144, 157-59
Resurrection
    of the believer, 32, 34, 44, 48, 58-59, 72, 95, 101, 108, 110, 117, 129, 134, 142, 163-64, 190, 214
    of Christ, 170, 173-75
Rigney, 136
Riker, 187
Sacramental ontology
    See Christian Platonism
    and Participation
Sacraments, baptism and communion, 185-90
Sanctification, 89, 100, 122, 160, 167-69, 179, 194, 196-97, 200, 208-9
Schaff, 3, 77-78
Schreiner, 41-43, 45, 47
Smalley, 40, 167
Strange, 213
Strobel, 115-16, 119, 132-34, 136, 146, 148, 154
Sutanto, 55, 143-44
Swain, 4, 5, 47
Tabb, 52, 162
Taylor, 5, 139
Teleology, 65-66, 161
theōsis
    See Deification
Tradition, 1-5, 15, 22-24, 55, 61-62, 71, 80, 84-85, 92, 99, 101-3, 105-8, 111, 118, 120,

122-23, 126, 138-46, 154, 156-62, 170, 176, 185, 187, 214
Transfiguration, 38, 46-48, 95-96
Trinity, 6, 11, 19-20, 37, 47, 91, 102, 112, 132-133, 136, 147, 154, 155-56, 177-79, 181, 191, 209
Trueman, 7, 122, 140
Turretin, 9, 11, 53, 62, 115-22, 133, 174, 204, 212
Tyson, 13, 15, 140
Union, 20, 40, 44, 64, 66, 70, 88, 127, 140, 157, 159, 163, 167-77, 183, 188-89, 197

van Mastricht, 162
Vanhoozer, 184
Vidu, 98-102, 172
Virtue, 69, 171-72
Webster, 11-12, 194-95
Wenkel, 25-26, 28, 30
White, 47, 104, 170-74
Wittman, 31, 53, 155
Wright, 142, 187
Zwingli, 5

SCRIPTURE INDEX

OLD TESTAMENT

Genesis
1, *191*
1–3, *24*
1:26-28, *192*
1:28, *202*
2:9, *24*
2:18, *202*
3, *24, 33*
3:1, *34*
3:8, *24*
3:15, *192*
3:22-24, *24*
6, *33*
6:11, *33*
7:11, *33*
9:1-7, *33*
9:16, *33*
11, *33*
11:4, *33*
11:8, *33*
11:9, *33*
12:1-3, *192*
15:5-6, *192*
16:7-16, *25*
17:6-8, *192*
26:4-5, *192*
28:1-22, *25*
28:13, *192*
32:22-32, *25*
32:30, *25*
35:1-15, *25*
49:10, *192*

Exodus
3, *27*
3–4, *25*
3:1, *27*
3:2, *27*
3:5, *25*
3:14, *25, 27*
17:1-7, *31*
20:12, *22*
20:18-21, *29*
24:9-11, *35*
24:12, *27*
24:14, *27, 34*
32, *27*
33, *27, 28, 31, 69, 108*
33–34, *25, 26, 29, 36, 45*
33:3, *27*
33:4-6, *27*
33:10-11, *27*
33:18, *28, 29, 35, 36, 42, 52, 53, 107*
33:19, *30*
33:19-23, *28*
33:20, *30, 55*
33:22, *30*
33:23, *30*
34:4, *30*
34:6-7, *28*
34:6-8, *46*
34:8, *28*
34:29, *28*
34:29-35, *46*
34:30-35, *29*
40:34-38, *25*

Numbers
6:25-27, *52*
12:6-8, *27*

Deuteronomy
32:43, *192*

Joshua
5:13-15, *25*
5:15, *25*

Judges
13:8-25, *25*
13:23, *25*

1 Samuel
16:1-13, *192*

2 Samuel
22:50, *192*

1 Kings
18:20-38, *46*
19:8, *46*
19:9, *46*
19:9-18, *26*
19:10, *46*
19:11-12, *46*
19:12, *46*
19:19-21, *46*

Job
19:23-29, *31*
19:26, *31, 60, 166*

Psalms
2:12, *31*
11:7, *52*
16:11, *20*
19:1-6, *42, 73, 158*
23, *190*
27:4, *2, 19, 42, 52, 54, 180, 202*
31:16, *52*
36:9, *51, 87*
50:7-12, *9*

Scripture Index

67:1, *52*
67:4, *191*
80:3, *52*
80:7, *52*
80:19, *52*
117:1, *192*
119:135, *52*
148:1-14, *158*

Ecclesiastes
3:11, *20*

Song of Solomon
3:1-8, *68*

Isaiah
6, *25, 37*
6:1-7, *47*
6:5, *38, 50*
7:7, *53*
7:17, *53*
11:10-11, *192*
19:24-25, *192*
20:4-5, *33*
24–27, *28, 31, 32, 34*
24:1, *32*
24:1-20, *32*
24:3, *33*
24:7, *34*
24:14-16, *33*
24:16, *33*
24:23, *32, 34, 35*
25:6-9, *32*
25:8, *34, 53*
26:19, *32, 34*
27:1, *32, 33, 34*
27:12-13, *32*
32:17, *53*
33:17, *183*
49:10, *53*
53, *37, 47*
53:4-6, *158*
65:16, *53*
65:19, *53*

Jeremiah
2:12-13, *197*

Ezekiel
1:4-28, *26*
1:28, *26*

Joel
3:16-21, *31*
3:18, *31*

Zephaniah
3:14-20, *31*
3:16-17, *32*

Zechariah
14:9, *32*

Apocrypha

4 Ezra
7, *52*

New Testament

Matthew
1:1-17, *192*
5:8, *58, 196*
5:29-30, *196*
8:11, *53*
8:23-27, *38*
16:18-19, *188*
16:19, *208*
17:1-13, *26, 38, 45*
17:5, *47*
18:15-20, *208*
18:18, *188*
22:1-10, *53*
22:37-40, *82*
23:23, *144*
25:21, *83*
28:19, *188*

Mark
4:35-41, *38*
9:2-13, *38, 45*
9:7, *47*
13:32, *174*

Luke
2:52, *174*
5:8, *38*
8:22-25, *38*
9:28-36, *38, 45*
9:34, *47*
10:42, *80*
14:16-24, *53*
15:11-32, *7*
22:16, *190*

John
1:1, *37*
1:11, *37*
1:14, *37*
1:18, *55, 56*
4:24, *9*
5:26, *11*
10:16, *193*
12:36, *37*
12:36-43, *47*
17:5, *110*

Acts
17:24-27, *18*

Romans
1:20, *42, 73*
2:10, *132, 133, 134, 136*
3:21-26, *158*
6:1-11, *189*
6:5-14, *196*
8:18-26, *201*
8:19-25, *166*
8:20-22, *33*
11:36, *18*
13:1-2, *22*
15:8-13, *192*
15:9, *192*
15:10, *192*
15:11, *192*
15:12, *192*
15:16, *194*

1 Corinthians
1:7, *41*
1:10-17, *41*
3:1-23, *41*
4:6, *106*
5:1-13, *41*
6:9-10, *196*
6:10-11, *196*
6:12-20, *41*
8:1-13, *41*
10:1-22, *41*
10:4, *31*
11:17-34, *41*
11:26, *189*
12–14, *41*
13, *41*
13:8-10, *41*
13:10, *41*
13:12, *1, 38, 40, 42, 59*

Scripture Index

14:1, *41*
15:27-28, *110*
15:35-44, *166*

2 Corinthians
1:20, *35*
2:17, *36*
3:12–4:6, *26, 36, 49, 57, 183, 184*
3:13-15, *49*
3:14-15, *184*
3:15, *49*
3:18, *36, 58, 124, 183*
3:18–4:6, *42, 131*
4:2, *36*
4:4, *49, 184*
4:5, *36*
4:6, *31, 36, 37, 49, 124, 130, 131, 183*
4:7-18, *200*
4:7–5:10, *199*
5:1, *53*
5:4, *201*
5:8, *58, 163*
5:9, *190*
5:16, *168*
5:16-21, *192*
5:17, *131*
5:21, *158*
6:10, *199*
11:1–12:10, *100*
12:2-6, *100*
12:11-13, *100*

Galatians
3:27-29, *189*
4:4-5, *175*
4:16-18, *192*
5:1, *196*
5:15-21, *158*
5:16-26, *196*

Ephesians
1:3-14, *159*
1:14, *53*
4:13, *198*
5:22-24, *22*
5:27, *53*
6:1-3, *22*

Philippians
1:22-23, *59*

1:23, *190*
4:1, *193*

Colossians
1:12, *53*
1:15, *37, 56*
1:17, *158*
1:18-20, *127*
2:2, *206*
2:8-15, *100*
2:19, *185*
3:1-11, *196*

1 Thessalonians
2:19, *193*
4:1-7, *196*
5:8-11, *196*

2 Thessalonians
2:15, *22*

1 Timothy
1:17, *55*
3:2-7, *22*
6:12-16, *196*
6:14, *53*
6:16, *55*

2 Timothy
3:16, *23, 42*
4:1-2, *53*
4:7-8, *196*
4:8, *53*

Titus
2:11-14, *196*
2:12, *53*

Hebrews
1:3, *37, 158*
8, *36*
11:27, *56*
12–14, *196*
12:1-2, *196*
12:1-29, *201*
12:2, *202*
12:12-14
12:28, *201*
13:7, *22, 61*
13:17, *22*

1 Peter
1:4, *53*

2 Peter
1:1, *43*
1:4, *167, 196*
1:9, *44*
1:12, *44*
1:13, *44*
1:15, *44*
1:16-18, *45*
1:16-21, *43, 44, 57*
1:19-21, *48*
2:14-16, *44*
3:1-13, *44*
3:1, *44*
3:4, *44*
3:11-13, *196*

1 John
2:15-17, *196, 197*
2:18-19, *39*
2:27–3:8, *75*
3:1, *39*
3:1-3, *39*
3:1-6, *196*
3:2, *38, 39, 40, 42, 52, 58, 76, 107, 131, 168, 169*
4:12, *55*

Jude
3, *23*

Revelation
4:10-11, *34*
5:6-14, *34*
6:9, *60*
7:9-12, *192*
7:9-17, *202*
7:13-17, *34*
8, *58*
12:3-5, *34*
12:17, *34*
18–19, *33*
18:1–19:10, *33*
18:16-18, *33*
19:6-8, *33*
20, *49, 163*
20:1-6, *49*
20:2, *34*
20:4, *60, 190*
20:4-6, *163*
20:7-10, *34*
20:11-15, *58*
20:12, *34*

20:13, *34*
21, *190*
21–22, *34, 49*
21:1-2, *50*
21:1-8, *50*
21:1–22:5, *202*
21:3, *50*
21:4, *34, 50, 58, 190, 201*

21:8, *50*
21:10-11, *50*
21:18-20, *50*
21:21, *50*
21:23-24, *34, 51*
21:27, *50, 58*
22:1-2, *51*
22:1-5, *136*

22:2, *24*
22:3, *34, 58*
22:3-4, *60*
22:3-5, *49, 52*
22:4, *52, 54, 58, 190*
22:4-5, *163*
22:17, *51*
22:20, *200*

I enjoy GOD
I delight in GOD
I will see His face
(To live is Christ
To die is gain)

(Ps. 27:4 - to gaze upon the beauty of the LORD)

p.179 - prayer is spiritual oxygen